AFGHANISTAN

Highway of Conquest

AFGHANISTAN

Highway of Conquest

BY

ARNOLD FLETCHER

Cornell University Press

ITHACA, NEW YORK

10648

First published 1965

Library of Congress Catalog Card Number: 65-17709

PRINTED IN THE UNITED STATES OF AMERICA

BY VAIL-BALLOU PRESS, INC.

Preface

AN unhappy nation, according to Thomas Carlyle, is one with too much history. By this definition Afghanistan should be unhappy indeed. Moreover, those who have set down its crowded history have rarely been its friends. All too often they have been globetrotters or British army officers, retired. The former have often seen little, understood less, and invented a great deal. The latter frequently carried on their research as an adjunct to invasion, and were thus hardly capable of objectivity. And many drew the longbow just as their ancestors had done at Crécy.

This book is an attempt to correct a distorted picture. Its concern is the history of Afghanistan as a nation from its beginning in 1747 to the present. Although the importance of the region in the history of Asia goes back for thousands of years, any detailed attention to its panorama of vanished peoples and crumbled empires is beyond the scope of this work. Since some acquaintance with its earlier background is necessary for any understanding of contemporary Afghanistan, one chapter is devoted to a short review of its earlier history. For the same reason a rapid survey of Afghan ethnic groups is also included. Both these chapters are necessarily anything but exhaustive. Many volumes could be written on Afghan ancient history and ethnology.

The research on which this book is based was carried on during a three-year period while the author was employed by the Afghan Ministry of Education, and on subsequent visits made possible by the generosity of various foundations. Most non-Afghan sources were examined; of these the collections of the India Office Library and the British Museum proved the most valuable. In addition, the author was able to study the manuscripts and materials available in the Afghan ministries of press and education as well as in the Museum of Kabul. Even more important, for the section dealing with the modern history of Afghanistan, were conversations with almost all the Afghan leaders of the past twenty years, including prime ministers Sirdar Shah Mahmud and Mohammed Daoud; foreign ministers Sirdar Ali Mohammed and Mohammed Hashim Maiwandwal; Abdussatar Shalizi, Zalmai Kahn, Dr. Abdul Kayeum, Mir Ansari, and a host of others too numerous to mention. Their kindness and candor are deeply appreciated.

This book is primarily concerned with political history, and more particularly with the internal development of Afghanistan and its reaction to outside forces. Social and economic factors have had less importance in Afghan history than in other countries, since up until about thirty years ago they were relatively static. Thus Mountstuart Elphinstone's *Account of the Kingdom of Caubul,* written a century and a half ago, was still the most authoritative work on Afghan society at the beginning of the twentieth century. The fact is partly a testimony to the genius of that author, but it also indicates the slow pace of social and economic change in Afghanistan. The past thirty years, however, have witnessed the appearance of an amazing dynamism, and the country is still changing rapidly.

An inescapable problem in any work on the Middle East or central Asia is that of giving Arabic, Persian, Pushto, or Turkish words an English transliteration. Writers on these areas have maintained a stubborn individuality, with scant heed to their predecessors. There are, of course, a number of sounds in these languages which have no English equivalents. The author has not attempted any systematic solution but has simply rendered words containing these sounds in their most common transliterations or, with apologies, as they sound to him.

Deep appreciation must be extended to my wife, Fern, for her encouragement. Lorraine Eckardt and Shannon Stack also aided greatly in checking the manuscript as did the Editorial Department of Cornell University Press.

The author knows many Afghans, whose friendship he prizes. To them and to all the Afghan people, for whom hospitality is a cultural imperative but whose courtesy and kindness have far exceeded this requirement, this book is affectionately dedicated.

ARNOLD FLETCHER

Sherman Oaks, California
April, 1965

Contents

Illustrations

AFGHANISTAN

Highway of Conquest

I

The Land

A simple Afridi boy am I
Far from the hills of home.
—AFGHAN SONG

THE NAME Afghanistan, to many outsiders, suggests a country remote, little known, and presumably exotic—if only because the Persian suffix *istan* ("land of") is so frequently an appanage to the names of improbable and fictitious places. Despite Afghanistan's crowded past and present importance, few Westerners have an accurate idea of its location, and for most, the people and the policy of the country are a mystery.

This contemporary obscurity has resulted partly from a geographical position so far outside the usual circuit of tourism that before the advent of air travel Afghanistan was difficult to visit. Mostly, however, the situation has come about because of the country's nineteenth-century political position. Caught between two aggressive rival powers, British India and Czarist Russia, the Afghans, as fiercely independent a people as any on earth, countered the double menace by developing an unnatural xenophobia and closing their borders to all but an occasional visitor.

The isolation that earned Afghanistan the title of the "hermit kingdom" was justified. All through the nineteenth century British and Russian agents skulked in the Afghan hills or roamed the border bazaars, engaging in espionage, subversion, and assassination. To romantic British authors, these activities might be known as the Great Game; but to the Afghans they were a deadly serious matter, and losing their national independence was an ever present possibility. It was primarily for this reason that Afghanistan discouraged foreign visitors and, with few exceptions, barred its own citizens from foreign travel. This policy ended about thirty years ago, and the country is just now beginning to emerge from the isolation that was its inevitable consequence.

In truth, the lands that make up the nation of Afghanistan have been highly important in the past of Asia. They have been at the center of powerful empires, and at times a buffer between rival powers. The region has always been a major corridor of travel, through which have passed many of the migrations and invasions that have shaped the political structure of Asia. The list of historic personalities who were born or who lived in Afghanistan is a long one and not the least of its people's complaints is that many of these figures are usually identified as Persians. The list includes Zoroaster, Roxanne (the bride of Alexander the Great), Firdausi, Sultan Mahmud Ghaznawi, Bayezid, Ansari, Farukhi, Khusro, and Jami. Timur-i-Leng (Tamerlane) was born just north of the borders of modern Afghanistan, as was ibn-Sina (Avicenna), the greatest of Moslem philosophers.

Afghanistan's interest is not limited to that of the historian or antiquarian. A compact nation-state with an area of about 250,000 square miles, it has existed as an independent or semi-independent country for over two centuries. It has a population of between twelve and fourteen million virile and aggressive people, who in their time have provided kings for Iran and India.[1] Bordering the Soviet Union for over seven hundred miles, it lies along the route from the main mass of Asia to the Indian subcontinent. The Afghan government is now engaged in a thoroughgoing program of modernization, and the moves it has made toward responsible and democratic government are hardly exceeded by any nation in Asia.

In shape, Afghanistan is an irregular quadrilateral, located in the North Temperate Zone between 29° 30′ and 38° 30′ north latitude, and between 68° 30′ and 75° east longitude. It is bordered on the north by Soviet Asia, more particularly by the "republics" of Uzbekistan, Tadjikistan, and Turkmenistan. On the west and southwest are Iran and Iranian Baluchistan; on the east and southeast are Pakistan and Pakistani Baluchistan. In the northeast a long slender salient of Afghan territory touches China, but because of the elevation and the lack of roads there is almost no intercourse between the two countries.

Afghanistan forms the eastern section of the raised land mass known to geographers as the Iranian Plateau, which is high above sea level. In the north it slopes toward the Amu Darya River, in the east toward the Indus plain, and in the south toward the deserts of Baluchistan. In a country three-fifths of whose total area is mountainous, by far the most impressive physical feature is a massive folded range bearing the sinister name of the Hindu Kush (Persian for "killer"), which bisects Afghanistan from northeast to southwest for about 450 miles.[2] The Hindu Kush is the western extension of India's arched mountain roof, and though lower than its sister ranges—the Karakorams, Pamirs, and Himalayas—it is one of the highest and most impressive ranges in the world.

Made up of young mountains composed largely of granite, with associated gneiss and mica slate, the Hindu Kush is treeless through much of its extent—a condition produced in part by the ravages of thoughtless men and hungry goats. The stark brown battlements, rising into the blue of usually cloudless skies, provide a backdrop for most of Afghanistan's scenery. In many ways they also separate the Middle East and India from high Asia, and most of the leading events in the history of Afghanistan have taken place south of their towering heights.

The Hindu Kush is threaded by passes which have witnessed many developments in Asia's past. Of those running from east to west the most important are the Anjuman, Khawak, Parandev, Salang, Kaoshan, Chaharder, Kharzar, Shinar, Haji Gak, and Ak Robat—all tortuous mountain trails winding among peaks and precipices.[3] They have been trodden by pilgrims to the shrines of the Buddha, by the footsore phalanx of Alexander the Great, by Mongol riders with their yak-tail banners, by Indo-

Aryans with their cattle and their Vedas, by Turks, Tatars, and Huns, and by a host of forgotten peoples. They have witnessed the passing of countless caravans bearing the wares of India, Persia, and China; and today they bear the trucks that haul much of Afghanistan's export and import trade.

Since these passes can be traversed even by armies through part of each year, they were the chief reason for Afghanistan's past importance; through them or around the western flank of the Hindu Kush have come almost all the invasions of India.

The section of the range to the north of Kabul, the Afghan capital, is called Koh-i-Baba ("father mountains"); a northern ridge farther to the east is known as the Safed Koh ("black mountains"). The extreme western part is called the Parapomisus—a name that was applied to the entire system by the geographers of ancient Greece.

Among other mountain chains that have prompted Westerners to dub Afghanistan the "Switzerland of Asia," some are spurs of the Hindu Kush, and some are independent of it. One of the latter is the Suleiman (Solomon) Range, which runs along the eastern frontier and separates the Afghan highlands from the Indus Valley. These mountains—probably the original home of the Pushtoon Afghans, the founders of the nation—are also pierced by passes, including the Shorawak, Bolan, Gomal, Tochi, and Paiwar, and the Khyber's twenty-seven miles of storied violence.

Afghanistan is dry, with an average rainfall of only about ten inches, and must therefore depend for irrigation upon its rivers, of which there are a number born in the mountains and hurrying down to the north, east, and south. The Amu Darya (the Oxus of antiquity), forms the border between Afghanistan and the Soviet Union for hundreds of miles.[4] Other important streams are the Kokcha, Hari Rud, Helmand, Arghandeb, Murghab, and Kabul. All are rushing torrents in spate, slowing to a trickle in summer when their water is taken off for the Afghan fields. Except for stretches of the Amu Darya, none is navigable.

Afghanistan's few lakes are more odd than economically important. Sarikul, close to the Soviet border, is sixteen thousand feet above sea level, fifteen miles long and a mile wide; for most of the year it is a block of ice. Band-i-Amir ("dam of the Amir") consists of a series of small lakes about fifty miles west of the valley of Bamian in the Koh-i-Baba Mountains. The dam to which they owe their existence was built by no Amir but is a natural formation of mineral deposits. These are beautiful lakes and should prove a major tourist attraction.

Afghanistan also contains rocky hills, plateaus, and narrow alluvial valleys, with some steppeland in the northwest and deserts in the south. Harsh and desolate though it is, much of the landscape has an impressive beauty. The towering mountain peaks, craggy hills, and dusty mesas, relieved by narrow ribbons of green in the valleys, offer a panorama which ranks in beauty with any in the world, and may be expected to draw many visitors to the country.

Although the climate of Afghanistan varies with the elevation and the location, it is everywhere extremely dry. Its remoteness from the ocean deprives the region of the moderating effect produced by large bodies of water, with the result that the winters tend to be extremely cold and the summers oppressively hot. Except in a few places, however, the heat is not as debilitating as in humid India, and the winter cold is mitigated by daily sunshine.

For administrative purposes, Afghanistan has been divided since March 1964 into twenty-nine districts known as Wolus-Wali. So far as an understanding of the influence of geography on Afghan history is concerned, however, these arbitrary divisions are less important than the eight large and distinct sections that make up the kingdom of Afghanistan: Bactria, the Hindu Kush, the Hazarajat, the Arachosian Plain, Kabulistan, the Hari Hud Valley, Jalalabad or Nangrahar, and Badakshan.[5]

Bactria, often called Afghan Turkestan, lies north of the Hindu Kush and extends to the Amu Darya and the Soviet border. This territory is largely a vast level plain, and at one time had a dense population and an extensive irrigation system. But since it was always a natural target for nomads from the north, it suffered repeated devastating invasions. From the worst of these, by the Mongols in the thirteenth century, it has never fully recovered. Mazar-i-Sharif ("sacred tomb"), the most important city of the region, is supposedly built on the site of the grave of the Caliph Ali, close to the ruins of the ancient city of Balkh.[6]

The Hindu Kush has already been described. Adjoining it to the south is the Hazarajat, a vast tableland broken by innumerable scattered mountain ranges, in the center of Afghanistan. The inhabitants of this inhospitably bleak, treeless, and desolate area eke out their living in narrow valleys along rivers whose banks in places rise directly from the bed of the stream.

In the southwestern part of Afghanistan, known as the Arachosian Plain, are the relatively fertile districts of Kandahar and Zamindawar. Watered by the Helmand and Arghandeb rivers, they are the chief source of Afghanistan's dried fruit exports. The southern section, Sistan, is sandy desert, sparsely inhabited and unproductive, although the ruins of many cities and towns suggest that it was much better watered in the past.[7]

Kabulistan is the collective designation of a number of plateaus surrounding the capital city of Kabul. They and Kabul itself are about six thousand feet above sea level, with a wholesome and temperate climate. Watered by the Kabul and a number of other rivers, the entire region is fertile and densely populated. Kabulistan is the seat of Afghan government, of the University of Kabul, and of much of Afghanistan's industry.

Badakshan, in the extreme northeast, is a mountainous area, much of it covered with forests, and noted in Marco Polo's time for its ruby mines. Wakhan, the adjoining strip of Afghan territory that touches the border of China, is a forbidding, seldom visited land of mountains and glaciers, notable chiefly as the habitat of the mountain sheep, *Ovis poli.* West of Badakshan is the district of Kataghan (once known as Tukharistan), the site of most of Afghanistan's cotton production. The Turki or Badakshani horse has been bred here for centuries—an animal whose reputation for speed and endurance once brought a Chinese army to the area with orders to obtain a supply for the Chinese emperor.[8]

The valley of the Hari Rud, lying in the northwest of Afghanistan and extending to the Iranian border, is an ex-

tremely fertile area whose largest city, Herat, once had a
population of perhaps a million people—far more than its present sixty or seventy thousand. Here the mountains dwindle into
rounded hills dotted with pistachio trees, affording in the past
an excellent route for India-bound invaders who wished to
avoid the mountain passes. Like Bactria, it has repeatedly
suffered devastating invasions.

Jalalabad or Nangrahar (known in ancient times as Gandhara) lies in eastern Afghanistan facing Pakistan. Lower than
most of the rest of the country, it has a number of fertile districts and a climate rather like that of India, pleasant in winter
but oppressively hot and damp in summer.

The overwhelming majority of Afghans are agricultural and
pastoral, and many of them live on a subsistence basis. Although
not much more than 10 per cent of its total land area is under
cultivation, Afghanistan, with a relatively small population, has
been spared the famines that have plagued its neighbors, and it
is safe to say that by Asian standards most Afghans are well fed.
Wheat is the most important crop and bread the staple of
Afghan diet, giving rise to the Afghan proverb, "Warm bread
and cold water are the two gifts of Allah." Other grains and
vegetables common to temperate countries are grown, and the
country is noted for its grapes and stone fruits.

Pastoralism, which remains important in the Afghan economy, is a way of life followed by true nomads as well as by
sedentary agriculturists who supplement their crops by raising
sheep, cattle, or goats. Even the latter frequently practice
vertical nomadism with the seasons. The sheep is by far the
most important food animal, and mutton is the staple Afghan
meat; the cattle are of poor quality both as meat and as milk
producers, for lack of selective breeding and because they are
usually turned out to forage in meager pasture lands. Camels of
the two-humped Bactrian type are common; so are dromedaries
and a cross between the two. On the backs of these animals
much of the merchandise of the country is still transported,
particularly to the many districts not reachable by motor roads.

Afghanistan is the home of the incorrectly named "Persian"
cat, as well as of the Afghan hound now popular with Western

breeders. Dogs of various other strains, popular with the nomads, are mostly huge, shaggy, and formidable, a terror to the wolves and sometimes, unfortunately, to the innocent traveler. The patient and indispensable donkey still performs much of Afghanistan's labor; horses also are common, especially in the north.

Wildlife in Afghanistan is varied and plentiful except in tribal lands, where rifles are no less essential than a shirt on one's back. The ibex, markhor, and ounce or snow leopard are found in the mountains, and the Persian gazelle abounds in the lowlands. A few tigers still roam the reed beds along the Amu Darya and the forests of Badakshan. Wolves, particularly in the winters, are a problem for the herdsmen and even occasionally, according to reports, a danger to human beings. Jackals and foxes are found throughout the country; there are hyenas in southern Afghanistan, and several kinds of bears in the wooded sections of the east.

The average Afghan is passionately fond of hunting, but few have any interest in fishing—with the result that trout and salmon teem virtually undisturbed in Afghan rivers, as do the giant sturgeon of the Amu Darya. Snakes appear to find the elevation and climate unpropitious, although an occasional krait or cobra turns up in the east. Insects, particularly flies and mosquitoes, are as obnoxious as they are elsewhere in Asia.

This brief description scarcely does justice to Afghanistan's enormously varied geography, but may serve as an introduction. Without question Afghan history has been strongly influenced by the location, topography, and climate of the country. Its function as an artery of travel has already been mentioned. Quite probably its mountainous terrain and its extremes of climate have favored the development of those aspects of character—love of freedom, loyalty to clan or tribe, and physical stamina—that have made the Afghans' role in the history of Asia far larger than their numbers would appear to warrant.[9]

II

The People

Oh Gods! From the venom of the
Cobra, the teeth of the Tiger, and
the vengeance of the Afghan—deliver
us.—HINDU SAYING

AFGHANISTAN is largely an ethnic mystery. The geography
that has made it a corridor of travel in Asia has also brought to
it a series of visitors—Indo-Aryans, Sakas, Parthians, Persians,
Kushans, Greeks, Mongols, Huns, Turks, and others whose
names have vanished from legend. Many of these were tran-
sients; others halted among the Afghan hills, where the long
process of blending and adaptation, in the absence of written
record, makes tracing their ethnogenesis almost impossible.

In recent years scholars have begun to examine the Afghan
ethnic groups; but anthropometric and serological evidence is
still scanty, and historic sources are fragmentary and inconclusive. Thus the question of Afghan origins has evoked more
controversy than consensus.

Nevertheless, any attempt to understand their history demands some knowledge of the varied peoples who comprise the
Afghan nation. Loyalties and rivalries among these groups are
fundamental to the Afghan past, and remain a problem in the
present. Students of the pluralistic societies of the Middle East
have noted in members of its ethnic enclaves what might be

9

called an "ethnic personality." Carleton Coon observes, for example:

I do believe that ethnic groups do possess standard types of personality at least in the Middle East. . . . Within reasonable ranges and allowing for probable errors it is possible to predict what persons of different ethnic groups would do under given situations in which outsiders were involved, and I would not be surprised that heredity and environment were involved, each force, in certain respects, limiting the other.[1]

Without accepting the suggestion made by Professor Coon that genetic determination is involved, it must be admitted that visitors to Afghanistan for over a century have consistently noted among the Afghan people different sets of behavior patterns, with evident variations even in sections of the same ethnic group. Thus it was possible for British recruiting officers working among the tribes on the Afghan frontier to receive detailed instructions as to which tribesmen they were to recruit and which they were to exclude. These instructions were not the products of anthropologists or psychologists, but they did reflect the experience of a century.

Although every citizen of Afghanistan is an Afghan, in a historic sense the name belongs to the people known as Pushtoons, Pukhtoons, or Pathans.[2] These latter speak a language called Pushto or Pukhto, of the Iranian branch of the Indo-European linguistic family and thus related to Persian, Baluchi, and Kurdish, although not derived from any of them. Pushto and Pukhto are dialects of the same language, differing chiefly in that a letter pronounced as a sibilant in Pushto becomes a guttural in Pukhto. Some linguistic authorities maintain that Pushto was the original form and Pukhto a later development; accordingly, for the sake of clarity and since the Durranis, the dominant tribe in Afghanistan from its inception, are Pushto-speakers, the words *Pushto* and *Pushtoon* will be used throughout, even in the occasional references to the "hard" dialect and those who speak it.

The origin and meaning of *Afghan,* once a synonym for Pushtoon, are unknown. One of its first recorded appearances is the *Hudud-al-Alam* ("Regions of the World"), a work of uncertain authorship which appeared around A.D. 980 and contained a tantalizing reference to "Saul, a pleasant village on a mountain. In it live Afghans." [3] The name occurs again in the writings of Mohammed ibn-Ahmad al-Biruni (circa A.D. 1060), who comments, "In the western frontier mountains of India live various tribes of Afghans." [4]

The casualness of these remarks is the more surprising since the Afghans (Pushtoons) make up almost half the population of Afghanistan and have dominated the nation since its beginning. Moreover, al-Biruni lived and wrote at the court of Sultan Mahmud Ghaznawi, whose armies were largely composed of Pushtoons. Most probably the name *Afghan* was originally applied to only a few of the Pushto tribes and later adopted by all of them. This development must have been fairly recent, for as late as A.D. 1809 the name Afghan was "known to the Afghauns themselves only through the medium of the Persian language. Their own name for their nation is Pushtoon, in the plural, Pushtooneh." [5] The name *Pushtoon* appears to have greater antiquity, even though its rarity in the writings of the past is likewise remarkable. Herodotus on a number of occasions mentions the Paktuike or Paktues, whom he describes as serving Xerxes in Greece, wearing skins and carrying the bow.[6] Some authorities consider these people to have been Pushtoons; others are less certain. The incompleteness of Pushtoon ethnography applies equally to many other Afghan ethnic groups.

According to their own tradition the Pushtoons originated in Palestine in the days of King Saul from whom they claim descent through a son Irmia (Jeremiah), and a grandson, Afghana.[7] They maintain that they grew great in Israel, where they were favorites of David and Solomon, and where the latter assigned them to guard the temple from the assaults of jealous demons. To aid them in this task, Solomon, master of the djinns and afreets, taught the Afghans Pushto, the language of hell. The statement is confirmed by the Prophet Mohammed, according to Afghan tradition, and may be said to acquire some faint credence from the nature of the language itself.

At this time there appeared a wicked magician, Bukht ud-Nasir (Nebuchadnezzar), who scattered the tribes of Israel and sent the Afghans, as the most obstreperous, far to the east, to the lands of Sham or Syria. From here they migrated to the mountains of Ghor in western Afghanistan, where they settled, adhering to the one God although surrounded by countless idolaters. In the time of the Prophet Mohammed, the legend continues, a chief of the Afghans, Qais or Kish, visited Mecca and embraced Islam, receiving the new name of Abdul Rashid. He returned to Afghanistan to convert his people; and from him, through his sons Sarban and Ghurghusht, and a daughter, Bibi Matto, all the present Pushtoons are descended.

This romantic genealogy aroused much interest in Victorian England at a time when the fate of the Ten Lost Tribes ranked as a public issue hardly less burning than the Balkan question. Modern scholars, however, point out that Pushto is an Indo-European rather than a Semitic language, and that its Semitic words are Arabic accretions. There is no mention of Afghana or the Afghans in either Hebrew or Arabic records until long after the time of Mohammed; when they do appear in the latter, the Afghans are usually called Suleimani, an indication that their homeland was in the Suleiman Range rather than in the western mountains of Ghor. Also, it has been a common practice in Moslem lands to invent genealogies connecting their people to Mohammed or the other prophets of Islam.

There is still no complete agreement on Pushtoon origins. Afghan scholars often trace them to the people of ancient Bactria, but a number of non-Afghan authorities believe the Pushtoons arrived from the north at a later date. Quite probably they were once a small group centered in the Suleiman Mountains, who were later joined by migrants who adopted their language and customs. There is some evidence in the writings of Arab geographers that the Ghilzai, today one of the larger Pushtoon tribes, are at least in part descended from the Khalaj or Khallukk, a people of Oghuz Turk or Epthalite Hun background.[8]

Although no census has been taken the Pushtoons are estimated to number about six million in Afghanistan, or about half its population, plus about five million living east of the Afghan border. They have been the dominant people in

Afghanistan since its beginning as a nation and the country is, in fact, a Pushtoon creation. Within Afghanistan they are largely concentrated in the east and south, although in recent years a number have been settled north of the Hindu Kush.

Regardless of their dispersal, Pushtoons exhibit strong similarities both of custom and of ethnic personality. The tribes, subtribes, and clans into which they are divided are invariably agnates and usually bear the name of an eponymous ancestor with the addition of *i* ("of") *zai* ("sons of") *khel* ("band of") as, for example, in *Waziri, Mohammedzai,* or *Suleiman Khel.* Loyalty to the tribe or clan varies from group to group but is usually strong; at the same time all Pushtoons have an extreme pride in their Pushtoon identity.

Pushtoons in the past have shown little interest in trade, industry, or urban living. Today they are mostly sedentary agriculturists; but about one million are nomads, moving over considerable distances with their black tents, their camels, and their flocks of sheep. These Kuchis carry on extensive commerce with the settled folk through whose lands they pass, exchanging animal products for grain, and they are also a problem for the non-Pushtoons because their tempers are uncertain and they often go formidably armed. A number are camel merchants who bring their wares to otherwise inaccessible parts of the country.

Settled Pushtoons are rarely sharecroppers or tenant farmers of the type common in the Middle East. They are most commonly freeholders, but a number are landlords, employing non-Pushtoons as tenants or laborers—a status that may have contributed to the independence and sense of personal worth and dignity that are typical of the Pushtoon personality.

Since their first recorded appearance, the Pushtoons have been characterized as turbulent, warlike, predatory, and revengeful. Ibn Batuta, who met them in A.D. 1333, said they were "mostly highwaymen"; [9] Timur-i-Leng, a century later, concurred—praise from Caesar indeed. The Pushtoon poet Khushal Khan-i-Khattak described his people as "malevolent, ruthless, and contentious." [10] Adam Olearius in the seventeenth century began a string of the usual unfavorable European comments by calling them a "self-conceited, insolent, cruel, and barbarous people. They slight others for no other reason than that they are not so rash as themselves in hazarding their lives without any necessity." [11]

Statements like this could be multiplied, particularly those from the memoirs of British soldiers and officials of the nineteenth century. They contain, however, only a shred of the truth. Pushtoons have undoubtedly been aggressive, belligerent, and prone to feud and faction—traits that might logically be expected in the circumstances. Since the Pushtoons have always reacted violently to foreign pressure or any threat to their freedom, the reports of invaders could likewise hardly be expected to show much objectivity.

A different point of view was expressed by Mountstuart Elphinstone, who in 1809 headed the first official British mission to Afghanistan. A scholar and linguist, Elphinstone gave a description of the Afghan character that remains sound to the present day. He found them "fond of liberty, faithful to their friends, kind to their dependents, hospitable, brave, hardy, frugal, laborious, and prudent; and they are less disposed than the nations in their neighborhood to falsehood, intrigue, and deceit." [12]

Physically the Pushtoons appear to be of mixed Mediterranean type with many Nordic features, although any definitive conclusions must await further anthropometric study. It is safe to generalize that they are predominantly brunette whites, dolichocephalic, and of slender build with prominent facial features. Many are handsome by Western standards.[13]

The second largest ethnic category in Afghanistan consists of the Tadjiks, who are scattered throughout the country but concentrated mainly in the north and west. Between two and three million Tadjiks live in Afghanistan; others live in Iran, the Soviet republic of Tadjikistan, and the Chinese province of Sinkiang. Although the Tadjiks are spoken of as a distinct group, recent investigation seems to indicate that they are actually several peoples who share no more than a name, a language (Persian), and sedentary living habits. Those in the west are often called Heratis, and probably have the same ancestry as the people of eastern Iran. Those north of the Hindu Kush are usually referred to as Parsiwans or Farsiwans ("Persian-speakers"); they show considerable Mongoloid admixture and are probably descended from a group of settlers from ancient Iran known as the Sarts. The "Mountain Tadjiks" described by Soviet ethnologists appear to have been among the earliest inhabitants of the region, and may indeed be autochthones.

Tadjiks have few traditions about themselves or their origins, other than that they came from Arabia and derive their name from the Arabic word *taj* (for "ornament")—a sign that they were once "ornaments of the Prophet Mohammed." In fact, however, *Tadjik* is an Arabic term, which appears originally to have denoted a non-Arab Moslem, but which by the fourteenth century had come to mean a Persian-speaking sedentary Moslem—a definition that still fits the Tadjik well enough.

Tadjiks are not tribal, nor do they seem to have much pride in their ethnic identity, possibly because they have lived under the Pushtoon hegemony for two centuries. They are mainly agriculturists, often working as tenant farmers or laborers, although some are to be found engaged in trade or handicraft in Afghan cities. They are not belligerent except for the mountain Tadjiks of Kohistan, north of Kabul, who are considered to be as aggressive as Pushtoons.

The scanty anthropometric studies made thus far of the Tadjiks of Afghanistan indicate that they are brachycephalic, and identify them with the Alpine division of the Caucasoid race. They are brunette whites and usually of slender build like the Pushtoons, but with more oval faces whose features appear less pronounced. As has been noted, many northern Tadjiks show traces of Mongoloid admixture.[14]

Pushtoons and Tadjiks have lived together with a fair amount of harmony for several centuries. A number of Tadjiks now hold high governmental posts, and others have served as Wazirs or ministers in the past, among them Abdul Majid Khan, who was minister of national economy for many years. Nevertheless, neither intermarriage nor social intercourse between the two peoples is common except in the cities, where tribal and ethnic affiliations have weakened.

In northern Afghanistan, between the Soviet border and the

Hindu Kush, live approximately a million Afghans whose speech derives from the Ural-Altaic linguistic family. Of these by far the largest group are the Uzbegs, who number about 800,000. Originally the name was applied to Turkic tribesmen who entered Afghanistan in the middle of the fifteenth century, one of whose early leaders was Uzbeg Khan, a descendant of the great Genghis Khan. The Uzbegs of today are a mixture of these Turco-Mongols with the population of Iranian agriculturists whom they found in the area. Thus the modern Uzbegs have either Mongoloid or Caucasoid features or a blend of the two. They tend to be brachycephalic with yellow-white complexions and broad cheekbones, and occasionally with epicanthic eyefolds. They are more stocky in build than Pushtoons or Tadjiks, and some of them are corpulent, as the latter peoples seldom are.

The Uzbegs have given up the tribal affiliations and nomadism of their Turkic ancestors and are sedentary agriculturists, although some have become successful merchants and artisans. Their language, a form of Turkish called Uzbeki, apparently derives from the Chagataian Turkish of medieval times.

In Afghanistan the Uzbegs have a reputation, probably undeserved, for indolence and procrastination. They intermarry freely with their Tadjik neighbors but rarely with the Pushtoons, who consider them somewhat less than social equals. But neither they nor the Tadjiks are subjected to any active discrimination, nor is there any real hostility between either group and the Pushtoons.

The other major Turkic group in Afghanistan, the Turkomen, number about 200,000 and are found mostly in the northwest. Most authorities believe they are descended from the Oghuz Turks who entered the area in the eleventh century, although they may have other strains in their ethnic background. They speak various Turkish dialects of a Western type.

Unlike the Uzbegs, the Turkomen are still pastoral, tribal nomads, the more important tribes being the Salor, Sariq, and Tekke. They have few contacts with other Afghans and have had little importance in Afghan history; in fact, many thousands have only recently arrived in Afghanistan as refugees from Soviet collectivization.

On the other hand, they have a distinct economic role as breeders of the karakul sheep, whose pelts—known as karakul, astrakhan, or Persian lamb—are the main Afghan export; and Turkomen women are weavers and dyers of the deep-red "Bokharan" rug which is another noted product.[15]

The Hazaras ("thousands") of Afghanistan are an interesting people whose homeland, the Hazarajat or Hazaristan, is the central mountain massif west of Kabul. Here they number about 600,000, and smaller groups are found in Bamian, in the Koh-i-Baba Range, and in Badakshan. The Hazaras are easily recognizable because of their Mongoloid features, which have aroused the curiosity of many foreign visitors. The usual explanation for this Mongoloid enclave in a predominantly Caucasoid country, that their ancestors were the soldiers of Genghis Khan, is found in almost every modern work on Afghanistan as well as in the semi-authoritative pages of the *Encyclopaedia Britannica*. Students of the Hazaras, however, are united in discarding this hypothesis. There is no evidence that Genghis Khan left a garrison in the region, little reason for him to have done so, and little likelihood that he would have selected the Hazarajat even if he had. One plausible suggestion is that the ancestors of the Hazara include Mongol soldiers who passed through the country in the thirteenth and fourteenth centuries, Chagataian migrants who pushed down from the north, and Mongol tribes who in the fifteenth century entered the Hazarajat from the south, conquering and intermarrying with a mountain Tadjik population.

Caution must be exercised in adopting this hypothesis, however, for there is also some indication that the name *Hazara* was used in the country before the arrival of the Mongols and that there may have been Mongoloid people in the Hazarajat for centuries prior to the Mongol conquests. Additional investigation may yet reveal that the original Hazara ancestors were a still earlier people.

Whatever their origin, the Hazaras resemble the Mountain Tadjiks in customs, though not in build. They are like the

Buriats of modern Mongolia in having coarse black hair, yellow to yellow-brown complexions, brachycephalic heads, broad faces, prominent cheekbones, and a heavy incidence of the epicanthic eyefold. Unlike the Tadjiks, they are divided into tribes, of which the more important are the Besud, Dai Kundi, Polada, Dai Zangi, Jaghuri, and Uruzgani. Almost all are sedentary agriculturists and speak a peculiar Persian dialect called Hazaraghi.[16]

Alone among the major ethnic groups in Afghanistan, the Hazaras are members of the Shia sect of Islam, and more precisely of the Ithna Ashariyah or "twelver" branch, whose beliefs they share with the majority of Iranians. No doubt this theological difference contributed to the hostility that existed between the Hazaras and their neighbors up to the twentieth century, and to the inferior social and economic position that they still hold. More probably, however, their racial difference was equally important, if not more so, since the Shia Kizzilbash of Kabul do not share their lowly status.

Hazaras have a reputation for physical strength, endurance, and industry in tasks that do not require much mental ability. Thousands of them leave their marginal homeland for Afghan cities, where they are employed as manual laborers and often as servants. In the past they were preferred as slaves "above any other people," and suffered severely from the raids of the Uzbegs, who had a sinister and deserved notoriety as man-stealers.[17] A number who enlisted in the British army in India proved to be brave and dependable soldiers and were usually assigned to engineering units.

North and west of Hazaras live a people called the Chahar-Aimak ("four tribes"). They are estimated to number between two and three hundred thousand, and are divided into the Jamshidi, Firozkohi, Timuri, and Taimani tribes although the Timuris are not always included among the Chahar-Aimak, and a tribe known as the Hazara is sometimes also listed. Many of the Chahar-Aimak are nomadic or seminomadic, those of the north living in the familiar yurt of central Asia and those of the south favoring a yurtlike tent. They speak Persian of a type known as Herati, and unlike the Hazaras of the Hazarajat, with whom they were long at odds, are members of Sunni Islam.[18]

Still another interesting people in Afghanistan are the Kafirs, now usually known as Nurs or Nuristanis, of whom perhaps one hundred thousand live in the eastern province of Nuristan and across the border in Chitral. In the nineteenth century it became known that a strange people living in this remote and mountainous area were fairer of skin than their neighbors, spoke a strange language, and were non-Moslems, as the name Kafir ("ingrate" or "infidel"), given to them by the Afghans, demonstrated. The romantic conjecture aroused by these circumstances and abetted by Rudyard Kipling in *The Man Who Would be King,* led to the suggestions that the Kafirs' ancestors might have been ancient Greeks or possibly Christians.

Unfortunately for this romantic theory, an intrepid Englishman, Sir George Scott Robertson, who visited the Kafirs toward the close of the nineteenth century, found no Greek or Christian affinities beyond a fondness for wine and goats. It was not long afterward that Abdur Rahman, the Afghan Amir, sent three converging armies into Kafiristan and subdued the Kafirs, who had previously given proof of their manhood by collecting Moslem heads. Many Kafirs were converted to Islam, and their country was renamed Nuristan ("land of light").

The Nurs consist of two main groups, the Black Coats and the White Coats, who are subdivided in turn into a number of tribes. In language they are of the Indic branch of the Indo-European stem, closely related to Dardic. Their religion, a combination of animism and polytheism, featuring ancestor worship, animal sacrifices, wooden idols, and grave effigies, has almost disappeared in Afghanistan and is vanishing in Chitral. Their social customs include a system of potlatch feasts much like those of the coastal tribes of the American northwest.

The Nurs, who live in villages and carry on a mixed agricultural and pastoral economy, are remarkable mountaineers. In at least one respect the old rumors were true, for they have a strong minority strain of blondism and many Nordic traits, especially among those of the upper social strata. The Nurs travel infrequently, and their remote country is seldom visited by Afghans and even more rarely by foreigners.[19]

Almost all of the small but important Afghan ethnic group known as the Kizzilbash live in the city of Kabul. Their origin is no mystery; their ancestors were a garrison left in the city by the Persian conqueror Nadir Shah Afshar, somewhere around A.D. 1745. Like their leader they were of Turkish rather than Persian background; the Kizzilbash ("red head") derives from the red Haidar cap once worn by Persian soldiers to signify adherence to the Shia sect and the cause of the Caliph Ali. Afghan Amirs, recognizing the value of this cohesive group and its dissociation from Pushtoon tribal loyalties made them into a household cavalry, thus assuring their protection from religious hostilities. Today the Kizzilbash are almost exclusively urban and frequently well educated, and often hold important positions in Afghan government or trade.

The foregoing are the major Afghan ethnic groups, but there are many others. Afghan Jews are still found in the cities, although in recent years a number have left for Israel. Some Hindus and Sikhs live among their ancient enemies, mostly in southern and eastern towns or cities. There is a fairly large Arab population in northern Afghanistan, and bands of nomadic Baluchis roam in the south. None of these groups, however, have had much influence on Afghan affairs.

Any attempt to describe Afghan culture and customs in detail would be beyond the scope of this work. There are, however, certain fundamental aspects of that culture without which any understanding of Afghan history would be impossible. These are religion, tribalism, and the code of Pushtoon law known as Pushtoonwala.

Almost all Afghans are Moslems, Islam is the official creed of the country, and Islamic law, as interpreted by the system of Abu Hanifah, is the legal code. Within Afghanistan, as in other pluralistic societies of Asia, Islam has been a major unifying force, whose traditions underlie Afghan folklore, literature and customs.

Probably about 80 per cent of all Afghans are members of the Sunni sect of Islam, which accepts the legitimacy of the four Khalifa or successors of the Prophet Mohammed. Most of the rest belong to the Ithna Ashariyah division of the Shia branch of Islam, which holds that Abu Bekr, Omar, and Othman were impostors and that the spiritual authority of Mohammed passed to his son-in-law Ali and thence to a iine of imams or spiritual leaders. The Hazaras are Shia Moslems, as are the Turi Pushtoons, some clans of the Orakzai Pushtoons, and the Kizzilbash of Kabul.

This doctrinal difference, which has caused as much trouble in the lands of Islam as the controversy between Catholics and Protestants in the West, remains a divisive force in Afghanistan even though it has not produced the bloody confrontations that have occurred in other Moslem lands. Probably, however, it contributed to the hostility with which the Hazaras were regarded by their neighbors and the willingness of the Pushtoons to hold Hazara slaves; for the Pushtoons, unlike the Uzbegs, are inclined to consider the institution of slavery immoral.

The Pushtoon Afghans in particular have been described as fanatics in religion, and a number of authors from Kipling to Michener have pictured them as antagonistic or even violent toward the infidel. Without question, their attacks on British personnel stationed on the Afghan border were frequent and often fatal. Moreover, among the eastern tribes a number of mullahs or Moslem priests once owed their authority less to theological training than to a gift for inflammatory preaching, zealously promising Paradise to whoever fell on behalf of the faith. Viewed objectively, however, the Afghans' reputation for fanaticism is a vast exaggeration.

According to the occasional Christian visitors prior to the first British invasion of the country in 1839, the Afghans were among the most tolerant of Moslems. Charles Masson and Alexander Burnes wandered unharmed through the country, entering mosques, visiting holy places, and in general enjoying all the privileges that would have been granted a Moslem. And when Masson, berated by an old lady for eating during daylight hours of the month-long fast of Ramadan, explained that he was a Christian, she not only apologized but brought him more food.

Constant British pressure after 1842 provoked Afghan leaders to countermeasures that used religion as a unifying device and as a means of preventing Afghans from succumbing to promises or bribes. The British occupation of Afghan territory led to a number of attempts at assassination, some of them successful. That these were the product of nationalism rather than religious fanaticism is strongly suggested by the fact that British civilians were never their victims; in fact, a British missionary roamed for years in parts of the Afghan hills where a British officer would have been shot on sight.

During the past thirty years many foreigners have visited Afghanistan, and in the early 1960's at least four thousand were living there, employed either by the Afghan government or as members of foreign missions. The few instances of insult or injury to these people have occurred as a result of nonreligious factors. Indeed, it would almost certainly be safe to say that more injury has been done to Afghans by the visitors than vice versa.

During the partition of India, when communal violence swept the neighboring North West Frontier Province, none of the Sikh or Hindu merchants in Afghanistan met with harm, and those from India who were fortunate enough to reach the Afghan border were given sanctuary. And despite a general Afghan sympathy with Arab feelings toward Israel, the colony of Afghan Jews continues to live in safety and to conduct business as usual.

From these illustrations it may be seen how tenuously based the legend of Afghan fanaticism is in reality. By nature the Afghans are a hospitable and friendly people, willing to accept almost any sort of behavior from a foreigner, however much it may clash with Afghan customs or religious beliefs. The so-called fanaticism in the past was almost always directed at the agents of a threatening imperial power, and was mild compared to similar actions by contemporary "freedom fighters."

This is not to imply that Afghans fail to take their religion seriously. The pervasive pattern of Islam underlies much of their personal and social life, and is a unifying factor among a people of great ethnic diversity. In rural Afghanistan the rate of literacy is low, so that often the village mullah is the only person able to read or write; he not only teaches the children and officiates at marriages and funerals, but is the arbitrator of disputes. Some of these men, it is true, are more familiar with superstition than with the Koran, and are apt to mulct their followers. But many others are sincerely devoted to Islam and to works of charity, giving protection to the poor and serving as a restraint upon unruly passions.

Tribes and tribalism are important in Afghanistan particularly among the Pushtoons, whose tribes vary in organization and in the degree of loyalty they command, but are strong and even at times divisive forces in the nation. Some of these tribes are large—the Yuzufzais, Durranis, and Ghilzais each have at least a million members—and others number no more than a few thousand. Of a multitude of terms denoting subdivisions four are commonly used: The Ulus or Kaum is the entire tribe. The Khel constitutes what might be called a subtribe, whose members live in the same general area. Next comes the clan, also called Khel, whose members live close together and often hold land in common. The smallest unit, the Kor or Kahol, is a family group whose members are all related.[20]

The degree of loyalty to the tribe varies considerably. Among the Ghilzai, for example, it has been weakened by intertribal feuds and rivalries. On the other hand, the Durranis, even though they are divided into a number of subtribes and are dispersed over a wide territory, were able in the past to unite in a common cause—one reason for their hegemony over Afghanistan since its beginning as a nation.

The leaders of a tribe are known as khans or maliks—titles that are partly hereditary but can be won by outstanding individuals regardless of family. In some tribes the authority of such men is strong, and in others it is virtually nonexistent; but it is never absolute, and for any khan to adopt a policy not supported by the majority of his tribesmen would be both unusual and dangerous. Most tribal decisions are reached by a tribal Jirga or council, sometimes composed of khans, maliks, and elders, and sometimes of almost all the male members of the tribe. Some tribes, especially among the eastern Pushtoons, are so egalitarian that the decision of a Jirga is frequently defied by a tribesman supported by a numerous and powerful family.

Living with the tribes are a number of nontribesmen known as *hamsayah*—a word literally meaning "neighbor" but more exactly rendered in this connection as "client." These people have an inferior social position and take no part in tribal decisions, but they are under the protection of their hosts and any offense to them would be avenged no less stringently, or in some cases, even more so, than if they had been tribesmen.

Among the tribes and throughout Afghanistan as a whole, the most important unit is the extended family, which for any individual comprises all relatives by blood or marriage. Theoretically the oldest male is its dominant member, but in practice the position may be taken by anyone of accepted ability or position, and sometimes by a woman. Interfamily rivalries and hatreds exist, particularly in situations complicated by plural marriages and antagonistic half brothers but any instance of need places all members of a family under strong social pressure to render assistance. This includes economic necessity, and Afghans who as a result of illness, injury or any other cause cannot earn a living are certain of support by the affluent members of the extended family.

Undoubtedly the strongest determinant of the ethnic character of the Pushtoon Afghans, and an influence on non-Pushtoons to some degree, is the code of custom known as *Pushtoonwala* or the "law of the Pushtoons." It covers three separate injunctions: *nanawatai* (literally, "I have come in"), or sanctuary; *badal,* or retaliation; and *mailmasti,* or hospitality. *Nanawatai* calls for protection to be extended to anyone, even an enemy, in search of refuge, and for mediation on behalf of a person wishing to make peace with someone he has injured. Its most extreme form occurs when a woman sends her veil to a man, imploring his assistance for herself or her family; to ignore such an appeal would be almost unthinkable. *Nanawatai* is declining in importance, but is still powerful among the tribes; in 1962, for example, the Afridis, traditional guardians of the Khyber Pass, closed that important route for a time in retaliation for the arrest by his own soldiers of a Pakistani colonel who had sought refuge in an Afridi hamlet.

Badal calls for revenge or retaliation for injury or insult to oneself or to a member of one's family. The nature of this retribution varies among the tribes; in some it can be settled by money payment or the intercession of elders, and in others only personal vengeance will suffice. The variation, incidentally, is not proportionate to the sophistication of the tribesmen. The Waziris and Mahsuds, probably the fiercest of Pushtoon tribesmen, are often willing to accept a money payment, and in any event will direct their anger at the specific offender. The far more sophisticated Afridis, on the other hand, usually insist on personal revenge, and regard all members of the offender's family as equally involved.

Personal retaliation with its concomitant of blood feuds has been practiced in many places, but in few as scrupulously as among the Pushtoon Afghans. Like the concept of the extended family, it arose from the need for protection in lands where law-enforcement agencies were absent, and it still acts as a deterrent upon predatory behavior. But it also encourages feuds and enmities which may last for generations, and is one of the reasons why the Pushtoon people, for all their pride of ethnic identity, have found unity so difficult. Naturally it has declined wherever the Afghan government has established law and order, but it is still real enough that Afghans, generally even those of the urban and educated classes, take any insult, injury, or slight with extreme seriousness.

Mailmasti or hospitality, among some of the tribes, is considered almost a sacred duty. To an Afghan the person and property of a guest are inviolable, and his comfort and pleasure are the host's chief concern. Quite possibly the Afghans are the most hospitable people in the world; no one is more despised than a niggardly host, and to invite away a guest in another's house is literally a mortal insult. As a social imperative, the open-handed hospitality found throughout Afghanistan is almost absolute.

Pushtoonwala is fading as Afghanistan replaces tribal loyalty with nationalism. Nevertheless, it remains a powerful force in the behavior of Afghans, including both the non-Pushtoons who are outside its provisions and the city-dwellers who have discarded their ethnic affiliations.

No brief summary can do justice to the complexity of Afghan customs. By way of generalization, it may be said that the cultures of India, Iran, and Turan are all reflected to a degree in that of Afghanistan. The heaviest influence is that of Iran and the Middle East; somewhat less important is the culture of India, and still less so is that of the Turanians to the north. To all of the cultural patterns thus adopted the Afghans, and above all the Pushtoons, have added their unique stamp, to produce an Asian nation unlike any other.[21]

III

Ancient Afghanistan

> The Earth has her hillsides
> and her uplands, hers is
> the wide plain.
> —ATHARVAVEDA

ALTHOUGH the prehistory of the lands of the Hindu Kush, the site of modern Afghanistan, is still largely unknown, promising investigations have now been begun. That in the western part of the Iranian Plateau man has lived since far back in the Paleolithic period has been amply demonstrated. Additional investigation in the Afghan hills and valleys will probably unearth Neolithic settlements like those of Tepe Siyalk, Tepe Hissar, and Bakun in neighboring Iran.

Some authorities believe, indeed, that the domestication of animals and agriculture may have begun on the Iranian Plateau. Cattle, goats, and sheep were all native to these uplands and wild prototypes of both emmer and einkorn, the two kinds of domestic wheat, are found there most notably at altitudes between two and three thousand feet above sea level.

Concerning the Afghan past, one thing is certain: for many millenniums people have lived in high Asia, on the plateaus and around the oases of the north. From time to time groups of these, under pressure of increased population, drought, or unknown factors, have migrated—some to the west, others across the Amu Darya River, surmounting the barrier of the Hindu

Kush or avoiding it by swinging around its western flank and emerging at last on the fecund Indian plain. Little is known of this process; but at some time in the second millennium before Christ, the people known to us as Indo-Aryans moved through the valleys of Afghanistan with their cattle and their sacred Vedas.[1] Somewhat later, other peoples of the same linguistic stem entered what is now Iran, and from among them the Medes (Madai) and their kin the Persians (Parsua) settled there. The Medes, led by Cyaxares (Uvakhshatra), established a powerful empire that dominated their Persian cousins. In 612 B.C. they destroyed Nineveh; two years later they had brought the power of Assyria to an end. The Medes in their turn were overthrown by the Persians under their king Cyrus (Kurush) the Great, whose rule by 550 B.C. embraced a vast territory including what is now Afghanistan.[2]

Fortunately for later historians, Cyrus and other Achaemenid rulers were fond of counting their blessings publicly and in permanent form, and their inscriptions on rock contain the first recorded mention of the Afghan lands. On the tomb of Darius the Great at Naqsh-i-Rustum, on the rock at Behistun, and at Susa are listed the satrapies or districts into which the Achaemenid empire was divided. These included Haraiva or Aria (modern Herat), Hauravatish or Arachosia (Kandahar), Sugudu or Sogdia (the land between the Amu Darya and the Jaxartes), Chorasmia (Khiva), Bactria or Bakhtrish (the land between the Hindu Kush and the Amu Darya), Thattagush or Sattagydia (the modern Hazarajat), and Gandhara (the Jalalabad and Peshawar valleys).

Bactria, with its capital Bactra (later Balkh), was one of the most important of Achaemenid provinces. It was here, in what was known as the "land of a thousand cities," that Zarathushtra or Zoroaster lived and taught around the middle of the sixth century B.C. under the protection of Vishtaspa, at first an independent king and later a satrap in the empire of Cyprus.[3] And among the soldiers who fought at Marathon in distant Hellas were those of Bactria wearing headdresses "very much like the Median."[4]

In the year 331 B.C., the lands of Afghanistan were lit by the brief flare of a human meteor. When Alexander of Macedon defeated Darius Codomannus at Gaugamela, his troops captured the records of the Persian army. From the lists of the troops and the orders given by Darius we know that the left flank of his army was largely composed of soldiers from Afghanistan; the cavalry on the extreme left were from Bactria, and those toward the center were Arachosians and hill Indians (possibly Pushtoons).

Pushing eastward to secure the empire that was now his, Alexander entered Afghanistan near the site of modern Herat, then marched south to Sistan, east to the site of modern Kandahar, and north across the Hindu Kush to Bactria. He returned to the area around modern Kabul—bringing with him Roxanne, daughter of the satrap of Bactria as his wife—and then sent his army along the Kabul River into India, while with a picked detachment he moved through the Kunar Valley into the area of modern Swat. Of that passage little record has been preserved in the region aside from legends and the epithet, Sikander Zulqarnain, "Alexander of the two horns," signifying fortune. It is probable that both the legends and the name date only to the advent of Islam. Chiefs of Roshan, Shignan, Wakhan, Chitral, and Gilgit once claimed him as an ancestor, but this is probably no more than a tribute to his reputation.

Alexander's death in 323 B.C. brought a struggle for his empire, the eastern portion falling into the hands of his cavalry commander Seleucus Nikator, who founded what came to be known as the Seleucid dynasty. At about the same time the powerful Mauryan state was developing in northern India, with Patna as its center. With Bactria in the hands of the Seleucids, Afghanistan became the meeting place of Seleucid and Mauryan territory.

The Seleucids now attempted an experiment. Thousands of Greek colonists were persuaded or ordered to come to this distant outpost, and Greek garrisons were placed on guard against the nomads of the steppes and the Mauryans of the south and east. From the Seleucid point of view the plan was a failure: the Greeks were successful colonists, but their penchant for schism was as evident here as it had been in Europe. By the middle of the third century B.C. the Seleucid governor of Bactria, Diodotus, was asserting his independence, an action that was continued by his son and successor, Diodotus II.[5]

For over a century the native people of northern Afghanistan were subject to an independent, Greek-ruled state, usually known as Bactria, which successfully resisted Seleucid attempts to regain control. Around 187 B.C., Bactrian armies led by King Demetrius annexed Aria, Arachosia, and Zaranka. Four years later they seized Gandhara from the Mauryans, and soon afterward the capital at Patna fell to an army led by the Bactrian general Menander.

During the period of Mauryan power, Indian influences were at work in southern and eastern Afghanistan, including Buddhism, which had the strong support of Asoka (264–227 B.C.), the greatest of the Mauryan rulers. In cave monasteries hollowed out of canyon walls, thousands of Buddhist monks devoted themselves to the contemplative search for enlightenment. Buddhism remained a major religion of Afghanistan for many centuries before it was finally extirpated by Islam.

Although by 170 B.C. Bactria held extensive territory, including northern India, Sind, and Afghanistan, it collapsed no less rapidly than it had risen. Demetrius, extolled by Chaucer as "grete Emetreus, the Kynge of Inde," was killed, presumably in battle, around 167 B.C., and in typical Greek fashion, after his death the empire disintegrated into a number of quarreling states which were easy prey for nomads of the north.

The nature of the nomad hordes that destroyed Bactria is still a subject of dispute, although scholars of the past and present have outlined their movements. The first people to cross the Amu Darya were the Sakas—a branch, apparently, of the Scythian nomads who in ancient times had ruled the Eurasian steppes from the Hungary plain to Mongolia. Entering Bactria, the Sakas pushed westward but were checked by their ethnic cousins the Parthians, who had occupied Iran and established a kingdom there. Thwarted, the Sakas turned to the east and occupied a region which still bears their name, Sistan or Sakistan. From here, according to the abundant evidence of coins, they extended their control over southern Afghanistan at least as far north as Ghazni, and reached Gandhara somewhere around the beginning of the first century B.C.

The Sakas are believed to have ruled for about a century before they were overthrown by the Parthians, who had reached the peak of their power, and who apparently, shortly after the beginning of the Christian era, came by the same route that had previously been taken by the Sakas themselves.

The Parthians' rule was also brief. Somewhere around A.D. 75 they were eliminated as a power in Afghanistan and northern India by still another horde from the north, the Yueh-chi, who were ancient enemies of the Sakas. After a defeat by another powerful horde, the Hiung-nu, these latter had wandered slowly westward and southward. At the Bactrian border they halted, and it was here that Kujula Kadphises, the leader of one of five tribal groups, gained control over the entire horde. His tribe was known to the Chinese as the Gui-shang, and under its name he established what was later known to the Romans as the Kushan dynasty.

Kujula Kadphises established control over northern Afghanistan, and around A.D. 60 seized Gandhara from the Parthians. His son or grandson, Wima Kadphises, established control over all of Afghanistan, and the next and most famous of the Kushan rulers, Kanishka, seized most of northern India. Under Kanishka the Kushan kingdom became powerful, while Parthia was greatly weakened. The result was an increase of trade between Rome and Asia, now that the Parthians' hostility toward Rome no longer barred the path from Europe to the Orient.

In his capital of Purushapura (the modern Peshawar), Kanishka appears to have become a convert to Buddhism, and the religion continued to spread through the valleys of Afghanistan. It was during this period, around A.D. 150, that art in the style once known as Greco-Buddhist but now—and more properly—as Gandharan, had its flowering. Some scholars still trace the inspiration for the sculptures of this period to the Greco-Bactrian kingdom, but the prevailing opinion is that the influence came from Roman Alexandria. At any rate, the style marks a transition from Hinayana to Mahayana Buddhism, with Buddha represented as a god rather than a sage, and many of the finest pieces have been found in Afghanistan, particularly at Hadda near Jalalabad.

The causes for the collapse of the Kushans are obscure. After Kanishka their kings included Vasishka, Huvishka, and Vasuveda; but around A.D. 230 the last of these was eliminated, and with him the Kushan power in Afghanistan, by the Sassanid dynasty of Persia.

Since the fall of the Achaemenids the Persians had been in eclipse. Their resurgence was led by Ardishir, a Persian vassal of the Parthians, who rebelled and decisively defeated his former rulers in a battle at Hormuz around A.D. 226. Ardishir then turned to the east; Bactria, Arachosia, and Gandhara were added to his dominions. There is some evidence that he invaded India and reached Sirhind; but according to Ferishta, he was persuaded to retire by the offer of an enormous tribute in gold, jewels, and elephants.[6]

For about two centuries Sassanid power was dominant in Afghanistan, although the Persians probably ruled there through the petty Kushan kings who had become their vassals. Then around A.D. 425 another horde appeared from the north: a people known as the Epthalites or "white Huns," whose record was written almost entirely with the sword and who left little else for the enlightenment of posterity.

The Epthalites first appear as vassals and allies of the Avars in Zungaria, although Chinese sources indicate that they originated somewhere north of China. Breaking away from the Avars they migrated west into the lands north of the Amu Darya and then turned south into what is now Afghanistan. After extending their control over that territory they conquered northern India, and from a center that was either at Badghis, close to Herat, or in Badakshan, they waged frequent and often successful wars with Sassanid Persia. But in the end they were defeated by the Persians under Khusrau I Anushirvan, in alliance with the Turks, to disappear from history as precipitately as they had entered it.[7]

This final defeat of the Epthalites, around A.D. 568, marks a historic turning point in the region of the Hindu Kush. From it the Epthalites, Kushans, Sakas, and Parthians have all vanished as peoples, and no Afghan can say with certainty that any of them were his ancestors. A number of people in Badakshan claim to be descended from the Epthalites, although whether they are is uncertain to say the least. But in view of their numbers, none of these ancient peoples can have vanished altogether, and they are unquestionably the progenitors of many modern Afghans and perhaps even of whole ethnic groups. For this reason their ethnic and racial composition and their linguistic affiliations are of importance to the historian.

The Parthians and Sakas were almost certainly branches of the Scythian stem, and more particularly of that offshoot whose members remained above the Jaxartes, while the others, so well known to Greek historians, were migrating to the Pontic steppes. It is generally conceded that they were Caucasians, whose language was of the Iranian family.

Controversy over the racial origin of the Epthalites and Kushans continues. Some scholars maintain that the Kushan rulers, at least, were Turko-Mongols, but the prevailing opinion is that they were yet another branch of the Scythians. The Epthalites undoubtedly considered themselves Huns and were so considered by other people of the time; moreover, Soviet archaeologists have concluded that the Avars, with whom they were long associated, were predominantly Mongoloid. On the other hand, the Byzantine historian Procopius specifically referred to them as the only Huns "who have white bodies and countenances that are not ugly." [8] Quite probably W. W. Tarn approached the truth of the matter when he pointed out that every great horde must have been a "racial mixture."

The story of Afghanistan after the disappearance of the Epthalites is concerned with peoples who still exist as definite entities. For over a century the country was again dominated by the Persian Sassanids, while the Turks continued to move into the lands north of the Amu Darya, known ever since as Turkestan. Sassanid control appears to have been exercised through a kind of feudalism, and to have been limited further by a number of petty kings, of Turkish, Kushan, or Epthalite background, whose rule over small principalities was virtually independent.

One of the minarets of Herat, built in the fifteenth century by the Timuride princes.

Sabuktigin, who claimed descent from Yazdigird, last of the Sassanids—although, as his chronicler diplomatically put it, "only Allah knows the truth."

Whatever his lineage, Sabuktigin was a man of ability who dropped all pretense of ruling as a Samanid vassal, and who after twenty years had extended his control over much of Afghanistan, establishing what was known as the Ghaznawi dynasty. He was followed in 997 by a son, Ismail, and two years later by another son, the celebrated Mahmud.

Sultan Mahmud, the "image-breaker," and one of the most popular of all Moslem kings, led seventeen successful raids into India, earning both his title and the mountains of loot with which he decorated his capital. He surrounded himself with all the wit and wisdom of Islam, and it was at his behest that Firdausi composed the *Shah-Nama,* the Moslem epic. In apprehension, the distant Caliph gave Mahmud the titles of Yamin-ud-daulat ("right arm of the state") and Amir-ul-Millat ("leader of the faithful"). He was the greatest military captain of the time, and his capital at Ghazni was resplendent with marble palaces when the London of Edward and Harold was no more than a muddy village.[11]

A splendid site for a robber warlord, but less so for the capital of an empire, Ghazni declined after Mahmud's death in A.D. 1030. After a century it became involved in a war with Ghor, another mushroom state that had emerged in the mountains of western Afghanistan. The outcome was a terrible sack in A.D. 1149, which earned Ala-ud-din, the Ghori king, the title of Jehan-suz ("world-burner").

Ghor replaced Ghazni as the paramount power in Afghanistan until A.D. 1215, when it was conquered by Mohammed Shah, ruler of the Khwarizm Shahs from across the Amu Darya. The Ghoris apparently were an Iranian people, probably Tadjiks, whereas the Ghaznawis had been Turks even though their armies were largely made up of Afghans. Ghor's chief exploit was in the north of India, where Muiz-ud-din Mohammed Ghori and his general, Kutb-ud-din Aibak, established Moslem rule. Thus in a sense the vanished conqueror is the ancestor of

Pakistan.[12] For a long time the location of the Ghori capital, Firozkoh ("turquoise mountain"), was unknown, but it has recently been established with some certainty.

The Khwarizm Shahs, who ended Ghori rule in Afghanistan, were a remnant of the empire of the Seljuk Turks. Established in the oasis once known as Khwarizm and today as Khiva, they won out against another remnant of the Seljuk empire, with its center at Merv, and against the Khitans, who were originally from Manchuria and who ruled a kingdom in Kashgar known as the Kara Khitai.

This time the outcome was catastrophe. At the zenith of its power, the empire of the Khwarizm Shahs was overrun by an avalanche of destruction—the Mongol horsemen of Genghis Khan. This most brutal of all nomad invasions annihilated the armies of the Khwarizm Shahs, totally destroyed their cities, and left a wilderness behind. It was at this time, interestingly enough, that one last homeless, desperate detachment of the army of the Khwarizm Shahs ranged far to the west and came close to destroying the ancient city of Jerusalem

After his conquest of the lands north of the Amu Darya, Genghis Khan moved into Bactria, ravaging that prosperous territory to a degree from which it has never recovered. After Mutukin, the conqueror's favorite grandson, was killed under the walls of Bamian, the enraged Mongol destroyed every person in the valley surrounding it. From here an advance force of thirty thousand Mongol riders moved south toward Ghazni, where Jelal-ud-din, the son of the last of the Khwarizm Shahs, had raised a force of Afghan tribesmen. Here, unexpectedly, the Mongols were defeated. It was one of the few setbacks in their whirlwind triumph.

The defeat brought Genghis Khan himself to the scene, where Jelal-ud-din won the admiration of the Mongol general by a leap into a river as he fled to India. There and in Persia he continued a romantic career. Genghis himself halted at the Indus, after being warned by a unicorn, according to a Mongol account, against proceeding further—a development which, if true, would have justified India in adopting this mythical monster as its national emblem. It is more likely that Genghis feared the heat of the Indian plains and its effect upon his northern riders.[13]

For some time Afghanistan remained at least nominally under Mongol control. In A.D. 1247 Mangu Khan, a grandson of Genghis, appointed as governor of Herat a Ghori noble, Shams-ud-din, who seized the opportunity offered by the decline of Mongol strength in Persia to establish a new dynasty. Called the Kurt, it ruled the territory around Herat for almost a century.[14]

The year 1336 brought the greatest of the Turkish conquerors Timur-i-Leng or Tamerlane ("iron limper"). Timur, known to the East as the "Lord of the fortunate conjunction," was a chief of the Gurkan clan of the Barlas Turks, who lived north of the Amu Darya. After he had succeeded in uniting the Turkish tribes he began a career of conquest equaling that of Genghis Khan. Unlike the Mongol, Timur had an interest in art and culture, although admittedly he never allowed it to interfere with his passion for war.

His conquest of Afghanistan was carried out with difficulty. There was no scope for his genius as a tactician among the hills, and he found some of the tribes, particularly the Kafirs, impossible to subdue. In 1397 leaving a grandson, Pir Mohammed, in charge at Kabul, he pushed on to India and its easier targets, defeating the Indian armies with ease and leaving Delhi so ravaged that "for two months not a bird moved its wing."

Timur then returned to adorn his capitals at Samarkand and Bokhara with buildings constructed by Indian slaves and furnished with the spoils of their country. Directing his attention to the west and north, he continued his victories. At the climax of his career he defeated Bayezid, the "thunderbolt," the hitherto invincible Sultan of the Ottoman Turks. Timur's death in 1404 left his empire to Pir Mohammed.[15]

Following the pattern of its predecessors, by the end of the fifteenth century this sprawling state had become a jumble of squabbling principalities, each ruled by a descendant of Timur. From among these conspiring kinfolk appeared in 1483 another leader of genius in the person of Mohammed Zahir-ud-din, better known as Baber, "the tiger." A fourteenth-generation descendant from Genghis Khan as well as a fifth-generation one from Timur-i-Leng, Baber for a while seemed destined to reunite the Timuride Empire; but his attempt was finally blocked by the coming of the last of the nomad migrations from central Asia. Shortly before 1500 the Uzbegs, a Turkish people, began moving southward toward the Amu Darya. In 1503, with all hope lost, Baber with a small group of companions crossed the Hindu Kush, and "in the last ten days of the second Rabi without a fight, without an effort, by Almighty God's bounty and mercy, I obtained and made subject to me Kabul and Ghazni and their dependent districts." [16]

Baber was followed to Kabul by a restless band of "begs and braves" eager for action. In order to provide it, and also because one of his ancestry could hardly do otherwise, Baber led a series of campaigns against the Afghan tribes and against his remaining Timuride relatives. Finally he took his warriors to India, and in 1525 he defeated the Sultan of Delhi, who was an Afghan from the Lodi tribe. On April 27 of that year, when Baber's name was read in the great mosque of Delhi as Padishah, what was inaccurately called the Moghul dynasty had begun.

Baber died in 1530, and at his request his body was taken back to Kabul and buried "in the pleasantest place in the neighborhood." The simple tomb of this most amiable of Asian conquerors is there still, and bears the epitaph:

> A king from whose brow shone the light of God
> Was Zahir-ud-din Mohammed Baber Padishah.

The Moghul dynasty in India had its beginning almost simultaneously with the Saffawi dynasty of Persia; in fact, Baber and its dour founder, Shah Ismail, were well acquainted. For two centuries these dynasties were neighbors, rising to greatness and then declining at almost the same time. Relations between them were fairly stable despite the strain occasioned by the prevalence of the Shia creed in Persia and of the Sunni at the court of the Moghuls.

During this period Afghanistan was a buffer state once again, with Kabul in Moghul hands and Herat in those of the Saffawis. Kandahar, on the line between the two, changed hands several times. It was seized in 1595 by the Moghul Akbar, recovered in 1622 by Shah Abbas, recaptured by Shah Jehan in 1637, and in 1649 recovered by the Persians.

During this era of Moghul-Saffawi dominance, new forces began to stir in Afghanistan as the hitherto mutually antagonistic Pushtoon tribes for the first time made tentative attempts to unite. The first step in this direction was taken by the Yuzufzais in 1667. It was continued in 1672 by the Afridis who were joined by the Khattaks, Sherannis, and Ghilzai in claiming complete independence. Together they annihilated several Moghul armies, and they coined money in the name of their "king," Akmal Khan. They did, indeed, have all the attributes of sovereignty except unity. As soon as Aurungzeb, the Moghul ruler, put down the steel and seized the silver sword, the movement collapsed in a welter of internal treachery.

The next surge of Pushtoon power took place in Kandahar, where the Saffawis' declining power was in the hands of a Georgian prince, Shah Nawaz (Giorgi XI of Kartli)—whom Afghans describe as the "seed of Satan and a ravager of the people." In 1709 the Ghilzai, led by Mir Wais, chief of the Hotaki clan, descended from their northern strongholds, killed governor and garrison, and seized the city. At about the same time the Abdalis, another Pushtoon tribe, captured the city of Herat.

From these events the weakness of the Saffawis was obvious, Soon hosts of Ghilzai horsemen were making raids into Persia, looting, plundering, and meeting only feeble resistance. On one such expedition Mahmud, son of Mir Wais, with half-insane audacity led his troops to the very walls of the Saffawi capital at Isfahan. Here, to the astonishment even of Mahmud, the impotent Shah, Sultan Hussein, surrendered his throne to the invader.

Afghan rule at Isfahan was short. The Ghilzai were few and far from home; they were bitterly hated by the Shia Persians, as much for their creed as for their cruelty. The growing madness of their leader finally led to his murder by his own men and his replacement by a cousin, Ashraf. The new king was "modest and brave," but the damage had been done; after a defeat at

Zargan in 1730, the surviving Ghilzai fled to their death in the deserts of Baluchistan.

The hero of the Persian recovery was a certain Nadir Quli, "slave of the wonderful," who is known to history as Nadir Shah Afshar. An erstwhile bandit and the son of a shepherd of the Afshar tribe of Turks in northern Iran, Nadir legitimized his early career by becoming a soldier and rising to the command of the army of Tahmasp Mirza, son of the shah who had surrendered to the Ghilzai. Soon after the defeat of the Afghans, Nadir transferred the royal mantle from Tahmasp's shoulders to his own; for, as his chronicler put it, "the only shrine at which he worshiped was ambition."

After becoming shah, Nadir began a series of brilliant campaigns which have earned him the title of the Persian Napoleon, although in fact the Corsican might no less fittingly be called the French Nadir. Kandahar and Kabul fell before him in 1738; he then set out for India, where he defeated the enormous Moghul army with ridiculous ease. Loaded with the portable wealth of India, including the Peacock Throne, he returned home to an unending series of successful campaigns against the Sindi Amirs, the Ottoman Turks, and the Uzbegs of Bokhara. Always of a suspicious nature, however, he became increasingly paranoid and in 1747 fell beneath the scimitars of his own officers, the victim of a plot for which his own sadism was largely responsible. With his death the story of the nation of Afghanistan begins.[17]

IV

Ahmed Shah Baba

> The Rocks of Hind are pearls; the
> Rivers are wine; the Mountains are
> musk, but the People are pigeons.
> —AFGHAN SAYING

THE death of Nadir Shah, with which Afghanistan as a nation began, was an ominous portent. The Persian conqueror had speeded the disintegration of the Moghuls; but for all his ability, to which his rule gave ample testimony, he had not succeeded in establishing a new and powerful Persian state. On the contrary, the favored troops in his army, and those upon whom he most relied, had been Turkomen and Afghans. This, added to his cruelty, was one more cause for the hatred the Persians bore him.

At the time of Nadir's death, the elite guard of the Shah were a body of horsemen from the Abdali Afghan tribe, who had served him faithfully since the beginning of his career. On hearing of their leader's murder these Afghans forced their way into Nadir's tent to view his body. Apparently fighting erupted between the Afghans and the Persians and continued until the Afghans broke off and galloped for home, calling back curses on their former comrades.

As the Abdalis moved up the road past Herat they spread the news, calling for the chiefs of the seven Abdali subtribes to gather at Kandahar, which lay ahead of them. For they realized

clearly that the opportunity was at hand to further the interests
of the Abdalis and to organize a state. Their powerful rivals the
Ghilzai were still recovering from their ill-fated Persian adventure, and from the mauling they had received at the hands
of Nadir Shah. No danger was to be feared from the crumbling
Moghuls in India or the chaos in Persia. And after serving
under the iron discipline enforced by Nadir in all his campaigns, the Abdalis knew themselves to be masters of the art of
war.

At the shrine of Sheikh Surkh, near Kandahar, their chiefs
now met to elect a king. This was no easy process. For a time it
appeared that Pushtoon nationalism would be wrecked by
tribal jealousies, since each of the chiefs was willing to advance
his own candidacy but unwilling to support any other. Seven
meetings were held without decision. At the eighth, however,
Sabir Shah, a noted dervish, got to his feet. "Why all this ver-
bose talk?" he said. "God has created Ahmed Khan a much
greater man than all of you. He is of the most noble of Afghan
families. Maintain, therefore, God's work for His wrath will
weigh heavily on you if you destroy it."

The sirdars thereupon unanimously chose Ahmed Khan the
first king of the Afghans. Then Sabir Shah built a mound of
earth saying, "This is your throne," plaited a circlet of wheat
straw, and placed it on Ahmed's head, saying, "This is your
crown." [1]

At the time of his coronation Ahmed Shah was twenty-three.
His father, Mohammed Zeman Khan, had been the leader of the
Saddozai, the head clan of the Popolzais, and had been in exile
in Multan when Ahmed was born. At the age of fourteen
Ahmed had been captured by Nadir Shah, who was much impressed by the young Afghan's ability and had made him a
captain of the royal guard.

For all his personal merits and the prestige of his family,
Ahmed was still extremely young to be selected by the age-
revering Afghans. Although the Saddozai were the most hon-
ored of all the Abdali clans, they were not numerous, nor were
the subtribe of the Popolzais, which they headed, and who
totaled about twenty thousand. The Barukzais were by far the

largest of the Abdali subtribes; thus since basic Afghan loyalties
are always to the immediate unit, the most powerful Abdali
sirdar was Haji Jemal Khan, the chief of the head Barukzai clan,
the Mohammedzais.

In fact, not less than to his own personality and the prestige
of his family, the selection of Ahmed Khan was undoubtedly
due to the relative weakness of his own tribe. Willing to accept
a chief who might lead them to glory and power, the Abdali
leaders were unwilling to accept a despot. They chose Ahmed
as king in order not to lose too much of their personal power; in
short they were setting up a kind of feudalism rather than a
centralized state.

The personality and ability of Ahmed Shah fortunately compensated for the weakness of his position. Also the young king
was lucky. Soon after his coronation a huge caravan loaded with
revenue from the Punjab lumbered into Kandahar. The
caravan leader, Taqi Khan Akhtabeghi, one of Nadir Shah's
Persianized Turks, who had heard nothing of Nadir's death, was
promptly relieved of the treasure by Ahmed Shah.[2] Out of this
tribute, Ahmed was able to pay the trained soldiers who had
served with him in Nadir's army. He also used the money in
judicious bribes to calm the supicions of outlying chiefs.

The young king then attempted to organize his new nation,
on the Persian model, with allowances for Afghan temperament
and custom. He assigned Abdali chiefs to important posts, and
set up a royal council consisting of the eight most powerful
Abdali sirdars, whom he thereafter consulted on all major ques-
tions and whose advice he usually followed.[3] His aim was to
govern as "first among equals," and though this concept of government was rare in Asia, it proved successful.

As a rule Ahmed favored the Abdalis and tended to treat the
royal clan of the Saddozais as sacrosanct. But he was also careful
to conciliate the other Pushtoon tribes, offering them kinship
and equality with his own tribe in return for their loyalty. It
was he who changed the tribal name of the Abdalis to the one
by which they have been known ever since: Durrani, "of the
pearls." Reputedly he did so because of a dream, although the
name may simply have originated from the pearl earrings that

had been worn by the royal guard of Nadir Shah, which Ahmed had led.

Ahmed was astute enough to recognize that the individualism of the tribes was too strong to permit any truly central authority to be established. Indeed, much of the internal history of Afghanistan from his time down to the present has consisted of the struggle of the central government against tribalism. Once he had set up an embryonic Afghan state, Ahmed Shah looked about for ways to preserve it. He was aware that he had a talent for war and a people who appreciated such ability; he knew the weakness and the wealth of his neighbors, and he saw the wisdom of directing the restless energies of his subjects toward an exterior target. He made his first move toward the city of Kabul, to the north. Here Nasir Khan, a Persian mercenary, was acting as governor in the name of the dead Nadir Shah. Nasir had served both the Moghuls and Nadir faithfully despite a chronically deficient salary—no great matter in any event—and he now refused Ahmed's demand for surrender. Instead he raised a mixed force of Hazaras and Ghilzai to defend the city.

But unfortunately for Nasir, the Ghilzai and the Hazaras disliked each other more than they did the Durranis; and they made only a feeble resistance against the trained soldiers from the south. Kabul's Persian garrison of Kizzilbash were another story; but they too preferred the relatively civilized Durranis as their prospective rulers, and accordingly surrendered on a promise of equal status. Nasir Khan fled toward India, pursued by a body of Durrani horsemen who succeeded in capturing the fugitive's considerable harem. When the news reached Nasir Khan that his women and children had been treated with kindness, he returned and offered his submission to Ahmed Shah. The Afghan army then occupied Peshawar without opposition.

By this time the Moghul Empire was close to disintegration. After Aurungzeb, the Moghul shahs had carried on the dissipations of their predecessors but had lost the ability to withstand their effects. Kings and courtiers devoted much of their time and ingenuity to new and ever more exotic vices, with an occasional interlude of conspiracy—Shia against Sunni, the Persian party against the Turanian party, or brother against brother.

Traitors at the Moghul court kept Ahmed Shah up to date on conditions at Delhi. One of these was Shahnawaz Khan, Moghul governor of the Punjab. When he sent the Afghan invitation to invade India, Ahmed needed little urging. In December 1748 an Afghan army made up primarily of Durrani horsemen galloped out of Peshawar and raced toward Lahore. Meanwhile, for some unknown reason Shahnawaz Khan had changed his mind; and when the Afghans reached the Chenab River they found the Moghuls in their path. For two days the armies faced each other; on the third night the Afghans quietly moved up the stream, forded it, and ignoring the Moghuls, made for Lahore. It fell without opposition, but this did not save it from a fierce and bloody sack. After a feeble try at rescue, Shahnawaz Khan fled for Delhi with his soldiers leading the way.

Meanwhile the aged Moghul emperor, Mohammed Shah, had sent the main Moghul army under the command of his son, another Ahmed Shah, to relieve the original defenders. With what remained of Shahnawaz Khan's troops, it met the Afghans near Sirhind. Here, on March 11, 1748, the Afghans—whose total number was less than half that of the Moghul host—had the advantage, up until a soldier accidentally ignited the power train. The ensuing explosion killed hundreds of Ahmed Shah's Afghans, forcing him to withdraw his forces. He did so in good order, and the Moghuls did not pursue.

Cheered by this solitary triumph after a lifetime of defeat, Mohammed Shah died not long afterward. His son, the Moghul Ahmed Shah, whose accession to the throne came partly as a result of this purely fortuitous victory, proved to be weaker than his father. In the winter of 1749 the Afghan army once again crossed the Indus, and this time Ahmed Shah took especial precautions with his gunpowder. The new Punjab governor, Muin-ul-mulk, who marched to meet them, sent to Delhi for aid, and was ordered to treat with the invaders, offering the Punjab in exchange for peace. Satisfied, Ahmed Shah returned to Afghanistan richer by a province without losing a man.

After this success in the east, the Afghan king turned toward the west. In the fall of 1750, with an army of about 25,000 that included a force of Baluchis under their chief Nasir Kahn (a different man from the ex-governor of Kabul), Ahmed marched on Herat. This city, where Ahmed had spent his boyhood, was nominally under the control of Shah Rukh, a grandson of Nadir Shah, who from his capital at Meshed maintained a feeble rule based mainly on his grandfather's reputation. The real power in Herat belonged to Mir Alim Khan, an Arab chief of Sistan, who was represented by the governor, Mohammed Amir Khan.

It was the latter who replied to Ahmed Shah's demand for surrender by closing the city gates. Since the Afghan army consisted entirely of cavalry they were now in a dilemma; for Ahmed Shah, brilliant though he was as a tactician and cavalry leader, had no training in siege attack. It was his good fortune, however, that many of the city's garrison were Durranis, who soon induced the recalcitrant governor to yield.

Moving on to Meshed after this easy triumph, Ahmed found more walls, this time manned by hostile Persians. Accepting a hollow promise of allegiance from Shah Rukh, the Afghans then rode to Nishapur, at the time a rich and important city. Here they found not only more walls but a bitter winter as well. Somewhat foolishly, Ahmed persisted in a futile siege, while his men starved and shivered in the barren fields, until February when what remained of the army straggled back to the shelter of Herat. For the rest of the winter Ahmed remained there, re-cruiting a new force from among the Durrani tribesmen and the Chahar-Aimak to the north, and attempting to strengthen his weak artillery by the casting of a huge cannon, which fired a projectile weighing 472 pounds.

Early in the spring of 1751 the Afghan army again advanced on Nishapur, where the citizens were now less inclined to resist because the attack had come during the spring planting. They were further disheartened by the noise of the great cannon—which discharged one shot and then promptly burst. The city surrendered no less promptly, all unaware that the Afghans were once again in the midst of technical difficulties.

From Nishapur the Afghan king rode back to Meshed. He gladly left the once prosperous land of Khurasan, since it had now been so ravaged that booty was negligible. But he was enticed by the weakness of Shah Rukh—who for his own part was willing to promise anything in order to be left in peace, and readily ceded the provinces of Torbad, Bakhaz, and Khaff to Ahmed, with a promise to coin money in the name of the Afghan king.

Satisfied with this conclusion to a series of campaigns that had added little to his glory, Ahmed set out for Kandahar. Before leaving Herat he sent a force commanded by one Beghi Khan to the north of the Hindu Kush, where it made an attack upon the scattered Uzbeg khanates. In this way Maimana, Andkhui, Balkh, Bamian, and Badakshan were all seized with only token opposition. They agreed to accept governors loyal to Ahmed Shah, who in most instances were the same khans who had ruled them before. An especially important victory was the one over Sultan Shah, the Uzbeg khan of Badakshan, since it gained for the Afghans a shirt of the Prophet Mohammed, once the property of Bokhara. To this day it remains Afghanistan's most sacred relic, and rests in a special shrine at Kandahar.

Ahmed's invasion of Khurasan had been a side issue; Afghan aspirations, then as now, were primarily directed toward the east, and by December 1751 the Afghan army was already back in the profitable Punjab. Ahmed's reason for this invasion, if indeed one were needed, was that the revenue promised to him under the previous treaty had not been paid.

This time the Afghans met with difficulty. The Moghul commander, Muin-ul-mulk, was one of the few leaders of his own time and place who had courage and determination, and for four months he stoutly held out in the city of Lahore. The siege continued while sickness and starvation ravaged the city, and the Afghans raided the surrounding countryside. When at last Lahore surrendered, Ahmed Shah sent a mission to Delhi demanding the cession of the Punjab under threat of further invasion.

The Mogul Shah had neither the courage nor the means to resist, and in April 1752, he formally yielded to Ahmed's demand. Meanwhile, a unit of the Afghan army commanded by a

Durrani sirdar, Abdullah Khan, had ridden north into Kashmir; and as the Punjab fell to Afghanistan, he had no trouble in seizing that beautiful province.

For the next four years the Afghan monarch remained in Kandahar, attempting to organize a country that had grown into an empire. Within Afghanistan the tribes were sated with the wealth that the conquests had brought them, as well as somewhat weakened by the loss of some of their bravest men—as a result not so much of enemy action as of the cholera and dysentery that were inevitable to any military campaign at that time. In the Punjab the Afghan king made no attempt to rule directly or to incorporate the Punjabis as he had the Pushtoons. He appointed his old adversary, Muin-ul-mulk, as governor, and so long as the revenues kept flowing to the north he was satisfied.

When Muin-ul-mulk died in 1753, he was replaced by one of his widows, Mughlani Begum, who to attain such a post in a Moslem land must have been a woman of outstanding ability. But her sex suggested an easy target so far as the Moghuls were concerned; never reconciled to the loss of their richest province, in 1755 they retook the Punjab and deposed its lady governor. In answer to Mughlani Begum's call for help, Ahmed was back in November 1756; this time, ignoring the Punjab, he marched straight for Delhi. The Moghuls offered no opposition, and lives were saved thereby; but the capital suffered its worst sack since the time of Timur. For a month the Afghans prowled the streets, taking whatever they fancied in the way of gold and women. Ahmed Shah, with preoccupations of his own, made no attempt to halt these ravages, and it is doubtful whether he could have done so if he had tried.

For a time Ahmed contemplated emulating Baber, and making Delhi the center of his empire. The marriage of the niece of the Moghul Shah to Ahmed's son Timur was arranged, and the Afghan monarch added a daughter of Mohammed Shah to his harem. Coins were struck in Ahmed's name, and the khutba read in Delhi mosques proclaimed him emperor. But his plans were altered as the heat of the Indian summer brought an epidemic of cholera which decimated the Afghan army and as

Ahmed Shah, like most Afghans, found the humid heat of the Indian lowlands unbearable, he decided to withdraw to Afghanistan, leaving Delhi in the charge of Najib-ud-daula, the Moghul Nawab of Oudh and one of the many quislings at the Moghul court. Timur Mirza, Ahmed's eleven-year-old son, was named the Afghan viceroy of the Punjab, with a Barukzai sirdar, Jehan Khan, actually in command.

But at this time any sort of stability in India was an impossibility. The power vacuum left by the collapse of Moghul authority had not only brought on the Afghan invasions but had also opened the way for a resurgence of Hinduism. In the Punjab the Sikhs began to grow stronger; further to the south, the Marathas began to look northward. At this time the latter had firm control over the Deccan from their capital at Poona. They had changed greatly from their ways as simple bandits in the time of their founder, Shivaji Bhonsle, and now formed a powerful and aggressive state under the rule of the Peshwas, their kings.

When Ahmed Shah returned to Afghanistan in 1757, a body of Maratha raiders commanded by Raghunath Rao, a brother of the Peshwa, were approached near Delhi by several Moghul nobles, who apparently preferred the rule of Maratha Hindus to that of Afghan Moslems—or perhaps were moved solely by personal ambition. At any rate, the Maratha army advanced to Lahore, drove Timur Mirza and Jehan Khan from the country, and appointed Adina Beg Khan, one of the Moghuls who had worked with them, as governor of the Punjab. After collecting their usual *chauth* or tribute, they turned toward Delhi, and drove out Najib-ud-daula, the Afghan viceroy.

Ahmed Shah soon received messengers on horseback from Najib-ud-daula and Jehan Khan telling of the trouble in India. To the former he replied: "I am engaged this year in this country because on one side of me Nasir Khan has rebelled, while Darwesh Ali Khan of Herat has risen in revolt on the other. God willing, when I am free from the entanglement in this country, I will return and settle your business." [4]

The rebellion of Darwesh Ali Khan was a minor matter and quickly settled; the defection of Nasir Khan was more serious.

Nasir was the Khan of Kalat and the paramount chief of the Baluchis—a bold and able warrior whose cavalry had served in the van of the Afghan army from the beginning. Now, however, "the knife of ambition had cut the cord of loyalty"; renouncing allegiance to Ahmed Shah, he had declared himself an independent sovereign—a step that had a certain justice, since the Baluchis were not Pushtoons.

Ahmed Shah was not eager to enter the deserts of Baluchistan or to attack the elusive and propertyless Baluchis; but as a feudal ruler he was obliged to punish any breach of fidelity. Accordingly, a force of Durrani cavalry under the command of Ahmed's Wazir, Shah Wali Khan, was sent against the rebels.

Nasir Khan, having fought alongside these invaders for years, was not impressed. With a levy of troops from the Baluchi tribes he met the Afghans at Mastung, about seventy miles north of Kalat, and won a complete victory. This brought Ahmed Shah and the main Afghan army to the scene, whereupon Nasir Khan retreated behind the walls of Kalat, which had been carefully provisioned. Nasir's intimate acquaintance with Ahmed's weaknesses served him well; the Afghan army fretted before the walls in a futile search for forage in the barren countryside. In the treaty that was finally negotiated, Nasir Khan renewed his pledge of fidelity to Ahmed, agreeing to provide troops for foreign adventures and to protect Afghanistan from invasion, but stipulating that they were not to be used in Afghan domestic quarrels. Nasir Khan was also absolved from the payment of the yearly tribute—a condition that was perhaps the real object of his revolt.

Once these internal troubles were put down, Ahmed Shah once again directed his attention toward India. Realizing that the campaign against the Marathas would be more serious than any he had yet attempted, he issued a call to Jehad—holy war. A large army came flocking to his standard: Durranis and Ghilzai; the tribes of the east; Baluchis, Chahar-Aimaks, and Kizzilbash.

With a host estimated at sixty thousand horsemen and an infantry made up of many thousands of hillmen, all armed with matchlocks and long knives, Ahmed Shah in August 1759 advanced from Peshawar toward Lahore. Sabaji Bhonsle, the city's

Maratha commander, immediately withdrew and joined another Maratha general, Dattaji Sindhia, who was besieging a Moghul force at Shukartal.

On January 9, 1760, the Afghans forded the Jumna and attacked. After a brisk battle in which Dattaji Sindhia was killed, the Marathas retreated southward to join still another Maratha army near Delhi. The combined forces returned, only to be defeated in another battle, the survivors of which fled to the Deccan.

The Peshwa or Maratha ruler raged as the fugitives arrived; it was now plain that only the Afghans barred Maratha domination of India. Word was sent to all the Maratha chiefs to gather for a great crusade, and thousands of wiry riders spurred their ponies to the muster.

Sadashiv Rao, known as the Bhao, the ablest and haughtiest of Maratha generals, was in actual command of the host, although its nominal leader was Vishvas Rao, the Peshwa's sixteen-year-old heir. There were rumors that the latter was to mount the Moghul throne at Delhi. Probably the most valuable of the troops was a contingent of sixteen thousand free companions, armed and trained in the European fashion, and commanded by Ibrahim Khan Gardi, a Moslem soldier of fortune. Gardi had worked for the French general Bussy and had carefully studied French drill and tactics. His men were armed with muskets and bayonets and were well drilled. As a renegade Moslem, incidentally, Gardi was especially detested by Ahmed Shah and the Afghans.

As news of the Maratha onslaught sped northward, Ahmed Shah sought for allies. Many of the Moghuls and Rohillas joined him, including Shuja-ud-daula and thirty thousand soldiers from Oudh. The size of the opposing armies can only be conjectured, however, for though there were chroniclers in plenty, their reports show more flare for metaphor than mathematical accuracy. The probable number of fighting men on each side was about eighty thousand. But the Marathas were followed by mountains of baggage and a multitude of noncombatants, including the wives and children of the officers; this was a considerable departure from the customs of the Maratha founder, Shivaji Bhonsle, who had made it an offense punishable by death to bring a woman to a Maratha camp.

The Maratha host met no opposition as it lumbered north, although the Bhao alienated some of his Hindu adherents by his arrogance. A serious loss was the defection of Suraj Mal and thirty thousand Moslem-hating Jats. Suraj Mal's suggestion that the Marathas follow their traditional skirmishing tactics was contemptuously rejected by the Bhao. The rejection caused Suraj Mal to leave with his Jats, commenting as he did so that if the Bhao won he would probably make the Jats wash his loincloth.

Reaching Delhi, the Marathas occupied the city without meeting resistance. As the monsoons waned the Marathas moved to Sirhind, where they cut the Afghan line of communications. At the fortress of Kunjpura, an Afghan stronghold staffed by Rohillas (Afghans resident in India), the Maratha cannon breached the walls of the fort, and the defenders were slaughtered to a man. As a later chronicler mordantly noted, Ahmed Shah "expressed regret but no benefit came to those who had fallen." Actually the taking of Kunjpura proved the Marathas' undoing; for while they were dividing the treasure gathered in the fort, the Afghans had crossed the flooded river about twenty miles north of Delhi, placing themselves squarely across the Marathas' line of retreat. The Bhao immediately fell back upon the village of Panipat, where he pitched an enormous camp surrounded by a sixty-foot moat. The Afghans followed suit a few miles away, and the two opponents settled down to a vigilant wait.

Very quickly it became apparent that the chatter of the goatherd Surat Mal had not been empty. The Maratha host and its two hundred thousand camp followers soon ran short of provisions, and pestilence stalked the camp. The Afghans were in better shape; they had few followers, and thanks to the exertions of Ahmed Shah, who rode fifty miles a day, they were able to block all the Marathas' attempts at foraging.

The extended negotiations between the two armies, each of them conscious that defeat would mean destruction, were prolonged by the intransigence of the Rohilla Afghan leader Najib-ud-daula, who hated the Marathas for ravishing his homeland and for the massacre of his men at Kunjpura. Finally, on January 6, 1761, the Bhao wrote to a Hafiz Rahmat Khan, who had been acting as intermediary: "The Cup is now full to the brim and cannot hold another drop. If anything can be done, do it, or else answer me plainly at once; hereafter there will be no time for writing or speaking." [5]

In the dark of the early morning of January 13, 1761, the Bhao, "with the waters risen above his head," gave the order for battle. Each of the Marathas, who for two days had been without food, left one end of his turban hanging loose and painted his face with saffron as a sign that he meant to conquer or die. From the tents they had left behind came the crying of frightened women and bewildered, sleepy children.

The Afghans were at first unaware of the Maratha movement. As soon as his scouts galloped in with the news, Ahmed Shah rode out, without changing his sleeping robes, to learn whether the Marathas planned to attack or to retreat toward Delhi. As the dawn began to break, he could see the long lines of soldiery and hear the sound of conches and drums. Unhurried, he roused the Afghan camp and prepared the order of battle.

The two armies faced each other along a front extending for nearly eight miles. The Maratha right wing was composed of slender spearmen mounted on wiry ponies. In the center were the heavily armored horsemen of the Khas Paga, the household cavalry. On the left stood the infantry of Ibrahim Khan Gardi. In the rear of the center, under the branches of a black mango tree, the Bhao and Vishvas Rao watched from the back of an enormous elephant.

The Afghan wings were made up of Rohilla and Moghul horsemen, interspersed by tribesmen from the hills. The center consisted of Durrani cavalry mounted on powerful Turki horses. Ahmed Shah and his staff rode in the rear.

Battle began just before daybreak with an attack by Ibrahim Khan Gardi, who was slightly in advance as the Maratha line moved forward obliquely. His sepoys drove back the Moghul horsemen in their front, firing salvos of rockets and advancing in short rushes. This left a gap between the Afghan right and center, into which the Bhao sent the household cavalry with their shouted war cry of "Hur, Hur, Hurree." The line wavered and for a time the Afghan cause seemed lost; but the Afghan commander, Shah Wali Khan, leaped from his horse and called to his soldiers, "Our country is far off, my friends. Whither do you fly?" Thanks to his leadership and the quick action of Ahmed Shah in sending reinforcements, the line held.

All morning the battle went on, in swirling skirmishes that grew increasingly spasmodic as the famished Marathas' strength began to fail. At about two in the afternoon Ahmed sent to the Afghan camp for all the wounded, malingerers, and camp followers, ordering them on pain of death to come to the battlefield. With this motley force he launched an attack on the Maratha center, while the Durrani horse took the right wing in flank. With dramatic suddenness the battle was over—Marathas fleeing for life, Afghans in vindictive pursuit. Vishvas Rao was killed by a stray shot and the Bhao mounted a horse and galloped into the melee, to atone for his blunders by the death of a hero.

All through the night the rout continued, with the Afghan horses easily overtaking the Maratha ponies. Even the villagers, fired by memories of the tribute the Marathas had imposed, were seized with the lust for slaughter, surrounding and knocking down the retreating troops.[6]

Early the next morning the Afghans entered the Maratha camp, where twenty-five thousand women of the noblest Maratha families awaited their new masters, and where five hundred elephants and masses of treasure fell into Afghan hands.

This battle, the third on the field of Panipat, is known in Indian folklore as the Battle of the Black Mango Tree, and has been called one of the decisive battles of history. If the Marathas had won, some historians contend, they might have consolidated India under a rule that would have made its subsequent conquest by the British an impossibility. As it turned out, the power of the Peshwas never survived the disaster at Panipat, and though the Marathas underwent a resurgence, they never regained the position they had held beforehand. Whatever importance the battle may have had, there is nothing in the Marathas' history to indicate that they had the ability of the early Moghuls; they began as poor bandits and blackmailers and ended as wealthy ones, disliked equally by Moslems and by Hindus.

The Afghans, on the other hand, gained little at Panipat beyond glory and loot, both of them trivial items in the ledgers of history. The outcome of the battle marked the flood tide of Afghan power and from this time on Afghanistan was to suffer a steady decline.

In a sense the battle marked the end of an era, little as the combatants were conscious of the fact. The success of Ibrahim Khan Gardi's sepoys, although obscured by the Maratha disaster, was in fact a portent. The traditionally superior mobility and dash of horsemen had proved unavailing against discipline and gunpowder; at times during the battle, trained infantrymen had shown themselves able to outfight cavalry.

After his victory Ahmed Shah remained only briefly in India. His men were anxious to take their trophies home, and the approach of the summer filled him with foreboding. Accordingly he placed a puppet prince, Ali Gauhar, on the Moghul throne and returned to Afghanistan.

Even while Afghan and Maratha struggled for power, a new force had begun to exert itself in the Punjab—the military and religious brotherhood of the Sikhs. Originally a fifteenth-century attempt by Guru Nanak to reconcile Hinduism and Islam, Sikhism had begun as a small and pacific movement. But religious persecution by the later Moghul rulers caused Sikhism to become increasingly militant under the leadership of Hargobind. The change of character was completed by a grandson, Guru Govind Singh.

Ably led, Sikhism was further strengthened as many of the Jats, a Punjab people who were the sturdiest in India, joined its ranks.[7] As Moghul power declined, the Khalsa, the army of the Sikhs, moved toward dominance in the Punjab. Conflict with the Afghans, who considered this fruitful province their rightful territory won in battle, now became inevitable.

The Afghan army had no sooner left India in 1761 than the Sikhs were abroad, raiding and looting town after town, meeting with little resistance and with such favor by the native population that the Afghan governors were unable to check them. By the end of the year most of the Punjab was already under Sikh control, and Ahmed Shah was obliged to head back through the passes once again. With an army made up entirely of cavalry, he surprised the Sikh Khalsa near Luddhiana and administered a crushing defeat. He then marched on Amritsar, the holy city of the Sikhs, where his soldiers were ordered to destroy the temples and defile the holy places with the blood of cows—an action that had been urged by the Indian princes over the protests of the Afghan leaders, for as a chronicler remarked of the desecration, "Nothing is fiercer than a local hound." In the hope of conciliating the Punjabis, Ahmed then left a Hindu, Kabuli Mal, to govern in his name.

By the time he returned to Afghanistan the Sikhs were busier than ever, their numbers having been swelled by new recruits thirsting to avenge centuries of Moslem oppression. All through the Punjab cities were sacked, Moslems were slaughtered, and mosques were defiled or destroyed.

In 1764 Ahmed Shah returned after having requested Nasir Khan, the Baluchi leader, to invade from the south. Again the Afghans were victorious, and Ahmed Shah appointed a Sikh, Alha Singh, as governor of Sirhind. Again as soon as the Afghans retired the Sikhs reappeared, seemingly stronger with each new defeat. In 1766 Ahmed Shah once again returned, weary of marching and fighting these "bees without honey," and once again the pattern repeated itself. No matter how often they were victorious in open battles, the Afghans were powerless to crush a movement inspired by religious zeal and supported by most of the people of the Punjab. At last in 1769 Ahmed Shah prepared another attack, which if carried out would have been his tenth invasion of India. But this time he failed to cross the Indus. His soldiers were tired of futile warfare, and the king himself was ill. The plans for the invasion were canceled; the king returned to his capital at Kandahar.

Ahmed was now fifty. Worn out after a lifetime of battle, he knew that his rule must soon end. A malignant growth on his nose, from which he had suffered for some time, had left him increasingly ill. In February 1772, at a council of Durrani nobles, he named his second son, Timur Mirza, as his successor and turned over the government to him. He then traveled to a summer retreat in the Suleiman Mountains, where he died on April 14, 1772. His body was returned to Kandahar and buried in a tomb in the center of the city. The epitaph inscribed there begins, "The king of high rank, Ahmed Shah Durrani, was equal to Cyrus in the business of ruling."

The story of Ahmed Shah is one in which a father's reputation has suffered from the sins of his children. One of the most imposing figures in Asian history, a brilliant military commander, and the founder of a nation, he nevertheless remains almost unknown to the outside world. Endowed with all the qualities that make for successful leadership, Ahmed had few of the defects that sully the records of so many Asian rulers. He was deeply religious; in the cruelty that marked his attacks on Sikhs and Hindus he merely followed the custom of the time and the practice of his opponents. Toward his own people he was benevolent, free from pride of station, and approachable by the poorest. He substituted a simple salute of the hand for the servile obeisance common to Asia; he eased the criminal code, and forbade mutilation as a penalty.

Along with his political and military ability, Ahmed had talent as a poet and was a patron of learning, philosophy, and literature. His poetry has a certain resemblance to that attributed to David, another warrior king.

The kingdom built by Ahmed was to fall a long way from the greatness he brought to it. That Afghanistan still exists as a kingdom after two centuries of vicissitudes is due not a little to a monarch who is known not as The Great but by the warmer tribute of Baba, "Father." [8]

V

The Fall of the Saddozais

> An ungrateful son is a wart on a
> father's face—to leave it a blemish,
> to cut it a pain.—PUSHTO PROVERB

AHMED SHAH left eight sons. Timur Mirza, his favorite and
chosen heir, was second in age to another son, Suleiman Mirza.
At the time of his father's death Timur was in Herat. He left
immediately for Kandahar, and learned on the way that a group
of sirdars, headed by the old warrior Shah Wali Khan, had
nominated Suleiman as their candidate.

Fortunately for Timur, his father's prestige remained strong.
As the prince approached Kandahar the adherents of Suleiman
began to offer their submission to Timur—among them Wali
Khan, whose daughter was married to Suleiman and who had
apparently allowed family feeling to influence his judgment.
This reversal by the hero of Panipat did not prevent Timur
from having him executed—a resolute action which convinced
Suleiman's remaining followers that their cause was hopeless.
With their candidate they fled to India and exile.

The new Timur Shah had been born in 1746 near Meshed.
As his father's darling he had been carefully schooled in the art
of Afghan kingship and allied by marriage to a series of neighboring dynasties. He had much of Ahmed's personal charm; but
although he was a brave soldier, he had small interest in war or

conquest. Most of his energies were devoted to his extensive harem.

One of his first acts as king was to transfer the Afghan capital from Kandahar to Kabul. This move has often been interpreted as an attempt by Timur to remove himself from the center of Durrani power and the relatives of Shah Wali Khan. But there were other considerations as well. With Kashmir and the Punjab in Afghan hands, Kabul was nearer the geographical center of the realm. Also, the summer climate at Kabul was more temperate than at Kandahar, and Peshawar was pleasant and accessible as a winter capital.

Timur made few changes in the government organized by his father. The Durrani sirdars continued in their posts of authority, and so did the council of paramount chiefs. The Kizzilbash of Kabul were selected as the royal guard, and Timur was careful to pay the army well and on time—a practice sometimes neglected by later rulers.

Although Timur had had enough of battles, he invaded India five times—in 1774, 1779, 1780, 1785, and 1788—as a result of the constant challenge of the Sikhs. The rest of his campaigns were undertaken in response to threatened vassals who appealed for aid. Three times an Afghan army went to Khurasan to bolster up the feeble rule of Shah Rukh. Another army was dispatched to Sind after the Sindi Amirs of the Kalhora tribe had been deposed by Fath Ali Talpura. Here, however, Afghan reverses forced Timur to recognize Fath Ali as Amir of Sind in return for an empty promise of tribute.

Timur ruled for twenty years, during which there were only two internal revolts—a record for the entire history of Afghanistan. One of these uprisings was organized by a Durrani sirdar, Abdul Khaliq, with the support of the Baluchi ruler, Nasir Khan, and was suppressed with difficulty. The other was an attempt at a *coup d'état* engineered by Sahibzada of Chamkanni, a eunuch who commanded the palace guard and who was also a noted mullah, in conspiracy with Faizullah Khan, a malik of the Khalil tribe near Peshawar. Their plan was to assassinate Timur and replace him with Iskander Mirza, son of his exiled brother Suleiman. On the appointed day a number of Khalil tribesmen slipped into the royal palace at Peshawar and made a determined effort to reach the Shah. They were frustrated when Timur promptly climbed into a tower and bolted an iron door, until loyal elements of the guard could come to his rescue. The conspirators escaped to the hills, from which Faizullah Khan was lured by a promise of pardon, which was immediately violated.[1]

The memory of Ahmed Shah, which during the reign of Timur was still a powerful prop to the Afghan throne, no doubt tended to keep down internal disturbances. Another reason for the peacefulness of these twenty years may have been simply that the energy and aggressiveness of the Afghan people had been depleted by the unending campaigns under Timur's father.

Timur died suddenly at Kabul on May 18, 1793, under circumstances that caused his pious enemies to attribute the event to the judgment of Allah, while others pointed an accusing finger at one of the Shah's many wives. More probably, however, the cause was cholera.

Timur's reputation in his own country is not great. Afghan chroniclers tend to resent his failure to carry on the expansive policy of his father, and to condemn his indefatigable sensuality. Foreign writers have accepted this view, uncritically and rather unfairly. Viewed more objectively, Timur Shah appears as an able and tolerant ruler, whose reign was freer from internal dissensions than that of any other Afghan king. Under him the country enjoyed twenty years of peace and though he failed to bring home the loads of plunder that won glory for his father, an even more valuable trade and commerce developed in Afghanistan. Lieutenant Vigne, a British officer who visited Afghanistan about fifty years after Timur's death, commented, "The reign of Timur Shah was still remembered by the oldest inhabitants of Kabul as that in which the city enjoyed its greatest modern prosperity." [2]

So far as the complaints concerning Timur's lechery are concerned, there is no doubt that he indulged his prerogatives as a monarch with enthusiasm. He left behind uncounted numbers of children, of whom thirty-six were by legal wives. Twenty-one of these were sons, and upon their father's death each promptly advanced a claim to the throne.

Among this multitude the three strongest candidates were two whole brothers, Humayun Mirza and Mahmud Mirza, and a half brother, Mohammed Zeman Mirza. The first two were the governors of Kandahar and Herat respectively, and ranked first and second in age. Mohammed Zeman was fifth in age, but his position as governor of Kabul, in possession of the treasury and in command of the royal guard, made him a prominent contender. And whereas Humayun and Mahmud were the children of a Saddozai princess, Zeman's mother was a Yuzufzai— which meant that Zeman had support in the east and that his rivals were popular in the south.

A crucial factor in the contest was the position of the most powerful of the Durrani subtribes, the Barukzais. When Paindah Khan, chief of the Mohammedzai clan and thus head of the Barukzais, swung to Mohammed Zeman, his selection was assured. The various half brothers who had hastened to Kabul were persuaded to renounce their ambitions after a few days' confinement on a diet of bread and water; Humayun Mirza, who attempted to rally the support of the Durranis, was defeated and driven to Baluchistan, while Mahmud remained at Herat in watchful neutrality.

Zeman Shah, twenty-three years old at his coronation, had the courage and ability of his father and grandfather, but in him these qualities were marred by an overweening arrogance. He was determined to rule with absolute authority and to end the power of the feudal chiefs, with whom his predecessors had preferred to deal by means of a judicious mixture of conciliation and bribery. Such an attempt to extend the central authority was probably inevitable; but it began a struggle that was to last for forty years and to end by destroying the empire of Ahmed Shah.

This Afghan "time of troubles" was the consequence of basic weaknesses in the political structure that had been hidden by the martial successes of Ahmed Shah and the tolerant rule of Timur. One serious defect was the absence of primogeniture in Afghanistan. It was aggravated by the custom of plural marriage, which among the virile Afghans invariably produced a number of half brothers who were often conditioned by the rivalries and antagonisms of the harem and each convinced that his claim to power was as good as any other's.

Another weakness was the lack of any mystique of kingship in Afghanistan, and the ingrained individualism that kept such a concept from taking hold. To the tribal khans and maliks the king was in no sense a superior being; he was merely an equal who through fortune or family had acquired power.

In such a situation the Saddozais could have little hope of becoming the royal family of Afghanistan. Since the basic loyalty of any Afghan was always to the smaller unit, the Saddozais could count on constant support only from the Popolzais. The Mohammedzais, on the other hand, were assured the backing of the Barukzais, by far the strongest Durrani tribe.

Some writers, Afghan and foreign, have castigated the Saddozais for a lack of leadership, and have described them as weak and vacillating. This accusation is unjust. Indeed, if the Saddozais had accepted the privileges of royalty without demanding absolute power, they would have been able to maintain themselves on the prestige of their clan and its founder. It was the attempt to strengthen royal authority that brought about their downfall.

For several years after the accession of Shah Zeman, Afghanistan was troubled by intermittent civil war as now Mahmud and now Humayun attempted to seize control. Encouraged by these internecine struggles, the outer provinces still controlled by Afghanistan made sporadic moves toward ending their allegiance. Shah Zeman could probably have coped with these rebellions without much difficulty, had it not been that his departure from Afghanistan invariably brought a new invasion by his half brothers, which forced his return. Few kings have marched as many weary miles as Shah Zeman.

Like his predecessors, he was also troubled by the Sikhs, who had become a major power in the Punjab. After several abortive attempts to crush them, Shah Zeman sought a solution by appointing a young Sikh chief, Runjit Singh, as his governor in the Punjab—an error in judgment comparable to that of the fictional Dr. Frankenstein, although for a time the idea seemed to work. With the Punjab apparently secure, Shah Zeman returned to Afghanistan, where his presence checked the latest attacks of his rivals. With the situation apparently stabilized, the king now put into effect a plan that he had long contemplated.

That Zeman owed his position largely to the support of Paindah Khan, chief of the Mohammedzais, could hardly fail to rankle in a king so little disposed to the acknowledgment of favors. The upshot was that Shah Zeman began to remove Mohammedzais from the positions of importance they had held since the days of Amed Shah and to replace them with chiefs of other tribes. Many of these—including one Vafadar Khan, who was appointed Wazir—were Saddozais.

These actions aroused the suspicion of other Durrani sirdars, who were naturally well satisfied with the essentially feudal nature of the Afghan government. Finally a secret meeting was held to consider action and possible rebellion. News of the cabal—which included Paindah Khan, Mohammed Sharif Khan, head of the Kizzilbash, Sultan Khan of the Nurzai Durranis, and Rahim Khan of the Alizai Durranis—was brought to the Shah by the inevitable informer, and the king moved promptly; the men were all arrested and summarily executed.

Although it is difficult to see what was left for Shah Zeman to do under the circumstances, the move proved to have been suicidal. Fathi Khan, oldest of twenty-one sons of Paindah Khan, immediately fled to Persia, where with the promise of Barukzai support he induced Mahmud Mirza to make another bid for the throne. At Saadut, near Girishk, the center of Barukzai power, the two men were joined by Barukzai, Alizai, and Nurzai tribesmen. Kandahar was occupied without opposition, and the rebels moved toward Kabul. Here they were met by the royal army; but its commander was a Nurzai chief who had accepted the post for the purpose of betraying Zeman, and who promptly turned his soldiers over to Fathi Khan and Mahmud Mirza. The deserted shah fled toward Peshawar; but after having taken refuge with a tribal chief, he was surrendered to his pursuers in a rare breach of the Afghan law of sanctuary.

Blinded and imprisoned in Kabul, the fallen monarch finally escaped, probably with the connivance of Mahmud, and made his way to Bokhara. Here he was treated cruelly by the Uzbeg amir, Hyder Turi, who hoped to gain the Koh-i-nur diamond, which Zeman had hidden in the wall of his Kabul cell. Escaping once again, he fled to Herat, where his half brother Haji Firuz-ud-din was governor. Although the latter was a whole brother of Mahmud, he treated the fugitive kindly and sent him under escort to India, where he lived for fifty years as a British pensioner. To the end of his life he pined for his homeland, crying, "Kabul! Kabul! What is Kashmir to Kabul? I shall never see my homeland again." [3]

In the perspective of time it is easy to sympathize with Shah Zeman's attempt to centralize his government and to end Afghan feudalism. His failure was as much a result of circumstances as of lack of ability, and it is noteworthy that the Afghans have more respect for his memory than for any other of the sons of Timur Shah.

Meanwhile Mohamud Shah mounted the musnid, and promptly indicated that he did not plan to imitate his predecessor but was quite content to rule with the cooperation of the powerful chiefs. The most influential of these, Fathi Khan Barukzai and Shir Mohammed Khan Barukzai (the son of the old Wazir, Shah Wali Khan), divided authority between themselves while Mahmud settled back to enjoy the privileges of royalty.

The only serious menace to the new government was the whole brother of the deposed Shah Zeman, a young man named Shuja-ul-mulk, who governed the city of Peshawar. His mother's connections made him influential with the eastern tribes, as his brother had been. As a further advantage he held part of the royal treasury, which he used freely to gather a large and unruly lashkar of Afridi, Mohmand, and Yuzufzai tribesmen. With these he moved through the Khyber Pass in a bid for the throne. His men met the army of Mahmud, commanded by Fathi Khan, near Surkh Rud. In the battle that took place, the eastern tribesmen were victorious until they stopped to plunder the treasure of their own commander. The confusion introduced into their ranks, and undoubtedly into the mind of Shuja, gave Fathi Khan the opportunity to rally his troops and to drive the opposing forces from the field. Shuja took refuge among the Afridis at Tirah Bagh, and Fathi Khan occupied Peshawar without resistance.

For a time Shah Mahmud was apparently secure on the throne, although a revolt by the Ghilzai caused some concern. This powerful tribe had been willing to accept Durrani hegemony without opposition, the more since the government made no attempt to control the Ghilzai homeland but in fact left their tribes completely alone. Now, however, a group of Ghilzai led by Abdul Rahim, a descendant of the hero Mir Wais, raised a revolt, whose collapse in 1802 was at least partly due to the Ghilzai practice of plundering other clans of their own tribe.

At this moment the situation underwent one of those sudden shifts that can be so bewildering to anyone unfamiliar with the rivalries and the complexities of Afghan affairs. For some time there had been tension between the Pushtoons and the Kizzilbash of Kabul, an outgrowth of the natural antagonism between the Sunni branch of Islam, represented by the Push-toons, and the Shia branch, represented by the Kizzilbash, aggravated by the occasional use made by the Kizzilbash of their position as the royal guard for purposes of extortion. This discontent was exploited by Shir Mohammed, the Barukzai chief, who resented Fathi Khan's appointment as Wazir and was his personal enemy, despite their kinship as Mohammedzais.

With the chief mullah of Kabul, Syed Ahmed, as his stalking horse, Shir Mohammed took advantage of the execution of a young Pushtoon for the murder of a Kizzilbash to instigate a riot among the volatile Kabul citizenry. Shah Mahmud soon found himself besieged behind the walls of Kabul's Bala Hissar or "upper fortress." The revolt had been timed to take place while Fathi Khan was absent in Kandahar, and its leaders now invited Shuja to come to Kabul and ascend the throne.

The young prince left his hideout among the Afridis and hastened to Kabul, where he was joined by the insurgents and a number of volunteers from turbulent Kohistan. A few days later Fathi Khan arrived from Kandahar, only to see his troops desert to the enemy, for Shir Mohammed was also a Mohammedzai, with no taint of sympathy for the schismatic Kizzilbash. Fathi Khan with a few followers rode for Kandahar while Shuja entered Kabul in triumph.

As the newest addition to the growing list of deposed Afghan kings, Shah Mahmud was promptly imprisoned, although at the instance of Shir Mohammed—who tried to safeguard himself against changes in fortune—he was not blinded. Shah Shuja made no reprisals, in fact, except against the chief who had surrendered Shah Zeman—and his punishment of the latter was an action approved by all Afghans. Even Fathi Khan was rather contemptuously pardoned.

From 1803 to 1809 Shah Shuja ruled an Afghanistan that had suffered sadly from these dynastic struggles. His reign was made continually uneasy by incipient revolts and court intrigues. Most of these were sponsored by Fathi Khan, whom the king was unable to punish, since that sirdar was now careful to keep himself at Saadut in the heart of his tribal territory. One of these plots, a daring act carried out by Dost Mohammed, the youngest of Fathi Khan's twenty brothers, brought about the escape of Mahmud from prison.

Another problem for Shah Shuja was a growing rift with his Wazir, Shir Mohammed, who felt that the king owed his throne to him and who was anxious to wield royal power. In 1808, with Shuja absent on a campaign in Sind, Shir Mohammed carried out a coup that placed Shuja's nephew Kaissar Mirza on the throne. This time, however, the ambitious Barukzai overestimated his strength; his army was defeated by the returning troops of Shuja and his head was carried on a pole through the bazaars of Kabul.

This action was no less fatal to Shah Shuja than the execution of Paindah Khan had been to Shah Zeman; in both cases the victim had been the main prop to the throne. In the spring of 1809 Fathi Khan with Mahmud captured Kandahar and moved toward Kabul. Shuja, who at the time was in the winter capital at Peshawar, hastily marched through the Khyber and met the rebel forces near Gandamak. Here Fathi Khan won a complete

The mosque of Mazar-i-Sharif, reputedly the resting place of the Caliph Ali.

Afghan Turkomen playing Buzkashi, the "goat game."

victory, and Shuja fled to India. During the next three years Shuja made frequent but futile efforts to regain the throne, but he met with no support even from his former allies in the eastern tribes. In 1813 he gave up and retired to Luddhiana, in India, where he joined his brother Zeman on a British pension.

Mahmud, now that he was again Shah, followed a Saddozai custom: he became as indolent in prosperity as he had been energetic in adversity, and shared neither in the cares of government nor in the toils of war. Surrendering the affairs of state into the hands of Fathi Khan as his Wazir, he allowed the Mohammedzai chief to rule unopposed while he settled back to enjoy the delights of the harem and the wine cellar.

Fathi Khan, on the other hand, had boundless energy. In many ways an oddly contradictory personality, this kingmaker was an able administrator and general but was often guilty of rash and emotional behavior. Courteous, affable, and generous, he was indifferent to the enemies his position brought him; like many Afghans, he was addicted to nepotism, a trait which his twenty brothers were ready and willing to encourage. Nominal control over Baluchistan went to one of these, Rahimdil Khan; control over Kandahar to another, Poordil Khan, over Peshawar to Sultan Mohammed Khan, over Ghazni to Shirdil Khan, and over Bamian to Kohendil Khan. Dost Mohammed Khan, the youngest of the brothers, was placed in charge of the royal guard.

In 1811, the energetic Wazir led an Afghan army into Kashmir, which was controlled by Atta Mohammed Khan, the son of Shah Shuja's Wazir, Shir Mohammed. Fathi Khan was aided in this attack by Runjit Singh, the Sikh raja, who was now the most powerful man in the Punjab and who hoped to be given the governorship of Kashmir. Though in this the Sikh was disappointed, it was virtually his only reverse in a career of successful statecraft. The recovered province was placed in the hands of Mohammed Azim Khan, another of the Barukzai brothers. From this time on Runjit Singh dropped all pretense of ruling as an Afghan vassal.

For a few years Afghanistan seemed to be recovering stability under the control of Fathi Khan. Caravans once again plodded to India and to central Asia with some expectation of safe arrival; artisans and merchants began to reappear, and trade and commerce to revive.

When this promising security collapsed, bringing Afghanistan to a state of internal chaos, the cause—as has so often been true—was partly external. During the Afghan's previous internal squabbles, Persia had made a recovery under the Kajars, who established their dynasty in 1795. Khurasan, including the city of Meshed, was soon in Persian hands; the Persian rulers then began to look toward Herat, a district governed at the time by Haji Firuz-ud-din, the same man who had aided the blind Shah Zeman to reach India. The Haji, a whole brother of Shah Mahmud, was primarily concerned with religion, although he was well enough pleased to be in a position of power.[4] He had given a lukewarm support to Shah Mahmud, but had been careful to stand clear of the hatreds that had developed between the sons of Timur Shah.

In 1805 a Persian army commanded by Mohammed Khan Kajar moved on Herat and then withdrew after a mismanaged campaign characteristic of latter-day Persian armies. Nevertheless, Haji Firuz-ud-din was enough shaken by it that he agreed to pay Teheran a small yearly tribute, and at the same time to aid the Khurasan tribes that were resisting Persian control.

Encouraged by this gesture, Fath Ali Shah, the Persian king, decided to send another army against Herat, as a means of regaining some prestige after a series of inglorious defeats by Russia. In 1816 a large force was mustered at Meshed and placed under the command of Hussain Ali Mirza, a son of the Shah. The royal leader procrastinated to such an extent, however, that Fathi Khan was able to bring the Afghan army all the way from Kabul before the Persians arrived.

Haji Firuz-ud-din's welcome to these reinforcements was mixed. When he greeted Fathi Khan warmly but refused to allow the troops to enter the city, Fathi Khan became convinced that the Haji was not to be trusted. Acting with his usual precipitancy, he arrested the governor and took control of Herat. His seizure of the Haji was probably justified, and he had the prudence to send the latter to Kabul under honorary escort. But then the Wazir made one of those errors for which he was noted, in total disregard for its possible consequences: he seized the considerable treasury that Haji Firuz-ud-din had amassed at Herat, and sent his youngest brother, Dost Moham-med Khan, into the Haji's *zenana* (harem) in search of further spoils.

This rash act, the most serious possible by Afghan standards, was perhaps enacted on the initiative of Dost Mohammed, who at the time was the wildest and most daring of the Barukzai brothers, and was known as Gurkek, "little wolf." At any rate, the young sirdar undoubtedly went beyond his instructions when he tore a famous jeweled girdle from about the hips of a girl who happened to be the daughter of Shah Mahmud and the sister of the heir apparent, Kamran Mirza.[5]

News of this, when it reached Kabul, was infuriating to the Shah's son Kamran, who was already a personal enemy of Fathi Khan and who was also dismayed by the power his father's in-dolence had permitted the Wazir to exert. Kamran, as it hap-pens, was an unlovable character, who according to a contempo-rary was "fond of drinking spirits as well as bhang and opium and who spent the whole of his life in ornamenting himself and also in the company of boys whom he loved most tenderly." [6] Although Fathi Khan might well disregard such an opponent, he had failed to anticipate the effect of his breach of Afghan morality upon the sodden Mahmud. When Kamran was joined in his importunities by others of Fathi Khan's enemies at the Afghan court, Shah Mahmud roused from his torpor and ordered the Wazir's arrest. The commission was given to Kamran, who set out immediately for Herat.

Meanwhile the Afghans had defeated the Persians in an odd battle, which ended in the simultaneous flight of both sides. The Afghans, with a shorter distance to go, had soon reached Herat; finding themselves unpursued, they returned to the bat-tlefield as the Persians continued to gallop for distant Meshed. This dubious victory, sweetened by the capture of the Persian baggage, raised Fathi Khan's self-confidence to its zenith. To friends who brought messages of Kamran's purpose he scoffed, "I twice placed Mahmud upon the throne and his kingdom is now in the hands of my kinsmen; who is Kamran, therefore, that in a dream he should think of injuring me?" [7]

It was to prove a fatal boast. Kamran arrived and was greeted with respect by Fathi Khan. But a few days later Fathi Khan was called to an audience with the prince, seized by the latter's guards, and blinded on the spot.

It has been said that the dagger that put out the eyes of Fathi Khan also struck at the heart of the dynasty of Ahmed Shah. The twenty brothers of the Wazir were still at large and in posts of importance; they immediately forgot their own large personal ambitions, and made common cause against the Saddozais. Shirdil Khan, Poordil Khan, and Kohendil Khan, all sons of the same mother (who apparently was fond of the suffix *dil,* for "heart"; two other sons were Rahimdil and Mirdil) immediately left Herat and hastened to Saadut, the Barukzai center, where they were joined by thousands of vengeful tribesmen. Dost Mohammed Khan, whose action had started the trouble, left for Kabul, where he was able to induce the Kizzilbash, his mother's people, to drive Mahmud from the city.

After escaping to Ghazni, where he was joined by Kamran and the remnants of the army from Herat, the Shah advanced toward Kabul. Here he was met by the insurgent army commanded by Mohammed Azim Khan, second oldest of the Barukzai brothers. The battle was a fiasco; the troops of Mahmud deserted to the Barukzais, and it was with difficulty that the Shah regained the safety of Ghazni. Even here he was not safe, for the army of Mohammed Azim was approaching and the garrison was untrustworthy. In a rage of mutual recrimination, Mahmud and Kamran fled to the Saddozai stronghold of Herat, where with frightful cruelty they put the blinded Fathi Khan to death.[8]

With the collapse of the dynasty of Ahmed Shah, Afghan nationhood very nearly came to an end. Mahmud and Kamran continued to rule at Herat, where with the power in his own hands, Kamran treated his father with contempt, once depriving him of wine for a month. After Mahmud died in 1829—of poisoning by his son, according to rumor—Kamran followed the family pattern, devoting himself to narcotics and strong drink and placing the control of Herat in the hands of his Wazir, Yar Mohammed Khan. The latter, an Alikozai Durrani chief, candidly described himself as the wickedest man in Asia, and he was also one of the most able.[9] Keeping Kamran in a prolonged stupor of debauchery, he was soon master of the city and ruled as a supposed servant of the Saddozai until 1842, when he had Kamran murdered.

The ability of the Saddozai to hold Herat was the result of discord among the Barukzai brothers, whose unity had vanished with success. As individual members seized power, usually in areas where they had been governors, Afghanistan disintegrated into a number of petty states. Mohammed Azim Khan held Kabul; three of the "dil" brothers, Kohendil, Rahimdil, and Poordil, ruled Kandahar; Nawab Jabbar Khan held Kashmir; and Sultan Mohammed Khan governed Peshawar. Officially Mohammed Azim Khan was head of the family; but the rest paid little heed to his requests, and throughout the country the khans and maliks of the tribes did as they pleased. All the territory once held by Ahmed Shah that lay outside the borders of Afghanistan proper had ceased to pay any allegiance. At the same time the Sikhs, headed by Runjit Singh, began to harass the borders of their old Afghan enemies.

At this, the nadir of Afghan fortune, a new leader rose to prominence. Surprisingly enough, it was Dost Mohammed Khan; the youngest of the Barukzai brothers; he had acted as governor of Ghazni for Mohammed Azim Khan, and after the latter's death in 1824, had replaced him as the ruler of Kabul. He had apparently outgrown the exuberance of his youth, for he governed with skill and moderation. Not the least of his good qualities was a personality of outstanding charm, which won him many friends and the Afghan saying, "With the Dost a kind word goes farther than a rupee." An enemy described him as "a man whose shrewd sense and natural ability had been developed by the constant collision with character of every hue and intrigue of every form." [10]

Making no effort to extend his control, the Dost concentrated on restoring stability at Kabul, Ghazni, and Jalalabad. In 1837 he was crowned in Kabul, not as Shah but as Amir-ul-Muminin ("commander of the faithful").

VI

The Coming of the British

When the knife is over your head
you remember God.—AFGHAN PROVERB

WHILE the Afghans were undergoing their time of troubles, a new power had begun to grow which was eventually to dominate the plains of India. After a prosaic start as a trading concern, the British East India Company had been caught up in the confusion that followed the collapse of Moghul authority. The skill of its agents and the negligence of the Bourbons enabled the Company to gain control of Bengal and southern India, and after the defeat of Mir Kasim in 1764, left it the strongest contender for hegemony over all of India.

The British had heard many tales of the distant Afghans and were impressed by reports of their martial prowess, but the death of Ahmed Shah and the indolence of Timur reduced their apprehension over possible conflict with the Afghan horsemen. But they had another reason for uneasiness in the unpredictable forces unleashed by the French Revolution, and above all in the activities of a military genius by the name of Bonaparte, who was reported to have said as he led his army to Egypt, "La puissance qui est maîtresse de l'Égypte doit l'être à la longue de l'Inde." [1]

At about the same time a somewhat disreputable group of French adventurers descended on the courts of Indian rulers, each harboring a violent Anglophobia and a Gallic facility for expressing it. One such band even sailed from the Île de France (Mauritius) to the court of Tippu Sultan, the ruler of Mysore, where it addressed that surprised and sanguinary potentate as "Citizen" Tippu and promised him aid in defending the "rights of man."

Although these last failed to alarm the British, the menace of Napoleon was another matter. A message was promptly sent to the Company's representative in Persia, instructing him to take measures "for inducing the Court of Persia to keep Shah Zeman in perpetual check, so as to preclude him from returning to India." [2] Three lacs of rupees were also forwarded to oil the official wheels at the Persian court—a suggestion that more was needed having been vetoed by Lord Wellesley, who sensibly observed that "the plan for subsidizing the whole army of Persia is more extensive and expensive than circumstances seem to require." [3]

The Persian ruler was Fath Ali Shah—a not inconsiderable despot after a series of royal nonentities, and one who not only considered Herat a lost Persian province but also had Mahmud, the half brother of Shah Zeman, as a willing pawn—and he was amenable to the envoy's suggestion. Accordingly he helped Mahmud to invade Afghanistan with a small force, and in 1799 and 1800 he sent expeditions to Khurasan. These were blocked not without a good deal of effort by the harried Shah Zeman, whose Afghan army was obliged to shuttle back and forth between the threat of the Sikhs and of the Persians.

In 1800 Captain John Malcolm went to Teheran as an envoy of the East India Company, which by now had almost sovereign powers in dealing with Asian states. After protracted negotiations implemented by bribery, Malcolm concluded two treaties with Persia, which were ratified in January 1801. One of these was a commercial agreement, the other a stipulation that in return for British aid the Persians were to resist any French attack on India. The latter added:

If the king of the Afghans should ever show a resolution to invade India—an army overthrowing mountains, furnished with all war-like stores, shall be appointed from the State of the conspicuous and exalted, high and fixed in power [the Persian Shah] to lay waste and desolate the Afghan dominions, and every exertion shall be employed to ruin and humble the above nation.[4]

British interest in this clause of the agreement waned with Napoleon's setback in Egypt and the civil wars in Afghanistan. When Russia annexed the provinces of Georgia, Sheriwan, and Karabagh, the Persian Shah made a request for aid under the terms of the treaty; but the British refused, pointing out that their obligation concerned only the French.

Fath Ali Shah thereupon immediately approached the French, who in their turn sent a mission to negotiate a commercial treaty, and also an envoy, General Gardannes, to plan for a Franco-Persian invasion of India. This development brought a prompt reaction from the British. Captain (now Sir John) Malcolm was sent to Teheran as an envoy of the East India Company, and Sir Harford Jones as the official ambassador from Whitehall. At the same time an embassy headed by C. T. Metcalfe hurried to the Sikh court of Runjit Singh; and another led by Mountstuart Elphinstone journeyed to Peshawar, where Shah Shuja, the current ruler, was holding his winter court. This was the first official contact between the Afghans and the British or, indeed, any European power.

After a series of incidents produced by the attempts of Jones and Malcolm to outdo each other, a preliminary treaty was concluded between Great Britain and Persia in March 1809. By its terms all previous treaties between the Shah and European powers were annulled; no armies were to be permitted to pass through Persia toward India; the British were to remain aloof from Afghan-Persian disputes and were to provide arms in the event a European power attacked Persia.

This treaty was the result of Persia's anger over the treaty concluded at Tilsit between Napoleon and Czar Alexander II, which the Persians saw only as a sign that their professed friend had joined their inveterate enemy. The British more correctly interpreted the Franco-Russian accord as a measure directed against themselves. Indeed, it was an objective of the French to have the Russians send an army into Persia, there to be joined by a French army arriving by way of Constantinople, with which, after securing Persian reinforcements, it would march on India.

This scheme, like Napoleon's invasion of Egypt, was based more on imagination than on any knowledge of the logistical problems it involved. No less than his British opponents, who were classical scholars to a man, Napoleon had in mind the historic invasion of Alexander the Great. What both sides failed to realize was that the phalanx could travel where the Grand Army would disintegrate.

A short time after the conclusion of the Anglo-Persian treaty, the mission headed by Mountstuart Elphinstone reached Shah Shuja's winter court in the city of Peshawar. Elphinstone, one of the brighter stars in the galaxy of nineteenth-century British Indian officialdom, made a favorable impression upon the Afghans, and was much taken by them in turn. His *Account of the Kingdom of Caubul,* based on investigations made during the course of his mission, after a century and a half is still one of the best works on Afghanistan and the Afghans, and gives a picture of their hospitality and courtesy before these qualities had been marred by foreign aggressions.

Shah Shuja was willing to treat with these strangers, of whose power he had heard. In the treaty that was concluded, the Afghans agreed to oppose any French invasion of India, and the British to furnish all possible aid in such an eventuality. As it happened, the treaty was meaningless; Shuja was a fugitive before the year was out.

After Waterloo, the interest of the British in Persia and Afghanistan waned, to the annoyance of the Persian Shah. His pride was galled further when relations with Persia were transferred from London to British headquarters in India. Moreover, the East India Company's aggressive expansion for some time included a good deal of activity in the Persian Gulf, ostensibly in pursuit of the many pirates that infested those waters, but too close to Persia's shores for the comfort of its rulers.

For some reason the British were tardy in recognizing the threat of Czarist Russia, although it too was now persistently expanding its activities abroad. Theoretically, Russian-Persian relations had been stabilized in 1813 by the Treaty of Gulistan; but border incidents had been common, and in 1825, Russian troops occupied the province of Gokcha, which in the following year brought a declaration of war by the Persians and an attack by the Persian army led by Abbas Mirza, oldest son of the Shah.

After having been badly beaten in a series of battles, the Persians called for British assistance, which was refused. The British contended that the treaty of 1809 applied only in the event that Persia was attacked, whereas in this instance the Persians had been the aggressors. Helpless against Russian arms and discipline, the Persians capitulated. In 1828 they signed the treaty of Turkmanchai, which ceded the districts of Erivan and Nakshivan to the Russians and agreed to pay them an indemnity. Not long after this, a British envoy, Colonel Mac-Donald, took advantage of the Persians' chronic need for money, which the indemnity had made acute, to arrange—in return for the sum of 200,000 tomans—for the abrogation of the clause in the Anglo-Persian treaty concerning British aid. The cash was pleasing, but behind the action the Persians read a desire to desert a faltering ally; so, in disappointment and disgust, the Persians once again turned to Russia.[5]

Muscovy on the march was happy to oblige; Russians soon thronged at the Persian court, and rubles replaced rupees in Persian pockets. Abbas Mirza, the Persian heir apparent, had become especially pro-Russian—oddly enough, considering his defeats at Russian hands—and it was partly at his instigation, as well as at the urging of the Russians, that the Shah began to consider a campaign in the east. In any event, Persian pride was tender just then as a result of uninterrupted reverses at the hands of the Turks as well as of the Russians, and a divided Afghanistan promised less formidable opposition. Herat in particular seemed ripe for conquest, since the Heratis were not known for their belligerence and the Saddozai rulers of the city could expect no help from the brothers of Fathi Khan in the east.

With this motivation the Persians undertook several campaigns, but the condition of their armies was one of ludicrous ineptitude, and each venture proved a dreary fiasco. An extensive operation in 1833, led by Mohammed Mirza, the son of Abbas Mirza, was interrupted by the death of the latter. A year later the Shah followed his son to the "house of immortality," and Mohammed Mirza himself mounted the throne as Mohammed Shah. No less pronounced a Russophile than his father, the new ruler was under the influence of Count Simonich, an able Russian ambassador, and was supported by Russian money.

At about this time the British became aware that the old menace from France had been replaced by one that might prove more substantial. Although the attitude had been slow in developing, "that by the end of 1837 Russophobia was a major element in British opinion is not open to doubt." [6] This shift in British thinking was accompanied by a change in British officialdom. In London Palmerston became foreign minister in the cabinet of Lord Melbourne, and the influence of his sometimes thoughtless belligerence was soon apparent in Asia. At about the same time, Lord William Cavendish-Bentinck resigned as governor general of India. He was replaced by George Eden, later Lord and Earl of Auckland, who as a loyal Whig had served twenty undistinguished years in Parliament and who owed the appointment either to this or to the fact that his uncle was Lord Minto.

The many judgments written of Auckland have usually had a strong partisan coloring. At best he seems to have been, in the words of a contemporary, "a loyal party man, a steadfast supporter of Reform, and a sufficiently capable politician and assiduous official in normal times; but he was diffident, without experience in affairs of action, vacillating and quite ignorant of the East." [7]

When Auckland arrived in India, full of apprehension concerning Russian designs on India, Afghanistan was still divided. Dost Mohammed was consolidating his position at Kabul, however, and was looked upon as the most capable candidate for the empty throne, although his efforts in that direction were continually blocked by increasing pressure from the Sikhs.

Meanwhile, at Luddhiana the exiled Shah Shuja had been carrying on intrigues with a persistence that impressed Captain Claude Wade, the British political resident, who informed Auckland that the exile would be a better deterrent to Russian plans than Dost Mohammed. Auckland, who knew next to nothing of the situation, consented to advance Shuja's pension so that the latter could raise a mercenary army. Having mustered such a force—always an easy matter in India—Shuja made his way to Sind, where he defeated the Sindi Amirs and levied a contribution of 500,000 rupees.* This enabled him to increase his army and to invade Afghanistan by way of Bolan Pass.

The Barukzai brothers were startled by this recurrence of the Saddozai, a specter that had been laid for twenty years; but their fear was less of Shuja than of the British backing that was already common knowledge. According to Mohan Lal, a British secret agent who was then in Kabul, "It was known among the inhabitants that he was assisted by the British Government of which they were greatly afraid. The Sardars, who had no fear in their hearts, said that Shah Shuja could never keep his throne in Kabul as long as the Barukzai chiefs were alive." [8]

Shuja's army was made up of Punjabi Moslems, including a regiment of infantry trained in the European manner and commanded by an Anglo-Indian adventurer named Campbell. Largely because of the efficiency of the latter, Kohendil Khan and the Durrani forces from Kandahar were defeated in a battle at Khojak Pass; whereupon Shuja advanced and placed Kandahar under siege.

At Kabul, meanwhile, Dost Mohammed—who had a strong force ready for service against the Sikhs—was receiving frantic pleas for support from his brothers. Concerned over the British attitude, he wrote to ask Wade the extent of his government's commitments to Shah Shuja. Wade answered coldly that the British looked with favor upon Shuja's attempt to regain his throne but had no plans for active intervention.

* At this battle, one exceedingly fat Sindi chief made a dash for a boat that he had prudently provided. Unable to climb in, he gasped, "*Rish bageer* (Seize the beard)"—thus originating the name by which he and the battle were afterward known.

Reassured but still puzzled, the Dost moved in forced marches toward Kandahar. Early in June his army met that of Shah Shuja, and for several days the two forces engaged in a desultory struggle complicated by the fact that many of the combatants had been bribed by both sides. When finally Shuja's money gave out, the Saddozai fled to India, leaving his army to make terms with the victors.

This inglorious campaign had important side effects. One of these was that the withdrawal of Dost Mohammed from Kabul provided Runjit Singh with an opportunity to move up and occupy Peshawar, thus bringing Sikh rule to the mouth of Khyber Pass. Another was that the initial success of Campbell's corps showed the Afghans to be far less formidable than in the days of Ahmed Shah, and proved the ineffectiveness of their horsemen against trained infantry.

Following his victory the Dost made no attempt to incorporate Kandahar into his dominion. Leaving it in the hands of the "dil" brothers, he returned to his campaign against the Sikhs, whom he hoped this time, backed by a large and theoretically tested army, to drive across the Indus.

As the Afghan army moved through the Khyber, it was met by envoys from Runjit Singh, purportedly sent to discuss a settlement but actually to practice some judicious bribery. Among the envoys was one Josiah Harlan, who was probably the first American to enter Afghanistan, and whom the Dost received with honor.* Harlan repaid the latter's hospitality by inducing "his brother, Sultan Mohomed Khan, the lately deposed chief of Peshawar, to withdraw suddenly from the camp at nightfall with 10,000 retainers." [9]

Shaken by his brother's treason (although the two men had been personally unfriendly), the Dost returned to Kabul and began to gather another army. In 1837 this force, commanded

---

* Harlan, one of the colorful rogues wandering in Asia at this time, was born at Philadelphia in 1799. After leaving America because of troubles with the law, he served Asian rulers with entire impartiality. One of his assignments was as a surgeon in the British Indian army, a position for which he had neither training nor experience. He later became a colonel in the Union army during the Civil War and promoted a scheme to bring camels to the American southwest.

by Mohammed Akbar Khan, the Dost's oldest son, moved through the Khyber and defeated the Sikhs in a battle at Jamrud in which Hari Singh, the ablest Sikh general, was killed. The Afghans nevertheless failed to follow up this opportunity, and Peshawar remained in the hands of the Sikhs.

It should be noted that the Afghans were extremely concerned over their loss of Peshawar and the surrounding plain, both because of the richness of the province and because its Pushtoon inhabitants were basic to their own strength. Sikh rule, on the other hand, was always tenuous. Supported largely by an army trained by mercenary European officers, and the astuteness of Runjit Singh, the Sikh's hold on territory west of the Indus was maintained only by savage repression and continued military effort. Runjit Singh himself called Peshawar "a necklace of knives hung around my throat by Hari Singh."

Most probably the Afghans would have regained this lost territory once Dost Mohammed had stabilized his rule had the situation not been complicated by increasing interest of the British. The Dost, aware in a puzzled way of the antagonism of some of the British leaders, and of Wade in particular, in 1836 sent a letter to Auckland which read in part:

It may be known to your Lordship, that relying upon the principles of benevolence and philanthropy that distinguish the British Government, I look upon myself and country as bound to it by the strongest ties. The late transactions in this quarter, the conduct of the reckless and misguided Sikhs and their breach of treaty are well known to your Lordship. Communicate to me whatever might suggest itself to your wisdom for the settlement of the affairs of this country.[10]

Auckland did not reply until three months later, and then he wrote merely that he planned to send a commercial mission to Kabul. He concluded, "It is not the practice of the British Government to interfere with the affairs of other independent states; and indeed it does not immediately occur to me how the interference of my Government could be exercised for your benefit." [11]

The general trend of Auckland's thinking had been established by this time, partly from the advice of his subordinates and partly as a result of instructions from London. Even before replying to Dost Mohammed, he had been instructed as follows by the Secret Committee of the Board of Directors of the East India Company:

Judge as to what steps it may be proper and desirable . . . to take, to watch more closely than has hitherto been attempted the progress of events in Afghanistan and to counteract the progress of Russian influence in a quarter, which . . . could not fail, if it were once established, to act injuriously on the system of our alliances and possibly to interfere with the tranquillity of your own territory. . . . The mode of dealing with this very important question . . . we confide to your own discretion . . . as well as the adoption of any other measures that may appear to you desirable— should you be satisfied that the time has come for you to interfere decisively in the affairs of Afghanistan.[12]

The group of advisers to whom Auckland looked for direction was made up of Henry Torrens, John Colvin, William Macnaghten, and Claude Wade. These men were alike in being young and able, in their fluency as linguists, and in their wide experience of Indian affairs. But they knew little of Afghanistan, and followed Wade in tending to overestimate the Sikhs' power and in ascribing rather too much benevolence to Runjit Singh.

For some time the British had employed at the court of Dost Mohammed a combination agent and pseudo-envoy by the name of Charles Masson. This extraordinary figure was a mixture of linguist, numismatist, archaeologist, and hobo, who wandered through central Asia with as much aplomb as though it had been Hyde Park or Piccadilly Circus. Much respected by Dost Mohammed and the Afghan leaders, he had more knowledge of Afghanistan and its affairs than any foreigner.

Although Masson had let it out that he was an American, he was in fact a Briton, under an alias. Under his own name of James Lewis, he had joined and then deserted from the Bengal Artillery. This, unfortunately, was known to Auckland, who was accordingly not disposed to give much heed to Masson as an authority on Afghanistan.

Another British "authority," and one socially more acceptable, was Alexander Burnes, a thirty-two-year-old grandnephew of the Scottish poet, a captain in the Indian army, and a talented linguist. In 1832 Burnes had headed a mission to Afghanistan and Bokhara, and a book he had written on his travels had produced a sensation. He was extremely personable, and had left a strongly favorable impression on Auckland when the two met in London just before the latter left for India.

Burnes, unfortunately, had other less pleasing qualities: a temperament that alternated between moods of optimism and despair, and an ambition that made him reluctant to oppose his superiors even when he felt they were in the wrong. He readily took advantage of his position to indulge in various amatory adventures—which would not have been unusual for that time and place except for the surprising number of women involved. Masson was no doubt envious of Burnes, but he wrote sourly in his diary that he refused "to follow the examples of my illustrious superiors and fill my house with black-eyed damsels." [13]

Late in 1836, Burnes was sent to Kabul at the head of a mission that included two lieutenants whose surnames were Leech and Wood, and a Dr. Percival Lord. This was the "mission of commerce" mentioned by Auckland in his letter to Dost Mohammed, and although its ostensible purpose was to investigate the use of the Indus River for British trade, the underlying political intent was obvious. The mission arrived in Kabul in 1837 and was greeted with impressive ceremony.

Meanwhile, events to the west were adding to the importance of the mission. During the preceding year British influence in Persia had fallen so low that Mohammed Shah, the Persian ruler, was openly avowing that he planned to seize Herat. Although the British cared little about who occupied Herat, they did not fail to note that the Persians had been prompted by the Russians, and assumed that their intended move was the first step toward a Russian invasion of India. Probably the Russians had no such thing in mind, although the behavior of their agents in the field was often at variance with the words of officials in St. Petersburg. At any rate, early in 1837 the Persian Shah delivered to Yar Mohammed, who was now in power at Herat, a demand that the city accept Persian control. This ultimatum was refused, whereupon a large Persian army assembled and after some delay began a straggling march across the country. Four months later in November 1837, it reached the walls of Herat.

Both in London and in India the action of the Persians and the refusal of Mohammed Shah to heed British protests caused an alarm which in the perspective of time now appears completely groundless. It was believed, for example, that the Persian army was commanded by Russian officers—an absurd misapprehension, for although two divisions were commanded by foreign officers, Generals Boroffski and Semineau, the former was actually Polish and the latter French. The sole Russian officer was a convert to Islam, General Samsoun Khan, who had once been a sergeant in the army of the Czar.

The siege of Herat was carried out with the extraordinary bungling that characterized Persian military activities in the nineteenth century. According to a French general, J. P. Ferrier, who visited Herat shortly after the siege, the main endeavor of each of the Persian generals was to prevent the rest from achieving the slightest success, and that of the commander, Haji Mirza Aghazi, to avoid any necessity for becoming a military hero.

The Afghans, on the other hand, were ably led by Yar Mohammed, who had destroyed all the villages within twelve miles of the city before the arrival of the Persians, and had encouraged the defenders by a frequent use of the services of the public executioner. Since the Persians had also neglected the humdrum service of supply, their unfortunate soldiers were soon reduced to eating clover.

The defenders of the city were further heartened by the presence of a British officer, Lieutenant Eldred Edward Pottinger of the Bombay Artillery, who had embarked upon a private mission of investigation, disguised as a horse trader—a ruse that fooled no one. Pottinger's part in the defense of the city is now part of British folklore, though it is doubtful whether the "hero of Herat" was ever as important to that city as he later became to the British public. The Afghans see no reason nowadays to appreciate his efforts, and the jealous

Masson thought at the time that "the place would have been as well fought without him." Undoubtedly, however, his participation had a psychological effect upon the defenders, who supposed it to be a token of British support.

When the news of the Persian attack reached India, Auckland dispatched instructions to Burnes that changed the mission from a commercial to an openly political one and supplied him with intelligence for transmission to the Amir. The latter was to be told that the British could offer him no support against "our old friend and firm ally Runjit Singh," and advised him not to receive a Persian envoy who was reputedly on his way to Kabul. The message closed with the ominous declaration that "if he received with favor every emissary and every proposition the avowed object of which was to foment disturbances even at the hazard of his own independence, it is impossible but that the friendly feelings of the British Government must be impaired." [14]

This threat had been prompted by a report to the British from their agent Mohan Lal that the Dost had written to request aid from both the Czar of Russia and the Shah of Persia. The report was correct; indeed, the agent himself had helped draft the letters. Where Auckland and his advisers erred was in taking them seriously. As Masson and Burnes both realized, the Amir was merely hoping to prod the British into action. The policy of threatening to deal with their enemies was popular in Afghanistan, as it often is in countries surrounded by competing powers, to whom it may at times bring benefits and at times disaster. Burnes, hampered by a self-seeking ambition, was careful to confine such observations to the secrecy of his diary. Since he had, moreover, been given no plenary powers, the Dost was puzzled by this envoy who offered nothing more tangible than friendly advice.

At this time, a newcomer arrived in Kabul—a young man in the uniform of a Cossack lieutenant who had wandered up the road from Kandahar, and who purported to be an envoy of the Czar. He was not a Russian but a Pole, and his name was Jean Witkiwicz (spelled variously as Vilkovich, Vikovich, Vitkaviech, and Vitkavitch). After being deported to Orsk in 1823 for his part in founding a secret society of Polish patriots, he had learned Persian and Turki, aided Alexander von Humboldt in planning his expeditions to central Asia, and been given a commission in the Cossacks. When eventually he returned to St. Petersburg from his mission to Afghanistan he was received with honors. A week later he was found shot to death, his papers all destroyed—a suicide according to the government, a victim according to the skeptics. Every trace of his real purpose in Afghanistan died with him.[15]

To the Afghans an envoy without money or entourage was improbable. The Pole did carry two letters, however—one from the Czar, and one from the Persian Shah. Both were innocuous; the Shah said merely that Witkiwicz had paid his respects on his way through Persia, Nicholas I assured the Amir that Afghan merchants would be respected and welcomed in Russia.

The effect upon Burnes of the Czarist envoy's arrival, despite the caution with which the Afghans received him, was to bring on a fit of melancholy, for which his remedy was to bind his head with towels and make use of smelling salts. All this afforded Masson considerable amusement, since he was aware that the Dost had no faith in Witkiwicz at all, but had bidden the minister of court "to lodge him with Mohammed Hussein at the Nawabs and there will be two Lutiars (buffoons) together."[16]

Though Witkiwicz remained at Kabul, after a time Burnes emerged sufficiently from his depression to continue negotiations. Late in December he wrote Auckland his own recommendations for a policy in the best British interests. He was certain that Dost Mohammed was eager to conclude a treaty of alliance with Great Britain and willing to halt all communications with Persia or Russia. The only thing the Afghans asked of the British was their aid in inducing Runjit Singh to relinquish the city of Peshawar, for which the Dost was willing to pay an indemnity.

Burnes added his belief that the power and stability of the Sikh state were illusory, since they rested solely upon the aging frame of Runjit Singh. He was certain that the Sikh raja could easily be persuaded to give up Peshawar, which had brought him nothing but trouble.

The reaction in India confirmed the prudence of Burnes' habit of keeping his real opinions for his diary. Auckland immediately wrote to inform the envoy that he had exceeded his instructions, that he was not to concern himself with policy, and that the Dost was to expect no more than a "continuance of British good offices." Even this would be impossible, Auckland added, unless the Afghans made overtures of peace to the Sikhs and stopped all communications with foreign powers.

These instructions left Burnes in a hopeless position. The good offices beyond whose continuance he was empowered to offer nothing had, in effect, never begun. Rather than demand that the Afghans relinquish their sovereignty in the field of foreign affairs, on April 26, 1838, he departed Kabul for India, leaving Witkiwicz in possession of the field.

Without question the presence of the wandering Pole had strongly influenced the thinking of Auckland and alarmed the home government. Under instructions from Palmerston, Lord Clanricarde, the British ambassador to Russia, forwarded a strong note asking for a clarification of the purpose of Witkiwicz in visiting Kabul. This was answered on October 20, 1838, by the Russian ambassador to Great Britain, who asserted that the trip was due to the "restless activity of certain unaccredited and unrecognized individuals." [17]

It is still difficult to make out what lay behind this diplomatic denial. Without question the Czar's foreign office had been made uneasy by the growth of British hostility, particularly now that the Treaty of Unkiar-Skelessi in 1833 had brought the Russians close to a cherished goal, the Mediterranean. Most probably they were anxious to put any possible pressure on Great Britain and were surprised and pleased by the apprehensiveness of the British concerning Witkiwicz's visit. But if the Russians had intended serious negotiations with Kabul, they would no doubt have sent a more imposing embassy than the unattended, unfinanced Pole.

At any rate, Auckland and his advisers remained certain that the presence of Witkiwicz meant a serious threat to British India, and decided that British interests must be protected by immediate and drastic action. Their plan was to replace Dost

Mohammed by the exiled Shuja, who would then rule as a British puppet in the fashion established in the princely states of India.

This scheme originated in the mind of William Hay Macnaghten, head of the secret and political departments of the British secretariat; or so, at least, his colleagues declared in later years, with Macnaghten dead and unable to defend himself. The plan, which quite probably was his invention, met unanimous approval from other members of the council and was eagerly accepted by Auckland.

Having decided on a course of action, in May 1838 Auckland visited Lahore for a meeting with Runjit Singh. Here an agreement known as the Tripartite Treaty was signed on July 16 by Shah Shuja and on July 23 by Runjit Singh. Under its terms, Shuja was to relinquish all claim to territory held by the Sikhs, and Runjit Singh was to aid in Shuja's attempt to gain the Afghan throne. Shuja was to march on Kandahar along the route he had taken in 1834, while a Sikh army led by Timur Mirza, Shuja's oldest son, was to force the Khyber and advance on Kabul.

A few conversations convinced Auckland that the British could expect only paper promises from the Sikh leader. Actually, Runjit Singh was more concerned about safeguarding the Sutlej border with the British than about any threat from the Afghans. Looking at a map of India one day, he sighed and said prophetically, *"Ek din sab lal ho jaiga* (One day it will all be red)."* He was not averse to the destruction of Dost Mohammed, his most persistent enemy, and he realized that his refusal to participate might cause the British to reopen negotiations with the Amir; but he was determined to keep Sikh participation to a minimum. Aware of this hesitance, Auckland realized that the project must be a British effort. Acccordingly, on October 1, 1838, he issued at Simla a manifesto which set forth the reasons for the British action.

Few acts by an imperial administrator have been more roundly criticized than Auckland's, once his plan had actually gone down before the cold wind of disaster. But this almost unanimous condemnation was after the event. At the time his scheme encountered few dissenters, and the British public strongly supported it. The *Chronicle* represented the prevailing attitude when it said that "the course adopted by the Indian government, tending to erect Afghanistan into a barrier of our Eastern Empire, is such as is dictated by the soundest policy. . . ." [18]

The fundamental defect in the British action was almost certainly that it had been formulated by men all but totally ignorant of Afghanistan. Their considerable experience in India led them to equate Afghans with Indians, and this error was the cause of the troubles that followed.

"Auckland's Folly"

A true friend is a saddled horse.
—AFGHAN PROVERB

His Majesty Shah Soojah [sic] will
enter Afghanistan surrounded by his
own troops and will be protected by
a British army against foreign intervention and factious opposition. . . .
—SIMLA MANIFESTO

HAVING taken care of the diplomacy, Auckland turned to the
more difficult task of implementing the policy he had adopted.
Ferozepore was chosen as the point of assembly for an "army of
liberation" and Sir Harry Fane, commander in chief of the
Indian army, was appointed chief liberator. Six thousand men
were hastily recruited for the personal army of Shuja, most of
them Moslems from the martial Punjab, plus a number of
Gurkhas from Nepal, who had proved the value of their spirit
and the strength of their kukris in the Nepalese War and were
just beginning their career as the mercenaries of Asia. Twelve
thousand soldiers from the Bengal army composed the backbone of the force, and five thousand Marathas were enlisted at
Bombay to combat their old enemies.

Unsolicited thousands of the human kites and pariah crows
of India now appeared on the skirts of the spreading camp:

thieves, opium peddlers, prostitutes, hostlers, and beggars, all with ears cocked for the chink of gold and fingers twitching for the loot of the battlefield.

While young subalterns enjoyed themselves to the limit of their slender purses, their superiors spent the time in durbar. Shah Shuja, his long beard carefully dyed, arrived with a retinue of followers and the blind Shah Zeman. Next came Runjit Singh, "an old mouse with grey whiskers and one eye," followed by Auckland and British officialdom. The three courts provided prestige in plenty, the November weather was delightful, and spirits were high at the start of the "great adventure." Soon, however, "the spittle of argument was staining the carpet of accord," thanks to the obduracy of Runjit Singh. By some physiological miracle the brain of the wily Sikh had survived the mixture of brandy, opium, marihuana, and meat juice that was his daily potion, and his one eye (invariably a bright red) still saw more clearly than those of his allies.

Auckland had hoped that he could persuade the Sikhs to lead the main attack on Afghanistan; but he found that the Lion of the Punjab not only did not intend to enter the trap of the Khyber but also was opposed to the presence of British troops anywhere in his territory. After much discussion, the Sikh leader agreed to the formation of an expeditionary force at Peshawar, but insisted that the brunt of the invasion be carried by the British in the south.

At this moment news came that the Persian army had raised its siege of Herat and begun moving westward. With an army of thirty thousand men thus rendered unnecessary, Fane was replaced by Sir Willoughby Cotton, and one infantry division was placed in reserve at Ferozepore.

On December 10, 1838, Shuja and his personal levies moved out in the van, followed by General Cotton and the main force of about 9,500 soldiers. Although no count was made of followers, their number was undoubtedly enormous—twenty or thirty thousand men and women at the very least. No service of supply existed in the Indian army, and the British followed the ancient custom of dealing with private merchants who followed the troops. In addition, each British officer and soldier considered a staff of servants a necessity; one junior subaltern related that his tent was saved from being blown away by the efforts of his seventeen retainers. Finally, trudging in the wake of the army were a horde of India's pauperized population, including a number of "wives" picked up for the campaign. This tumultuous, completely undisciplined mass was given to sudden surges of panic, and the impossibility of providing even rudimentary hygiene made it a walking incubator for cholera, typhoid, and typhus.

At this time the efficiency of the British army in India had reached its nadir. To the businessmen who headed the East India Company, soldiers at best were no more than requisite nuisances, and officers' salaries were as low as their scale of living was high. Since the Burmese War of 1826 the troops had seen little action, and extended garrison duty had done nothing to develop rapport between officers and men.

The organization of the troops followed the European model, although with a deficiency of equipment. Both infantry and cavalry were formed in brigades of three battalions, one European and two sepoy. Dressed in the traditional red coats, white trousers, and tall shakos of the British army, the men were an inspiring sight in battle and a dismaying one in the heat of summer.

Artillery had not advanced far beyond that of the Napoleonic period. Most of the guns were horse-drawn; a few field batteries were pulled by oxen. The pack artillery that had long been a feature of Indian warfare was not used, since the elephant was considered unsuited for the Afghan uplands, and lighter pieces for horse or muleback were still uninvented.

Clumsy though the British army might be, it appeared a marvel of efficiency by comparison to anything the Afghans could boast. In fact, so greatly had the army retrogressed in strength since the days of Ahmed Shah that no longer did anything deserving of the name army exist in Afghanistan. The day of battles in which the issue was decided by swordsmanship was past; of the new requirements, discipline and the musket, the Afghans had none of the first and few of the second. Moreover, years of civil war had obliterated all but the last trace of Afghan nationalism, leaving little besides the old personal or tribal loyalties. Dost Mohammed, waiting anxiously at Kabul, was able to raise only a few thousand irregular horse, while the tribal chiefs remained aloof.

The first stages of the British march were uneventful. But after bridging the Indus at Bukkur and Shirkapore the men entered a waterless desert and began to suffer from thirst. (The little wooden kegs with which they had been provided were apparently the first official canteens in history.) Entering Bolan Pass, the army and the followers were harassed by Baluchi and Achakzai raiders, but the attacks were prompted by a desire for loot and were on a small scale.

After reaching Quetta on March 26, the army halted to await the arrival of the Bombay column, and Sir John Keane replaced General Cotton as commander. At the same time the troops were joined by Sir William Macnaghten, bearing the title of envoy from the Government of India to the court of Shah Shuja, and Alexander Burnes, who was to act as Macnaghten's assistant.

These appointments were part of the anomalous situation. Officially the British were neither invading Afghanistan nor at war with it, but were merely accompanying Shuja as an allied escort. The British taste for legality had seen to it that the military commanders had no authority except in military matters; the actual direction of affairs was in the hands of political officers.

The civil duties with which these "politicals" had been charged were ostensibly under the control of Shah Shuja, but were actually commanded by Macnaghten, and usually were executed by individuals according to their own judgment. Many of the latter had been hastily recruited from the lower ranks of the officers, with the result that generals found themselves taking orders from mere lieutenants—to the exceeding annoyance of the one and the vast amusement of the other.

As the British army moved through Khojak Pass and began its march across the sandy plains toward Kandahar, the local tribes proved more curious than hostile; the raids made by small bands of Ghilzai were prompted more by natural ebullience than by antagonism. The main casualties occurred among the camels; for contrary to popular belief, these ungainly beasts are a liability in unskilled hands, and during the course of the war over fifty thousand died on the way.

As the army neared Kandahar the Barukzai brothers who ruled the city fled to the west, and on April 24 Shah Shuja, accompanied by Macnaghten, entered the city in triumph. The latter, always an optimist, claimed an enthusiastic welcome; but according to a more observant British officer, though the crowds cried "May the Shah live forever," it was "not quite in the Vive le roi fashion." [1]

Nor was Macnaghten's belief that the Shah was popular in the south shared by the column led by Major General Willshire, which arrived on May 4. Forty of its men had been killed in combat, and hundreds of straggling followers had been murdered on the way. In general the Kandaharis stayed aloof from Shuja's court; the few chiefs who came forward did so less out of loyalty than hunger for the gold mohurs that Macnaghten was lavishly distributing.

On June 27, after a month of heat and dysentery the army moved on toward Kabul, leaving a strong force in reserve at Kandahar. The soldiers perspired in temperatures up to 120 degrees as they toiled up the plateau leading to Ghazni, which they reached after twenty-four days of uneventful marching. Here the garrison was commanded by Ghulam Hyder Khan, a son of Dost Mohammed. The approaching soldiers were met by scattered fire from skirmishers equipped with matchlocks, who soon broke off and retreated behind the city walls.

At three o'clock on the morning of July 23, a small party of engineers crept to the northern or Kabul gate, where they placed a thirty-pound charge of powder without arousing the sentries. The explosion blew the gate apart and allowed a storming party to enter the city. According to the official account, after a brief melee at the gate "the Afghans took refuge in the houses, firing on the column as it made its way through the streets, and a good deal of desultory fighting took place." But this was British understatement. That what really occurred amounted to a thoroughgoing sack of the city is attested by the casualties: five hundred Afghans dead, seventeen of the British, As the sepoys poured through the twisted streets, "you soon saw Cashmere shawls, ermine dresses, and ladies' inexpressibles over the bloodstained uniforms of our men—the poor women themselves, in some instances, dragged out." [2]

The brilliant exhibition of courage and timing that characterized the storming of Ghazni confounded the Dost, who found his few adherents daily melting away. In a last fruitless attempt he sent one of his brothers, Jubbar Khan, known as the "Feringhee's friend," to negotiate with the British; but the move served only to confirm the weakness of the Amir.

On July 30 the British renewed their march on Kabul. At Argundeh the Dost attempted a stand; but his followers fled at the rumor of the British approach, and only a row of abandoned cannon remained to meet the army that trailed down from the Ghazni plateau into Kabul.

Determined to remove the greatest danger to Shah Shuja from the scene, the British immediately sent Captain Outram with eight hundred cavalrymen in pursuit of the Dost. But their quarry was a crack rider from a tribe of horsemen, and he had an ally in one Haji Khan Kakar, an Afghan chief who volunteered to act as a British guide and who proceeded to take the pursuers down every path but the right one. After a month of fruitless chase, Outram and his men returned to Kabul, and in return for his dubious services Haji Khan Kakar was exiled to India.

Meanwhile the British had reached the walls of Kabul, where on August 7 Shuja, with Macnaghten at his side, rode through streets he had not seen for thirty years. The crowds were respectful but quiet—behavior that was immediately taken by the sanguine Macnaghten for the "congratulations of his people." But once again, another British officer, either more discerning or more apprehensive, saw nothing but "stern and scowling looks." [3] No trouble developed; Shah Shuja mounted his throne without opposition, and sirdars began to appear with pledges of fealty.

At about the same time a British mission left Kandahar for Herat, commanded by Major D'Arcy Todd, and bearing cash instead of cartridges, with instructions to conclude a treaty of alliance with Yar Mohammed. The latter, however, relying on nobody but himself and seeing all other men in the mirror of his own personality, took the British gifts and a British subsidy, asked for more, promised much, and fulfilled nothing. His policy could hardly have been expressed more clearly than when he wrote the Wazir of Persia that he "tolerated the presence of the British Envoy from expediency although to give him his due he was by no means niggardly." [4]

In Kabul the rule of Shah Shuja proceeded smoothly against a backdrop of British bayonets. The country was quiet, the bazaar-keepers were doing a rushing business, and the soldiers and sepoys were behaving with decorum. The British were much impressed by the forthright manliness of the Afghans, and the Afghans in their turn admired the British, particularly for their love of sports.

Auckland received the news of this friendship with satisfaction, the more since it enabled him to reduce the military forces in Afghanistan. In September, accordingly, the Bombay column marched from Kabul to Kandahar and then to India, and one month later General Keane, now Baron of Ghazni, rode to India through the Khyber Pass. On the way from Kandahar to India the Bombay column was ordered to turn aside and attack Mehrab Khan, the Baluchi chief of Kalat. The Khan was picked as a victim because he had supposedly withheld supplies when the British army entered Afghanistan, although in fact the wastelands of Baluchistan provided so little food that its inhabitants had been reduced by the passage of the British to "feeding on herbs and grasses."

With traditional Baluchi bravery, the old Khan defended his city "at the head of his people, he himself with many of his chiefs being killed sword in hand." After the sack of Kalat a puppet chief, Nawaz Khan, was installed, and the city was left in charge of a political officer, Lieutenant Loveday. According to Masson—who, it must be granted, was rarely objective about British politicals—Loveday's behavior reached new depths even for that degraded service. At any rate his rule was brief; the son of Mehrab Khan instigated a revolt, and after unseating Nawaz

Khan put Loveday to death. The British were in no position to retaliate, and the sordid Baluchistan adventure ended as a fiasco.

At Kabul, meanwhile, Macnaghten had begun to organize the new government. The plan followed the precedent set in India for states the British wished to control rather than annex. Power was divided between Shah Shuja and the British, with the former administering civil and criminal law while the British retained control over foreign affairs, the army, and the tribes.

Dyarchy proved a blunder in Afghanistan. Since the Afghans had no mystique of kingship but obeyed their rulers solely because they had power, it was obvious to all, himself included, that Shuja's power was really in alien hands. The latter had lost none of his pride in exile, and bitterly resented his role as a puppet. The charge that he began to intrigue against the British at this point has not been substantiated, but of his wish to have them out of the country there can be no question.

Macnaghten, however, saw nothing but success, for the sirdars were respectful and the tribes quiet. Occasionally some clan, usually belonging to the Ghilzai, would cause trouble; but such outbreaks were local and easily halted by punitive expeditions or the exercise of bribery. There appears, in fact, to have been little real hostility toward the British.

A court very quickly grew up around Shah Shuja, composed of leading Durrani sirdars and a number of Barukzais who were apparently willing to accept the renewal of Popolzai hegemony. It was unfortunate but inevitable that the high positions were given to Shah Shuja's comrades in exile, who were apparently determined to compensate for previous reverses. Other important figures were Osman Khan Barukzai, a nephew of the Dost; Abdullah Khan, a chief of the Achakzai Durrani; and Aminullah Khan, a powerful malik of the Ghilzai.

The only menace to the situation was the continued freedom of the Dost. In an attempt to remedy it, a regiment commanded by the Dr. Lord who had accompanied Burnes on the Kabul mission was sent to Khulm, where the Amir had taken refuge, and whence he immediately fled to Bokhara. There he was imprisoned by the Uzbeg Amir, while Lord settled for the winter under the shadow of the giant Buddhas carved out of the cliffs of Bamian Valley, sending his troops on punitive expeditions against Hazara villages that refused to sell him their small store of food.

The winter of 1839 passed in quiet. The British enjoyed the brisk weather of mile-high Kabul, where the Afghans were impressed by the gyrations of British officers on skates—a new thing in their ancient land. The wives and children of British officers traveled to join their menfolk, and a small but active social life developed.

Trouble appeared again in the spring, when on the Kandahar-Kabul road the irrepressible Ghilzai began a series of raids that were difficult to stop and impossible to punish. Macnaghten, who believed in using bribery rather than force, promptly instituted a system of subsidies that pacified the Ghilzai maliks.

In July a more serious threat appeared in no less a person than the Dost, who with the connivance of the Uzbeg Amir had escaped from Bokhara, and who arrived at Khulm accompanied by a host of Uzbeg horsemen. Lord promptly called for reinforcements, which were sent to the number of eight hundred sepoys. On September 18 the combined British force met the Uzbegs in a valley close to Bamian, where the northern riders demonstrated their matchless horsemanship by heading for home at a pace the British found impossible to match.

After his disappointment with these allies the Dost fled to Kohistan, where he raised a lashkar of the region's belligerent Tadjiks. With Kohistan impinging on Kabul, this was a serious threat to the British; so General Sale with two thousand troops was sent to the assistance of Lord. On November 2 the British cavalry entered the Parwandarrah Valley, about forty miles north of Kabul, and were surprised to encounter the lashkar of the Dost. The tribesmen, mostly on foot, scrambled hastily up the surrounding hills, while with somewhere between forty and eighty retainers (depending on the account one happens to read) the Amir once again rode off.

With two squadrons of Bengal cavalry galloping after them, the Dost and his followers, concluding that escape was hopeless, turned and charged. But the cavalry, seemingly "spellbound by the demon fear," broke ranks and fled, leaving their British officers to face the attack alone. In the melee that followed, Dr. Lord and two lieutenants were killed, while the Dost, unpursued, made his way to safety. The Bengal soldiers, by way of excuse, blamed the quality of their sabers.

Despite this minor victory, the position of the Dost was now desperate. The tribesmen could not be induced to stand against the British regulars, and "there was no rest for the sole of his foot." Two days after the skirmish, the Dost met Macnaghten while he was riding on the outskirts of Kabul and surrendered his sword to the surprised envoy.[5]

Now that the Dost was in their hands, the British were as profuse in admiration as they had been dogged in pursuit—much to the dismay of Shuja, who would have preferred more practical if less sporting treatment. Indeed, the gracious personality and intelligence of the captive contrasted so favorably with the sullen hauteur of the Shah that from this time on many of the British officers, including Macnaghten, frankly regretted their role in the Afghan dynastic struggle. After a short stay in Kabul, the Dost was sent in exile to India accompanied by Sir Willoughby Cotton. General Sale remained in charge pending the arrival of the new commander, General Elphinstone.

Critics have argued that this was the time for the British to withdraw; but however sound this opinion might be in London, it was shaky in Kabul, where Macnaghten was well aware that the country was far from secure in the hands of Shuja. But the once approving British public had now turned against the Afghan "adventure," and the Tory press had begun making capital of an affair that seemed to be reaching no conclusion. The directors of the East India Company, moreover, were becoming restive over the expense of maintaining an army that was barred by circumstances from more direct control of the situation. In December Auckland received instructions either to withdraw from Afghanistan or to increase the number of British soldiers so that true pacification could be achieved.

Auckland did neither. Like Macnaghten, he was personally involved with the Afghan program, and to adopt either alterna-

The Kabul river in the heart of the city of Kabul. Sir William Macnaghten was killed close to this spot.

His Majesty Mohammed Zahir Shah, king of Afghanistan.

tive would have been to admit an error in judgment. Instead, he ordered the troops removed from the walled safety of the Bala Hissar, the citadel at Kabul, to a cantonment in the suburbs (to the satisfaction of Shah Shuja, who disliked their presence so close to his zenana), and encouraged British officers and men to bring their families to the city. The latter came with various eccentric companions, many of whom had strong missionary tendencies. According to Burnes, who was now governor of Kabul, "Every man comes here and makes a Barataria of his own; one man has proposed a constitution, another has gone to form a society for the suppression of vice among the Uzbegs." [6]

Despite these new arrivals the winter passed without incident, and the success of the British occupation appeared so complete that Macnaghten in a letter to Auckland spoke of a country that was "quiet from Dan to Beersheba." Underneath the surface, however, the banked fires of dissidence were smoldering; and the Afghans' attitude toward the British was changing from friendly curiosity to increasing dislike. Shuja was losing what few adherents he had once claimed, since it was obvious that he was a mere captive of the British. The position of the Shah was all the more difficult because he was deprived of the traditional methods of Asian statecraft, as well as badly served by courtiers who wasted no opportunity to enrich themselves, and who blamed whatever displeased their countrymen on the British. And in fact the Shah himself suffered at the hands of the alien political officers, who in their youth and inexperience displayed a callousness, and frequently a sadism, that are possibly unique in the annals of British imperialism. General Nott, the commander at Kandahar, caustically remarked that "the conduct of the thousand and one politicals has ruined our cause and bared the throat of every European in this country to the sword and knife of the revengeful Afghan and the Bloody Bellooch." [7]

Although Nott's irritation with the power of these fledgling officers led him into hyperbole, there was a good deal of truth in what he said. Actions such as that of one Captain Peter Nicolson, who destroyed a village of twenty-three people because "he thought they looked insultingly at him," could hardly be expected to inspire confidence in British justice.

Among other reasons for the Afghans' hatred was that the British were meddling with their women.[8] Quite naturally many of the British officers and men, not to speak of the sepoys, found celibacy a trial during the long term of duty, the more since many Afghan women were (as they still are) exceedingly pretty by Western standards. At this time Victorian morality had not yet arrived in India, and the native "housekeeper" was a fixture in the quarters of most British bachelors.

After the arrival of the British in Kabul, numerous liaisons were not long in developing between soldiers and Afghan women, some of which were legitimized by marriage but most of which were less formal. Although concubinage was common in Afghanistan, prostitution had been almost unknown until the arrival of these free-spending foreigners. Even more galling to local pride were the affairs between the British soldiers and Afghan married women. Early in the occupation Shuja executed a man who had killed his wife for adultery with a British soldier. The Shah's action was ordered by the British, and was a heinous breach of Afghan custom.

Another cause of resentment was the inflation produced by the easy nonchalance with which the British, following Macnaghten's lead, tossed away their government's money. Afghan merchants, whatever their antagonism toward the foreigner, were happy to accept his gold, while the poor of Kabul began to suffer as prices soared.

Finally religious fanaticism was aroused among the Afghans by the activities of missionaries and by the soldiers' thoughtless defilement of Afghan shrines. Before this time, non-Moslem travelers in Afghanistan had been unanimous in remarking on the Afghans' toleration toward other creeds, and in particular toward Christianity. From now on, however, the story was to be one of an antagonism toward the unbeliever for which Afghanistan later became notorious.[9]

In September Macnaghten received instructions that brought the simmering discontent to a boil. The Secret Committee of the East India Company, determined to check the expenditures of

this unproductive project, had issued orders that the subsidies to tribal leaders were to be discontinued. However,
Macnaghten might doubt the wisdom of this decision, the
orders were final. As soon as they were given, the tribes
promptly cut off communications between Kabul and India.

Macnaghten was not greatly alarmed, since revolts had
erupted before and as quickly subsided. Besides, he was looking
forward to leaving Afghanistan for a new post as governor of
Bombay. Even for its author, the excitement of the Afghan
adventure had long since palled.

VIII

The Khurd Kabul

A drum sounds sweetly—at a distance.
—PUSHTO PROVERB

AS a matter of economy, Richard Sale, who had been made a major general, had been ordered to return to India with his brigade. It was these troops that were now sent to punish the recalcitrant tribesmen and clear the passes.

On October 9, Colonel Monteith and the van met fierce opposition in the Khurd Kabul Pass, about seventeen miles outside Kabul. They were joined on the following day by Sale and the brigade, and after three days of heavy fighting the advance cleared the pass. They pushed forward, only to be halted five days later by renewed attacks. The tribesmen, Ghilzai and Shinwaris, were fighting with a skill and persistence they had not shown hitherto, covering the heights and pouring a steady and accurate fire into the British ranks. On October 22, the harassed troops were at Tezin, still no more than twenty-nine miles from Kabul.

Apparently the British officers were close to panic. In all previous clashes the Afghans had come on in uncoordinated cavalry charges, which melted away before the steady fire of the British infantry. Now both tactics and terrain had changed. The tribesmen were accomplished hillmen, more agile among the rocky crags than any plains-bred Punjabi or British Tommy; they clung to the heights and kept the enemy under constant fire. And many of the Afghans were armed with jezails, long guns resting on tripods, which outranged "brown Bess," the Tower musket of the soldiers.

Leaving the safety of Tezin, the troops were attacked again in the Jagdalak Valley by large numbers of Mohmands, Safis, and Khugianis who had hurried up to join the battle. Several times the British rearguard wavered, but it held together under the urging of its officers. The situation had become so touchy that a total of 120 dead and wounded were left behind. The sepoys were becoming demoralized, and the Afghan soldiers of Shah Shuja were openly fraternizing with the attackers.

On October 30, Sale's brigade reached the valley of Gandamak, where it halted to await news from Kabul. The message that arrived from Macnaghten reported that all Kabul had risen, and ordered the brigade to return at once.

Sale, who had been wounded, was appalled at the thought of again facing the deadly passes. With a timidity oddly at variance with his past and future career he called an officers' council, at which a decision was taken, over the protest of one captain, to disobey orders and continue toward Jalalabad. In his reply to General Elphinstone, who was now the commander in Kabul, Sale justified the step by pointing out that his ammunition was gone, his wounded impossible to move, the entire countryside up in arms, and the troops in Kabul already short of provisions. All of this was perfectly true, but it still does not explain Sale's recalcitrance; especially since his wife and daughter were still in Kabul. At any rate, on November 11 the brigade continued toward Jalalabad.

In Kabul the situation was grave. When the brigade left, the city had appeared quiet; Macnaghten had been preparing to depart, and the British were looking forward to the holiday season. Although friendly Afghans had brought repeated warnings that trouble was afoot, the British leaders had paid them no attention.

The chief cause of the disaster that ensued was the extraordinary ineptness of the British leadership, particularly among the military. The new commander, General William Elphinstone, second cousin of Mountstuart, was a superannuated veteran of the Napoleonic wars, ill with rheumatic gout and completely ignorant of Asia. Brigadier John Shelton, the second in command, was physically fit and personally brave but suffered from a personality disorder that was close to psychosis.

Under these men the British troops had been quartered in as unmilitary a position as possible. The cantonment was located in Sherpore, which today is a suburb of Kabul but at the time lay about a mile north of the city. About a thousand yards from the cantonment was the low hill of Behmaru, whose summit looked directly into the camp. All around were qalas, Afghan forts; one of them lay between the troops and the commissariat. The treasury and Burnes's residence were deep in the twisted streets of the city.

On November 2 the warnings of the friendly Afghans were proved to have been well founded. For some time a number of powerful sirdars at Shuja's court had been stirring up Afghan antagonism toward the British. Their leader was Abdullah Khan, chief of the Achakzai Durranis, a bold and energetic man who had become a particular enemy of Alexander Burnes. Aiding him were Aminullah Khan, a Ghilzai, and Zeman Shah, a cousin of Dost Mohammed.

The plotting of these men was an open secret, which Burnes and Macnaghten, knowing of the Afghan penchant for intrigue, treated with derision. Burnes and Macnaghten, incidentally, disliked each other, the former resenting his inferior position while the latter rejected most of Burnes's suggestions with curt comments.[1]

For some time Burnes had been threatening to exile a number of Durrani leaders who had corresponded with the Dost. This threat, as well as Burnes's protection of a number of Afghan women who had left their husbands to live with British officers, caused some of the Afghan leaders to join the conspiracy of Abdullah Khan. This fact was reported to the British by Osman Khan, Shah Shuja's Wazir. But for some reason no action was taken. On November 1, Mohan Lal, the British undercover agent who was still active in Kabul, went to the residence of Burnes and "told him that the confederacy has grown very high and we should fear the consequence. He stood up in his chair, sighed, and said, he knows nothing but the time has arrived when we should leave this country." [2]

Burnes was right; but that time had already run out. The next morning a hundred armed Afghans led by Abdullah Khan ran through the streets of Kabul, followed by a throng of the curious and the pugnacious. As they came they encouraged each other in the manner of mobs, and when the din of their approach reached Burnes at his residence, he ordered the gates of his compound barred and sent Macnaghten a call for aid.

Reaching the compound, the crowd began to hack at the clay of the walls, while the twenty-four male defenders fired through loopholes. As no soldiers appeared, the merely curious became combatants and the pugnacious grew bloodthirsty. Burnes and the little garrison fought desperately while they waited for help that never came, but at two in the afternoon they were overwhelmed. Burnes was killed instantly by a pistol shot, and no mercy was shown to anyone, Afghan women not excepted, who was found inside. The only survivor was an Afghan servant, Mohammed Hussein, who received twenty-six wounds.

The mob, now in a frenzy, turned next to the neighboring treasury and sacked it of its 17,000 pounds sterling. Here two captains, Johnson and Trevor, were not harmed and were allowed to go to the cantonment along with the latter's wife and seven children. Burnes was plainly the object of special hatred, because of his position as governor of the city, as well as the popular if incorrect belief that he was responsible for the British invasion, and his reputation for intrigues with Afghan women.

The immediate cause of the outbreak is still disputed. The British blamed the malice of Abdullah Khan, who according to their version had told a group of sirdars that they were to be exiled, and had circulated a letter he had forged, purporting to be from Shuja and calling for an attack on Burnes. The Afghans named as the instigator the head mullah of Kabul, Mohammed Shah Khan, who was supposed to have been visited by the spirit of a departed saint with instructions to drive out the infidels. Probably both stories contain some truth, but many of the crowd were undoubtedly motivated more by excitement and the lure of the lightly guarded treasury than by religious zeal.

No satisfactory explanation has ever been given for the lethargy of Macnaghten and Elphinstone, who listened to the roar of musketry from the city without taking a step to aid their countrymen. Shah Shuja alone sent a corps of Hindustani troops, commanded by the same adventurer, Campbell, who had served him in his unsuccessful invasion in 1834. The city was now completely aroused, however; everywhere its narrow streets and fortlike buildings swarmed with armed and furious Afghans. After savage fighting, Campbell retreated to the safety of the citadel.

For a few days there was a lull, although hundreds of Afghans streamed into the city from surrounding villages and the bazaar-keepers closed their shops. The British remained in their fatal apathy while the rebel sirdars were jockeying for position. After much argument, Mohammed Zeman Shah was chosen as leader, a tribute to the absent Dost Mohammed since power actually rested with Abdullah Khan and Aminullah Khan.

Meanwhile the story of the revolt in Kabul sped through the country, and around tribal fires the roar of the city mob became a war cry. In Ghazni, Musa Khan, a malik of the Suleiman Khel Ghilzai, raised the populace and drove the British commandant, Colonel Palmer, into the citadel with his garrison. A few days later a Captain Woodburn led 130 soldiers out on the road to Kabul, where they were killed to a man. In Charikar the strong garrison of Gurkhas and Punjabi sepoys was attacked by Kohistani Tadjiks led by a chief, Khoja Mir Khan. The Moslem Punjabis, after a show of resistance, defected to the Afghans, while the sturdy Gurkhas, far from home and in the midst of an alien religion, held firm. Finally Major Pottinger and Captain Haughton decided on a retreat, which was carried out in the middle of the night, leaving the sentries uninformed and doomed at their posts. On the way the mounted officers deserted their troops, to reach Kabul after desperate adventures, and the Gurkhas paid for their fortitude with death under the Afghan knives.[3]

It is easy to condemn this action by Pottinger, the "hero of Heart," from the safety of hindsight. But it must be admitted that the British officers had settled into a condition that can only be described as total funk. Lady Sale, a sharp-tongued observer who might better have been in command herself, noted in her diary the stupidities of the senior officers and the ineptitude of the juniors, and their reflection in the lowered morale of the men.[4]

At this time the Afghans were joined by a new leader, Mohammed Akbar Khan. The oldest son of Dost Mohammed and his father's favorite, the young sirdar had the Dost's personal charm along with considerable ability, which was marred by an ungovernable temper. That his mother was a Popolzai princess, sister to Shuja's queen, added to his authority as the acknowledged heir of Dost Mohammed.[5]

After Akbar's arrival the number and intensity of Afghan attacks upon the cantonment soon increased, while the British officers grew still more irresolute. Provisions were scarce in the now crowded city, and it was difficult for the troops to secure supplies. Snipers perched on the top of Behmaru Hill continued to fire intermittently into the cantonment, and a detachment sent to clear away this nuisance went unwillingly and withdrew at the approach of a few Afghan horsemen.

This fiasco was a culmination of the hopelessness that gripped the daily officers' councils. Over the opposition of Macnaghten and Pottinger, the officers called for immediate evacuation to India and negotiations with the Afghan leaders. These were opened by Macnaghten on November 25, and on December 11 a treaty was signed between the British and eighteen of the insurgent chiefs, in which the British promised to leave Afghanistan in return for provisions. Neither side kept the bargain; the British remained in camp and no supplies appeared.

Apparently Macnaghten still hoped to salvage something from the wreckage of the adventure. He knew that the Afghan insurgent leaders were not united, and that a struggle for power was going on among them; his long experience as head of the Secret and Political Department of the Indian government had given him considerable acquaintance with the operation of undercover activities and a strong faith in the use of bribery and intrigue.

Within Kabul itself, Shah Shuja was still safe in the Bala Hissar with a powerful force. The city's ten thousand Kizzilbash were not fond of their Pushtoon nighbors, and had taken no part in the attacks on the British; their chief, Sharin Khan, continued to give verbal support to Macnaghten without taking any action. Among the insurgent sirdars Mohammed Akbar was struggling to uphold the authority of his absent father; Moham-med Zeman Khan had his own hopes, and some of the Popolzais suggested retaining Shah Shuja as at least a titular monarch.

Among these cross-currents Macnaghten now moved with gold and promises. His intrigues were soon known to the Afghans, nor were they unexpected; but his evident participation in assas-sination was another matter. Rewards of ten or fifteen thousand rupees were promised to various desperate characters for the heads of rebel leaders, and were probably responsible for the deaths of two, Abdullah Khan and Mir Musjidi. Activities of this sort carried inevitable hazards.

On December 22 an emissary, Sultan Khan, rode to the British camp with an offer from Mohammed Akbar. The sidar proposed to deliver the head of Aminullah Khan, the last of the original rebel leaders; the British were to remain for eight months; Akbar was to be made Wazir and receive thirty lacs of rupees; and Macnaghten was to meet Akbar on the fol-lowing day to seal the bargain. This fantastic offer so delighted Macnaghten that he stepped straight into the trap. On the following morning the envoy, accompanied by three captains, Lawrence, Trevor, and Mackenzie, rode to meet Akbar by the side of the Kabul River. When some of the Afghans began to crowd around as the men were talking and Macnaghten spoke of this to Akbar, the sirdar answered, "No, they are all in on the secret." Then, according to Captain Lawrence,

No sooner were these words uttered than I heard Mohammed Ak-bar call out "Beeger" (Seize) and turning around I saw him grasp the envoy's left hand with an expression of the most diabolical ferocity. The only words I heard poor Sir William utter were "Az barae Khoda" (For God's sake). I saw his face, however, It was full of horror.[6]

While Macnaghten was struggling he was shot dead by Akbar, who used a pistol recently given him by his victim. Mackenzie and Lawrence were saved by two sirdars, who helped the officers to mount behind them and galloped free of the throng. Captain Trevor was killed when his horse stumbled and threw him under the Afghan knives.

Macnaghten has been denounced by critics for his role in the disaster, and his colleagues united in blaming him after his death. But Sir John William Kaye, whose history of the war is accepted as authoritative and who is extremely critical of many of Macnaghten's actions, noted that he acted with unfailing courage and constancy and quotes with approval a comment by Burnes that Macnaghten was an excellent man but out of his depth in the situation in Afghanistan.[7]

Macnaghten's death was apparently the result of Mohammed Akbar's passionate and emotional nature, for the original plan had been only to take him captive. Although Akbar later told Lady Sale that he deeply regretted his deed, the killing met with general approval from the Afghans, who regarded Macnaghten as the man primarily responsible for the British invasion.

When the British learned of the fate of Macnaghten, whose headless body was displayed hanging from a pole in the bazaar, they were completely demoralized; for the envoy, alone among the leaders, had shown resolution and energy. He was replaced as senior political officer by Pottinger, who was then advised to reopen negotiations with Akbar for withdrawal to India. Pottinger somewhat warily complied, and the professedly penitent Afghan leader agreed to a treaty, "to put away strife and contention and to avert discord and enmity." [8]

On January 6 the entire British contingent—army, missionaries, women, and camp followers—left Kabul for India. The weather was clear but bitterly cold. Pottinger's sensible suggestion that the soldiers be equipped with sheepskin jackets, and that their feet be bound with rags was rejected by the military.

Accordingly, at half-past nine in the morning the soldiers moved shivering out onto the road of retreat. Altogether they numbered 4,500, with 970 Indian cavalry, 2,840 Indian infantry, and 690 Europeans. About twelve thousand camp followers scrambled in the rear.

Despite the warnings of friendly Afghans who had advised pushing on without delay, the march was slow and camp was made only six miles from Kabul. The rear guard, in fact, failed to arrive until two in the morning.

The next day's march began at dawn, with camp followers pushing past the soldiers, to be joined in their panic by the Sixth Infantry of Punjabis. The cold was paralyzing, and these men from the steaming plains of India had only one desire—to be back where it was warm. Paced by this maddened throng, the army reached Butkhak at one in the afternoon. Here it was met by Mohammed Akbar, who called for a halt and demanded Pottinger, Lawrence and Mackenzie as hostages. Another terrible night found the camp huddled in the snow with the sepoys burning their caps and stripping the camp followers to the skin in order to clothe themselves.

On the third day, only twelve miles from Kabul, the army stumbled into the Khurd Kabul Pass. Carved by the Khurd Kabul River, the pass runs for seven miles between towering crags of iron and basalt; it is nowhere more than two hundred yards wide; and the road twists and winds with the river, which it crosses twenty-three times.

As the half-frozen British entered this gorge they fell under heavy attack from galloping bands of horsemen in the rear, and from the heights, where tribesmen crouched and fired into the throng. Several Afghan sirdars, Mohammed Akbar among them, rode in the van of the army and called on their countrymen to hold their fire, but to no avail.[9]

All day the killing continued until night brought merciful darkness but pitiless cold. With more than three thousand bodies lying stripped and frozen in the Khurd Kabul, almost all trace of discipline vanished. But it was during these hours of horror that one redheaded Irish private turned to a passing officer with the classic remark of the campaign: "Faith, Sorr.

Isn't this a conthrary country?" Some of the sepoys gave their
horses to women and children, and one who had been mortally
wounded handed his musket to a comrade, saying, "Run,
brother, run. It is government property."

The next morning at the first grey of dawn the survivors
moved forward without waiting command. Soon there came a
troop of Afghan horsemen led by Mohammed Akbar, who advised the British ladies and their husbands to come with him
inasmuch as he could not control the tribesmen. His offer was
accepted and those officers who were accompanied by their
wives went with him.[10]

Out of the weary, stumbling crowd drew the Forty-fourth
Queens Regiment, to be joined by about fifty files of the Fifth
Native Cavalry. Lengthening the gap between them and the
main body of the army, they pushed on to Kubbar-i-Jubbar, five
miles beyond the Khurd Kabul. The remainder moved on cau-
tiously while watching tribesmen clustered on the heights. In
the heart of the Khurd Kabul the British came to the Targh-i-
Taraki, a tiny defile only fifty feet long and ten feet wide. As
they crowded into this narrow passage, the tribesmen surged
toward them; penned in a struggling mass, soldiers and camp
followers were almost annihilated. Only a few stalwarts cut
their way through and hastened to join the advance at Kubbar-i-
Jubbar.

On the following day these survivors continued the retreat,
with Brigadier Shelton commanding the rear and courageously
repelling the tribal attacks. In the afternoon they reached
Jagdalak and took refuge in a ruined fort. Here they received a
message from Akbar asking that Shelton and a Captain Johnson
come to his camp and suggesting that the dying General
Elphinstone might accompany them. At the camp there was a
meeting with the Ghilzai maliks who had led the attacking
tribesmen. Akbar apparently did all in his power to induce these
chiefs to call off the attacks; Mohammed Shah Khan, a Durrani
sirdar, offered them 60,000 rupees if they could restrain their
men.

But Akbar's influence and the rupees were both unavailing,
for the maliks were completely unable to control their men.

After another day of continued attack the troops marched out, leaving behind seventy wounded. For a few miles they were unmolested; then they came to another small gorge, which was blocked by an abbatis of thornwood. Again the tribesmen swarmed to the attack, while many of the screaming camp followers were cut down by the maddened soldiers. Most of the cavalry took this opportunity to desert, followed by a fusillade of shots from their remaining comrades. Some of the stronger and more resolute troops managed to clamber over the barricade and continue toward Jalalabad. Twenty officers were left, with fifty men of the European Forty-fourth, six of the Horse Artillery, and about three hundred camp followers. The figures shed interesting light on the mechanics of survival, for considering their position as primary targets the number of officers is remarkably high.

This little band pushed forward, although they were slowed by the refusal of the men to leave their wounded comrades. On a hill close to Gandamak they made a stand. Here Major Charles Griffith, a hero throughout the retreat and the only remaining officer of rank, parleyed with the Ghilzai chiefs and secured their promise that the survivors would be allowed to continue unmolested. But then one of the tribesmen attempted to wrest a musket from a soldier and was shot dead, whereupon his infuriated clansmen overwhelmed the little band. Only a few were taken prisoner through the efforts of the maliks—one of them a sergeant who had wrapped the Union Jack around himself and appeared a person of importance.

Meanwhile a few of the cavalry had fought and galloped their way to Fatehabad, a village only sixteen miles from safety. Six of these men reached the village and five decided to rest—which meant to remain forever. The sixth, an assistant surgeon named Brydon, flogged his weary pony into the fort at Jalalabad with the news of the British disaster.*

* Brydon, a man "of pleasant face and rotund figure," is often described as the sole survivor of the Kabul field force. This is far from correct. In addition to the hostages held by Akbar, several soldiers who had been protected by kindly Afghans made their way to the fort at Jalalabad a few days after Brydon. Several hundred soldiers and camp followers who had been

While the soldiers of the Kabul army were meeting their deaths in the frozen passes, the crusty General Nott beat back Afghan attacks at Kandahar with relative ease. Here the Afghans followed their traditional tactics, which the soldiers, who were capably led and unhampered by the cold, easily repelled. In Jalalabad General Sale likewise held firm, protected by the walls and the Afghans' usual inability to cope with fortifications.[11]

The news of the Kabul disaster with its melodramatic overtones produced a shock of horror in Great Britain and was a contributing factor in the collapse of the decrepit Melbourne government. The Tories led by Peel had been loudly declaiming as absurd the fear of a Russian invasion of India through Afghanistan. After the election the new government promptly informed Auckland that he was to be replaced and that his successor, Lord Ellenborough, would arrive in the spring of 1842.

This was a final blow to Auckland, who, his sister reported, had aged ten years since the news from Afghanistan. He took no steps to improve the situation and awaited the arrival of Ellenborough with only one idea in his mind—to leave India forever.

Ellenborough reached Calcutta on February 28, 1842, and on March 15 announced a reversal of Auckland's policy: "To recover Afghanistan if it were possible would constitute a source of weakness rather than strength. The situation, nevertheless, calls for the reëstablishment of our military reputation by the infliction of some signal and decisive blow upon the Afghans." [12]

In order to carry out the last objective, two British armies were sent into Afghanistan, one to the relief of Nott at Kanda-

---

taken captive were later recovered and for years to come others continued to appear from the Afghan hinterlands.

Brydon, who was badly wounded, was unable to speak for several hours after reaching safety. His first words concerned his horse, which had been given him by a sepoy in the Khurd Kabul. It was dead. After surviving the disaster of the retreat from Kabul he was to be one of the survivors of the siege of Lucknow in the Sepoy Rebellion—surely enough adventure for any man.

har, the other to Jalalabad through the Khyber Pass. Then Ellenborough's resolution wavered, and on May 17 he ordered the
British forces to withdraw. An outburst of indignation goaded
him to reverse himself once again, allowing Nott to withdraw
by way of Kabul while the army at Jalalabad moved up to support him.

Meanwhile Afghan affairs were no less chaotic than before.
While Mohammed Akbar was besieging Sale at Jalalabad, open
war raged in Kabul between the supporters of Zeman Khan and
of Shah Shuja. With fighting inconclusive, and with both men
alarmed by the rising popularity of Akbar, they came to an
agreement in which Zeman Khan accepted Shuja as Shah in
return for the office of Wazir. Shuja then prudently assigned to
Mohammed Akbar the post of Sirdar-i-Sirdaranni (commander
in chief); but the latter, recognizing in the compact a threat to
his own authority and the cause of his father, refused to accept
unless the Shah came to Jalalabad—ostensibly to answer Akbar's
summons but actually to leave a country where his cause was
hopeless. As the royal litter left Kabul, it was met by a party of
Afghans led by Shuja-ud-doulat, a son of Zeman Khan, who
riddled the king with bullets and contemptuously flung his
body in a ditch.

This marked the end for the last of the leaders who only a few
years before had planned the Afghan adventure in Ferozepore:
Macnaghten, Burnes, and Shuja murdered; Auckland retired in
disgrace; Runjit Singh dead and already a legend. Shuja has
been the object of harsh criticism from Britons and Afghans
alike, but it should be said in fairness that he was a man of courage, persistence, and intelligence. His inevitable failure was in
part due to his overweening pride, but its chief causes were the
hostility of the Barukzais and Shuja's own impossible role as
a British puppet.

While the Afghans contended for power in Kabul the British
armies prepared to advance on the city. On August 9 General
Nott evacuated Kandahar and marched toward Kabul, with two
European and six Indian battalions; eleven days later General
Pollock with a force of 9,000 moved up from Jalalabad along a
grim trail strewn with bones. On September 13 Mohammed

Akbar made a stand at Tezin, but was easily routed by the British, who were stirred to fury by the mementoes of the previous winter. Skeletons were everywhere; "some were gathered in crowds under rocks as if to obtain shelter from the biting wind —in one case twelve skeletons huddled together in a little nook." [13]

Two days later the army entered a Kabul emptied of its inhabitants; after two days more, the army arrived from Kandahar. One of the first objectives was the recovery of Akbar's prisoners, who were being held at Bamian. Khan Sharin Khan, the Kizzilbash chief, volunteered to attempt their rescue and with six hundred horsemen galloped to Bamian Valley. The trip proved unnecessary, since before his arrival the Afghan officer in charge had freed the prisoners on a promise of 20,000 rupees. Thirty-one officers, ten women, eleven children, two civilian clerks, and fifty-two soldiers were left of the Kabul field force; all were English.

Nothing remained but revenge. The troops had been camped outside of Kabul, forbidden to enter the city, and instructed to act with propriety—a policy that brought some of the inhabitants trickling back. Then suddenly the soldiers were ordered to destroy Kabul, and they did it with thoroughness, sparing only the homes of the Kizzilbash. The Kabul bazaar, considered the finest in central Asia, was mined and burned; so was the mosque of Ali Mardane. The few inhabitants suffered with the buildings, as "every kind of disgraceful outrage was suffered to go on in the town." [14]

In addition, a strong force under General McCaskill was sent to the town of Istalif with its groves of mulberry trees and its crowds of refugees from Kabul. Here every male past the age of puberty was killed, and many of the women were raped by the sepoys. In the words of young Neville Chamberlain, "Tears, supplications were of no avail; fierce oaths were the only answer; the musket was deliberately raised, the trigger pulled and happy was he who fell dead. . . . In fact we are nothing but hired assassins." [15]

After leaving Istalif the force attacked and destroyed Charikar, returning content with a savage task ably done. Few of the victims in the towns had any connection with the tribesmen who had attacked in the passes.

With British military prestige now believed to have been restored, on October 12 the armies started for India, taking with them the blind Shah Zeman and the family of Shah Shuja. After pausing to demolish Jalalabad, the army entered the Khyber Pass and once again came under attack. Again the losses were heavy as the tribesmen continued their skirmishing tactics, and the rear guard was close to panic before it cleared the last of the hills.

The army crossed the Sutlej on December 18 and was greeted by Lord Ellenborough in ostentatious ceremony. In his speech the governor general pointed with pride to the gates of Ghazni which had been carried off by the troops, and which were reputed to be those of the Hindu shrine of Somnath, taken by Sultan Mahmud nearly a thousand years before.*

On its march through the Punjab the army was passed by a solitary horseman riding northward—Dost Mohammed Khan returning to Afghanistan and marking the epilogue of an unhappy chapter in the history of imperialism.

The subsequent careers of the British participants in the "Afghan adventure" are of interest. Sale redeemed his failure to return to Kabul by dying bravely in the Sikh War; Shelton survived a court martial, only to be killed two years later by a fall from his horse—at which his regiment turned out and gave three cheers. Pottinger's death of yellow fever in China ended what had promised to be a brilliant career. Neville Chamberlain became a field marshal and the grandfather of a prime minister; Henry Durand and John Lawrence became two of

---

* Ellenborough received the troops from a throne at the center of a formation in the shape of a five-pointed star. When the Duke of Wellington was informed of this he snorted, "And he ought to sit on it in a strait jacket."

Unfortunately Ellenborough had not examined the supposed gates of Somnath. His political opponents, who shortly did so, found them to be of deodar rather than the sandalwood of the originals, and to be carved with unmistakably Islamic patterns. In his speech he declared that "the insult of 800 years is avenged"; but in retrospect the shade of Sultan Mahmud would appear to have had the last laugh.

India's greatest statesmen; John Nicolson died the hero of the Sepoy Rebellion; Henry Lawrence was killed heading the defense of Lucknow. Henry Rawlinson deciphered the cuneiform writing of ancient Mesopotamia and became one of the world's outstanding authorities on Asian affairs.

No event in the history of the Afghan nation has exceeded the effect of this unfortunate war. The immediate costs were heavy. The British lost between fifteen and twenty thousand soldiers and fifty thousand camels, and, as camp followers were more expendable than camels, an undetermined number of Indian civilians. The Afghan losses were much greater, and possibly reached a total of seventy thousand.

Far more significant was the impact of the war upon the Afghans themselves, upon the way they were pictured to the outside world, and upon later British attitudes toward their nation. From that conflict sprang the legend of Afghan savagery, fanaticism, and treachery, a legend actively promoted by many of the British participants, and kept alive by the example of Rudyard Kipling for succeeding generations of British authors.

The persistence of this legend is somewhat surprising when the facts are examined objectively. On the basis of those facts the Afghans emerge with rather more credit than their opponents. Actually, for all the backwardness and emotionalism of the Afghan tribesmen, their actions were mild compared with those of modern resistance movements. Only a few prisoners were harmed, and no English women were raped—a fact that may have caused a certain subconscious resentment, if one may judge by the comments some of the ladies left behind. The destruction of the army in the Khurd Kabul was a ghastly affair, but most of the victims died with weapons in their hands, and the weather was as much responsible for the great mortality as the Afghan knives.

Many of the British actions are morally less defensible. The slaughter of the males of Istalif and Charikar; the execution of sixty Afghans on the first march to Kabul, with no more excuse than that they were rebels against their sovereign; the fact that no quarter was given to any Afghan on the return march to Kabul; the occasional practice of the sepoys of burning wounded Afghans; and the many rapes by sepoys and British soldiers set no example upon which to build a case against the Afghans. Macnaghten's murder has been frequently cited as a sample of their treachery; the fact that the envoy was on a mission of betrayal and had himself used assassination as a political weapon has been conveniently forgotten.

The effect of the war and invasion upon Afghan internal development was tragic. The cross-currents set up by the occupation, the shifts in the struggle for power, and the confusion of the fighting stirred up a rash of family and personal animosities which were not resolved for decades. Up until this time Afghans had been noted for their religious tolerance and their friendly attitude toward Europeans. Had the invasion never occurred, it is possible that Afghanistan would have adopted European ways at a rapid rate. The war blocked all this; it tinged Afghan hospitality with xenophobia and locked up the country in stultifying isolation for nearly a century.

IX

Afghanistan 1842-1880

> Do not grasp swordgrass, or if you
> do, grasp it tightly.—Pushto PROVERB

THE return of Dost Mohammed to Kabul ended the struggle for power in that city, and the Amir ascended the throne amid the congratulations of his people. At the same time, Kohendil Khan reappeared at Kandahar with a host of Durrani horsemen at his back and drove Safdar Jang, one of Shah Shuja's sons, who had been hoping to control that city after the British departure, into exile.

For a few years the Dost was fully occupied in the task of attempting to rebuild his ruined dominion and to control the passion and turmoil the British occupation had left behind. One of his major obstacles was his son, Mohammed Akbar, who emerged from the war a popular hero and whose disposition grew more vehement and erratic with age. Akbar had forgotten the ordered discipline of the British army; remembering only the frightened mob in the Khurd Kabul, he formed a war party composed of revenge-minded young sirdars at the court and pressed his father to attack India. The Dost had seen enough of British military might during his exile to be under no illusions as to the result of such a policy, but he found the sirdars hard to control. The Amir was also handicapped by the rumor spread by his enemies that he had become pro-British during his stay in India.

It was with difficulty that the Amir prevented the Afghans from aiding the Sikhs in the Anglo-Sikh War of 1845. His neutrality infuriated Mohammed Akbar, who from this time on disregarded his father's orders. After futile negotiations with the Shah of Persia, Mohammed Akbar organized a Ghilzai rebellion. Before it took place, however, he died with suspicious suddenness.

Thus ended the career of the "torch of Islam," an Afghan national hero. His erratic personality and his opposition to his father have been long forgotten, and he remains to the present day an Afghan symbol of national independence. Although he was certainly brave and intelligent, and possessed an extremely winning personality, his problem was that he was "blown about by violent gusts of feeling, bitterly repenting today the excesses of yesterday, and rushing into new excesses tomorrow." [1]

Soon after the death of Mohammed Akbar, the Sikh Khalsa, under the leadership of Diwan Mulraj Singh, sought revenge for its previous defeat. When hostilities broke out in 1848 the Sikhs knew that defeat meant national annihilation. Ready to grasp at any kind of aid, they turned to the Afghans with a promise to cede Peshawar and all territory west of the Indus in return for assistance. Such an acquisition would have meant the fulfillment of a major Afghan aspiration; accordingly, the Dost sent fifteen thousand Durrani and Kizzilbash horsemen under the command of Ghulam Hyder Khan, the younger brother of Mohammed Akbar and now the Afghan heir apparent. Galloping through the Khyber Pass, these troops occupied Peshawar and Attock amid the rejoicing of the Pushtoon population, free at last from domination by the hated Sikhs.

Having secured the territory, the Dost showed little interest in extending any further help to the embattled Sikhs. A number of the Afghans, however, were still embittered by memories of the Anglo-Afghan War; and five thousand of these were granted permission by the Dost to join the Sikh army facing the British at Gujerat. Here, on February 15, 1849, the hammer blows of the British artillery, abetted by the treachery of Sikh leaders, brought the Khalsa to its final destruction. Since the ground was unsuited for cavalry, the Afghan horsemen who formed the right wing of the Sikh army saw little action.

When these soldiers sped to rejoin the Dost they found that the news of the Sikh catastrophe had preceded them and that the Dost had withdrawn the Afghan army through the Khyber. The brief adventure had brought them nothing, for the British promptly moved up to occupy Peshawar, and the map of India was all red at last.

After the Sikh War the Dost concentrated on internal affairs. First he satisfied the restless spirits at his court by leading them across the Hindu Kush and against the tiny Uzbeg khanates which had long since renounced allegiance to the Afghans. Here for some years the Afghans carried on a relatively bloodless conquest, for the people were not hostile and were happy in most cases to exchange the justice of the Dost for the tyrannies of their former masters. By 1859 the land between the Hindu Kush and the Amu Darya again accepted the sovereignty of Kabul.

In 1855 Kohendil Khan, the last of the "dil" brothers, died in Kandahar, concluding a lifetime of mingled failure and fortune. The Dost, who had always supported his "shameless brother," felt now that family loyalty was satisfied, and Kandahar was joined to his enlarging dominion.

This left only the province of Herat outside the control of the Amir. Here in 1851 Yar Mohammed died peacefully in bed, while the cheers of his delighted subjects filled the air outside. His son, Syed Mohammed, who assumed power, had all his father's vices and none of his ability, although he did possess sufficient acumen to realize that he was detested by the population and vulnerable to the growing power of Dost Mohammed. Accordingly he approached the Persian Shah with the offer to rule as the latter's vassal, a move that brought immediate protest by the British. At first the Shah promised to agree to the latter's wishes and keep hands off Herat; but the presence in that city of his agents, well equipped with gold, and the mobilization of an army quickly convinced the British that the promise was an empty one.

At this time Herbert Edwardes was commissioner of Peshawar under John Lawrence, who as commissioner of the Punjab had already formulated his lifelong policy of having as little to do with Afghanistan as possible. Edwardes, on the other hand, believed that British interests could best be served by an Afghan alliance; and going over the head of his superior—a habit of his—he succeeded in persuading the governor general, Lord Dalhousie, of the merit of this view. Accordingly Dost Mohammed was invited to come to Peshawar, and he responded by sending his oldest son, Ghulam Hyder. The latter, a portly and placid man with much of his brother Akbar's charm, was instructed by the Dost to sign an innocuous three-point agreement guaranteeing mutual respect, which was concluded on March 30, 1855.[2]

Meanwhile in Herat, Syed Mohammed Khan had been deposed by Mohammed Yuzuf, a grand nephew of Shah Shuja. Fearing the advance of Dost Mohammed, who had occupied Kandahar, the new ruler followed the example of his predecessor and asked for Persian protection. Somewhat to his dismay, the offer brought a Persian army with orders to occupy the city, whereupon Mohammed Yuzuf compounded the confusion by hoisting a British flag and declaring that his first announcement had been a mistake—he was really a vassal of Great Britain. Prompt rejection of this gift by the British brought about the downfall of Yuzuf and his replacement by another Saddozai, Isa Khan. This internal turmoil allowed the Persian army to enter Herat without opposition, and led to the murder of Isa Khan by a band of drunken soldiers.

The apparently triumphant Persians were not aware of the change in the British government that had put its foreign policy once again under the direction of Lord Palmerston. Almost immediately a British squadron seized the island of Kharak in the Persian Gulf and landed an army at Bushire. These troops were commanded by Sir James Outram, another survivor of the Afghan War, and easily beat the Persians at Borasjun. The Shah, rudely shaken, sued for peace. By the terms of the peace treaty the Persians gave up all claims to Herat, and on March 4, 1857, they evacuated the city, turning over control to a Sultan

Ahmed Khan, also known as Sultan Jan, who was the son of Kohendil Khan and who had little liking for his uncle (and father-in-law) Dost Mohammed.

During this period of Anglo-Persian tension the Dost was again invited to come to Peshawar. This time he appeared in person, and a new agreement signed in January 1857 confirmed the provisions of the treaty of 1855, with a British promise to aid the Amir if he were attacked by a foreign enemy. The Amir agreed to allow a few British officers to enter Afghanistan until the Anglo-Persian War was concluded; after that the British were to maintain a Vakil, or native agent, at the Kabul court. At the conclusion of the treaty the Dost said, "I have now made an alliance with the British and come what may I will keep it till death." [3]

The British were soon to have reason to value the word of their former captive. On May 10, 1857, the sepoys at Meerut mutinied, and within a few weeks the British were struggling for survival against the troops they had trained so well. Afghanistan seethed with excitement as news of British reverses sped through the passes, and many of the khans and maliks called for a descent on India. But the Dost stood firmly behind the treaty. Without question the Afghan's inactivity aided the hard-pressed British; so did the fact that many of the 34,000 troops raised in the Punjab for service against the mutineers were Afghans. In a sense, the victim of Auckland was the savior of Canning.[4]

For the remainder of the Amir's life, relations between Afghanistan and the British were cordial. The old warrior, showing signs of age—once famed as a horseman he now rode an elephant—was finally able to unite his country for the first time since the death of his brother, Fathi Khan, in May 1863, when he entered the gates of Herat in triumph.

Nine days later Shir Ali Khan, the heir apparent (Ghulam Hyder having died), wrote to the Viceroy of India, "As death is the common lot of man, my revered father . . . died of a chronic illness at sunrise." [5]

Dost Mohammed Khan, the "Great Amir," must be given high rank among the rulers of Afghanistan, or for that matter of any country. After a shaky start, the "little wolf" settled down to a lifetime of effort directed toward unifying and pacifying his country; pursuing an unwavering course through adversity and exile, through faction and family intrigue, through foreign invasion and internecine war. Brave, humane, and tolerant, he gained the complete admiration of his enemies. His monument is the saying, still popular, "Is the Dost dead that there is no justice?"

Unfortunately for the stability of the government he left behind, Dost Mohammed had followed the pattern set by other Afghan rulers, and was survived by sixteen sons born to five mothers. Had Mohammed Akbar or Ghulam Hyder lived, the country would have had a peaceful succession; but their having died before their father meant a renewal of that Afghan curse, a struggle for the throne.

The third oldest living son of the Dost was Shir Ali Khan, a whole brother to Mohammmed Akbar and Ghulam Hyder and the favorite of his father, who had named him heir. The wishes of their dead father were of little concern, however, to Shir Ali's two older half brothers, Afzal Khan and Azim Khan, who promptly organized a revolt. In this they were aided by the position of Azim Khan as governor of Afghan Turkestan and by the backing of Abdur Rahman, an extremely able son of Afzal Khan. Nevertheless Shir Ali, bolstered by Dost Mohammed's prestige and by the royal treasury, was victorious.

The next year, 1864, brought another rebellion, this time from an unexpected quarter: its leader was a whole brother of Shir Ali named Mohammed Amin. Again the Amir won a victory, but at a heavy cost; for his favorite son, Mohammed Ali, after being unjustly upbraided for cowardice, plunged into the battle and was killed in a hand-to-hand fight with his uncle.[6]

The death of the prince cost the Amir his throne. Shir Ali was a manic-depressive; blaming himself for the event, he became temporarily unbalanced, and wandered through the streets of Kabul calling for his dead son. As a consequence the young Abdur Rahman came across the mountains with an army raised in Afghan Turkestan, whereupon the Amir, shaken from his madness, withdrew to Kandahar. Led by Abdur Rahman, the forces of Afzal Khan defeated Shir Ali at Sheikhabad, and again in 1867 at Kalat-i-Ghilzai. Shir Ali Khan then fled to Herat, and Afzal Khan became Amir.

Afzal Khan had none of his son's ability, and was harshly characterized as a "sot and an imbecile." [7] But that Abdur Rahman was a sufficient prop for the throne was proved once again by yet another defeat of Shir Ali, who had raised another army. Then suddenly fortune favored the deposed Amir; Afzal Khan died unexpectedly while Abdar Rahman was away with the troops.

Afzal's brother, Azim, who now announced his succession, was even less able than his dead brother, and had a reputation, dangerous in Afghanistan, for cowardice. Another deadly defect was his parsimony, especially since the contenders for the throne were all securing adherents by the usual means. The result was that Shir Ali, who had recruited another army, found Azim Khan's supporters hastening to his side. Deserted, Azim Khan fled for Persia, but died on the way; and Abdur Rahman crossed the northern frontier to seek refuge with the Russians.

This dynastic seesaw might have gone on indefinitely, since the tribal chiefs found it profitable and only occasionally dangerous. It was brought to an end, however, by the British. One cause of the confusion had been the refusal of the British to recognize any of the claimants to the throne, a policy that had originated with Lawrence. For some time opposition to this hands-off policy had been growing in India and London, and it won the day when Shir Ali approached the Russian military government in Turkestan. Once convinced of his error, Lawrence acted swiftly; he sent a message to Shir Ali recognizing him as Amir and forwarded a gift of 20,000 rupees and 3,000 muskets. This effectively ended the civil war, with Shir Ali firmly on the throne.

Free at last from family danger, the Amir was able to devote some attention to his ravaged country. Despite his emotional instability, the Amir was a capable man who recognized both the Afghans' desperate need for progress and the advantages of Western technology. Among his innovations were the establishment of the first Afghan postal service and the founding of the weekly newspaper *Shamsun-Nahar.**

In addition, the Amir attempted to organize a regular army on the European model. In this he was unsuccessful; though he set up a body of what appeared to be soldiers, the resemblance went no further than the uniform. It was impossible to recruit or to draft the belligerent Pushtoons, who found discipline and salary equally unappealing. Available draftees had to be collected from the Tadjiks and Hazaras, who were potentially good material—as the latter demonstrated in the British Indian army—but whose morale depended upon honest and efficient officers, and these were unavailable. Weapon training was nonexistent; so were staff operations, and the main activity of the officers was to extort as much as possible from the unfortunates they commanded.

Despite the efforts of the Amir, Afghanistan remained a case of arrested national development. Almost forty years of internal war and invasion had halted its progress; the power of the chiefs and the predatory tribes had risen as the authority of the Amir and the central government dwindled. In addition, the country had locked itself in an unnatural isolation, allowing few foreigners to cross its borders.

It is possible that some years of stability would have allowed Shir Ali to consolidate his rule; but once again outside forces over which the Amir had no control were to halt his country's progress. After the annexation of the Punjab in 1849 the interest of the British in Afghanistan had faded before their primary concern with the consolidation of their Indian empire and the influence of Lord Lawrence, who could not overcome the memory of a bone-strewn Khurd Kabul. As the years passed, however, and Britsh control over India was strengthened, new policies began to contend with Lawrence's in the minds of the British leaders. This change, which was clearly evident by 1868, came about largely because of the activities of Czarist Russia. Shortly after the Crimean War, a surging Russian drive pushed southward into central Asia, gobbling up the decayed khanates

* Azim Khan had briefly published the first Afghan newspaper, *Kabul*, in 1867.

that were the relics of once powerful empires. The tattered Uzbeg armies of Bokhara fled from Russian attack in 1863; two years later Tashkent and half of Khokand came under Czarist control. In 1867 Bokhara was further reduced and the province of Russian Turkestan was set up, with General Kaufmann, a fervent expansionist, as governor.

These moves caused concern among the British, even though they were inevitable, since the predatory inhabitants of the steppeland were impossible neighbors for a settled state. In addition, the Russian frontier areas were under military governors who paid little heed to the plans of the Russian foreign office.

Shir Ali was alarmed by these developments beyond his northern borders, and he was especially apprehensive over the letters that General Kaufmann persisted in writing him. In such a frame of mind he was happy to accept an invitation from the Viceroy of India, Lord Mayo, for a conference at Amballa. The talks there were unproductive; the British were in the final throes of the policy of "masterly inactivity," and though they asserted that they would view with severe displeasure any attempt to disturb the Amir's position, they added that they would never send a soldier to assist him.[8]

After Lord Mayo was murdered in the Andaman Islands by an Afghan convict, Shir Ali made another attempt to secure an alliance. But though Lord Northbrook, Mayo's successor, was more favorable to an Afghan alliance and promised aid in the event of unprovoked aggression, the Gladstone government repudiated this concession. Under direct instructions from London, Northbrook assured the Amir that the Russians contemplated no aggression, and that the British could not under any circumstances conclude an alliance with his government.

Shir Ali was bitterly disappointed. "The English," he wrote, "look to nothing but their own interests and bide their time. Whosoever's side they see strongest for the time they turn to him as their friend. I will not waste precious life in entertaining false hopes from the English and will enter into friendships with other governments."[9]

The Amir's resentment was deepened by other circumstances. Afghanistan and Persia, never friendly neighbors, had been squabbling about their Sistan frontier; when the matter was turned over to the British as mediators, the result, as usual, pleased neither party. Finally, when the Amir imprisoned his oldest son, Yakub Khan, for engaging in his family's penchant for revolution, he received an admonition from Northbrook. Greatly offended, Shir Ali answered that though the Viceroy's advice was undoubtedly based on "friendship and well-wishing," he had no right to interfere in Afghan internal affairs.[10]

In March 1874 Disraeli and the Tories replaced the government of Gladstone. The new cabinet, as energetic in foreign affairs as its predecessor had been lethargic, contained many members who had long chafed at the policy of masterly inactivity. One of these, Sir Bartle Frere, immediately prepared a memorandum setting forth a new policy toward Afghanistan, which called for the military occupation of Quetta and for the placing of British officers in Herat and Kandahar—a violation of promises made to Shir Ali by both Mayo and Northbrook.

The new policy was accepted by Lord Salisbury and in 1875 was communicated to Northbrook. But the Viceroy was neither Tory in politics nor docile in disposition. He replied that since the British had rejected the opportunity, which Shir Ali had once suggested, of establishing an agent in Herat, they could hardly now demand the reversal of the policy they had dictated. After an acrimonious exchange of cables, Northbrook resigned and was replaced by Lord Lytton, son of Edward Bulwer-Lytton and a poet under the pseudonym of Owen Meredith.

The new Viceroy had no knowledge of Asia, but compensated for that lack by a definite opinion on all subjects. He expressed himself as heartily in favor of the new policy:

Afghanistan is a state far too weak and barbarous to remain isolated and wholly uninfluenced between two great military empires. . . . It is our policy to cultivate on our north-western boundary a strong bulwark. . . . We do not covet one inch of [Shir Ali's] territory, we do not desire to diminish one iota of his independence. But we cannot allow him to fall under the influence of any power whose interests are antagonistic to our own.[11]

The Russians, undeterred by the change in the British political scene, continued their advance toward the Afghan frontier.

In 1875, when Kuddiar, the dissolute khan of Khokand, was overthrown by his subjects, the Russians annexed the state and renamed it Ferghana. This move left Bokhara and Khiva as the only independent states between Russia and Afghanistan, and the former was already under Russian direction. In the same year, after a march in heat as extreme as 149 degrees, a Russian army stormed the walls of the city of Khiva and annexed it and the surrounding territory. Sympathy for the Khivans should be tempered, however, for the Russians found 34,000 slaves within the city.

Now that Russian territory for the first time impinged on Afghanistan, the Amir was totally disturbed. He saw nothing that was likely to halt the expanding Russian state; in character much of northern Afghanistan was indistinguishable from the territory the Russians had already seized. Thus Shir Ali now communicated with General Kaufmann, with whose letters he had been bombarded for some time.

This step by the Amir has been interpreted as an attempt to force concessions from Great Britain, and it is true that just such a procedure has often been followed in Afghanistan and other countries rimmed by great powers. But in this instance Shir Ali was more interested in arriving at some accord with the Russians than in putting pressure on Great Britain; for the presence of his nephew, Abdur Rahman, at Kaufmann's headquarters was a serious threat.

The British had known for some time of General Kaufmann's letter-writing; indeed, both Mayo and Northbrook had assured Shir Ali that it was harmless. Lytton and the new government put a more ominous interpretation upon it, however, and were not willing to accept the assurance of Count Schuvaloff, the Russian ambassador to Whitehall, that it was merely a personal activity of Kaufmann's and had no part in Russian policy. The inscrutability of much of Russian policy, past and present, makes the real intent of the correspondence impossible to discover, though Kaufmann was unquestionably and notoriously independent in some of his actions.

On April 24, 1876, the new Viceroy wrote the Amir to announce that he was sending Sir Lewis Pelly as an envoy to

Kabul to "discuss matters of common interest." [12] Shir Ali answered politely but without equivocation that he must refuse this mission. Though he gave no reasons, his refusal was based upon a fear that he would be unable to protect a British envoy in Kabul, whose citizens could still recall the aftermath of the mission of Alexander Burnes.

Lytton was furious, and read into the Amir's letter a confirmation of his belief that the Afghans were seeking an alliance with Russia. Over the protests of three members of his council, he drafted a strong note to the Amir, containing a threat hardly veiled by the niceties of diplomatic language.

This note brought apprehension to the Kabul court, and the bazaars buzzed with rumors of British troops concentrating on the border. Shir Ali hastened to reply to the Viceroy with the suggestion that he explore the situation by consulting with Atta Mohammed, the British agent in Kabul. On November 10, 1876, Lytton met the agent at Simla. Here the Viceroy behaved with no little spleen, telling the agent that the Amir's position was "That of an earthen pipkin between two iron pots"—a statement neither diplomatic nor original. He instructed the agent to offer Shir Ali a four-point proposal: first, that the British would aid Afghanistan in the event of unprovoked aggression (the British to judge the necessity); second, that the British would recognize Abdullah Jan, one of the Amir's sons, as heir; third, that Afghanistan was to be opened to all Englishmen; and fourth, that the Afghans were to refrain from any foreign communications without British consent. [13]

This proposal was unrealistic and unfair; to accept it would have meant the immediate end of Shir Ali's rule and probably of his life. In desperation the Amir sent his Wazir, Nur Mohammed Shah, to India for another attempt at negotiation, which proved futile: the Viceroy would agree to discuss no other alternatives. Nur Mohammed, who was mortally ill with a chronic disease, pleaded in conclusion:

Matters have now come to a crisis and the situation is a grave one. . . . The British nation is great and powerful and the Afghan people cannot resist its power but the people are self-willed and independent and prize their homes above their lives. . . . You must

Her royal highness, Umairah, queen of Afghanistan.

The center of Kabul. The pillar commemorates the Afghan victory over the British at the battle of Maiwand.

not impose upon us a burden, which we cannot bear; if you overload us, the responsibility rests with you.[14]

At this time, circumstances far from Afghanistan were driving events toward a tragic conclusion. Russia, on the alert as always over the simmering unrest in the Balkans, watched with indignation as the Turks suppressed the Bulgarian revolt and went on to victories over Serbia and Montenegro. On April 24, 1877, Turkish refusal to accept arbitration brought a Russian declaration of war, and by January 1878 the army of the Czar stood before Istanbul.

The British reaction was violent. Parliament voted a war subsidy; a British fleet sailed for the Bosporus, and five thousand sepoys from Bombay were sent to Cyprus. Immediately the Russians countered by a threat to India. General Kaufmann, to his own delight, was instructed to mobilize an army in Russian Turkestan and to send a mission to Kabul; this he promptly did, informing Shir Ali in the meantime that if the mission was not received, Abdur Rahman would be sent across the border with full Russian assistance. General Stolietoff, six officers, and twenty-two men left Samarkand on July 14, 1878, unaware that the Congress of Berlin had begun the day before. Ignoring repeated requests from the Amir that it halt, the mission continued steadily, arriving in Kabul on July 22.

News of this Russian action was not long in reaching Lytton, for the British secret service had now achieved the high degree of efficiency that marked the later years of British occupation of India. The Viceroy, seeing his worst fears confirmed, cabled London:

There are three and only three courses open to us. To secure by fear or hope such an alliance with the present Amir as will effectually and permanently exclude Russian influence from Afghanistan. . . . Failing this to break up the Afghan kingdom. . . . To conquer and hold so much of Afghan territory . . . absolutely necessary for permanent maintenance of our Northwest Frontier. . . . I propose therefore in accordance with your instructions to send a British mission to Kabul.[15]

On September 10 a messenger galloped into Kabul with news that a British mission was arriving. He found the capital in mourning and the Amir in a fit of depression over the death of his son Abdullah Jan; and he learned also that the Russian mission had received orders to leave Afghanistan after the successful conclusion of the Congress of Berlin. At the same time the British mission, with 250 soldiers commanded by Sir Neville Chamberlain, and with Louis Cavagnari as political officer, had reached Peshawar.

On September 21, 1878, the mission advanced to Fort Jamrud at the mouth of Khyber Pass, where it halted while Cavagnari and an escort rode into the defile. Here they were met by Faiz Mohammed, the Afghan border commandant, who courteously but adamantly told them that they could not proceed until he had received approval from Kabul.

Quite obviously this was an attempt by the Amir to save face, and there can be no doubt that the mission would have been admitted after a brief check and further negotiations. But Lytton and the "war party" were in control at Simla and determined upon a military adventure; indeed, it is probable that the Viceroy heard of the halting of the mission with satisfaction. At least the spate of untrue reports which appeared, falsely accusing Faiz Mohammed of insulting and threatening Cavagnari, and the fact that Lytton disobeyed a directive from London specifically ordering him to send the mission by some other route than the Khyber seem to indicate that Lytton was seeking a *casus belli* rather than negotiation.[16]

Even so, the British government—with the exception of Lord Cranbrook, Secretary of State for India—was not eager for war, and some of its members were suspicious of Lytton's actions. But public indignation was added to the importunings of the Viceroy; Cranbrook finally won the day; and Lytton was instructed to issue an ultimatum to Shir Ali with an expiration date of November 20. When no answer was received, British armies crossed the Afghan borders, and thus began the second Anglo-Afghan war. Two days later, a message from the Amir arrived, pathetically dated November 19 and stating that the mission had his permission to proceed.

The Afghans in 1878 were less able to repel invasion than in 1839. The Amir had attempted to establish an army and had succeeded in building a uniformed mob, whose sole cohesive force lay in the tendency of its members to flee at the same moment. The tribes, the real strength of the country, had not acquired modern weapons but were still armed with knives and antiquated matchlocks.

British plans called for an operation by three armies. One in the north, commanded by Lieutenant General Sam Browne (who gave his name to the leather straps worn by officers in World War I), entered the Khyber and advanced toward Dakka; another in the center, led by General "Fighting Bob" Roberts, moved up the Kurram; a third, commanded by Lieutenant General Donald Stewart, followed the old route to Kandahar. The operations were well conceived and well executed, with only minor opposition in the Kurram and the Khyber.

Shir Ali attempted, as his father had done, to rally support, and met with equal failure. Despairing, he placed his son Yakub Khan on the throne and rode off toward Russian Turkestan, hoping to place his cause before a congress of European powers. His faith in European altruism was never put to the test, for the Russians refused him permission to proceed. Sick at heart, the Amir made his last ironic answer to the "sweet expressions" of the old siren, Kaufmann. Then, on February 21, 1879, he "obeyed the call of the summoner and throwing off the dress of existence hastened to the region of Divine Mercy." [17] The pipkin had indeed been crushed by the iron pots.

At the news of his father's death Yakub Khan hastened to open negotiations with the British, who were glad to call a halt. India was ravaged by famine and the invasion, though not bloody, was proving expensive. Besides, fickle public opinion in England had begun to shift at the news of the death of the friendless Amir. Accordingly, Louis Cavagnari met with Yakub Khan at Gandamak, and on May 20, 1879, signed a treaty which removed restrictions on British travel in Afghanistan and placed an envoy at Kabul.[18]

Following the Treaty of Gandamak the British army in the north was ordered to withdraw—a retirement that ranks with the most miserable in military annals. The weather was intolerably hot, and an epidemic of cholera swept through the troops. The central and southern armies were accordingly ordered to wait for cooler weather, and Cavagnari (now Sir Louis) was sent as envoy to Kabul with an escort of three British officers and seventy-five sepoys.

Cavagnari, though brilliant and courageous, was also hasty and arrogant, and had the political officer's usual penchant for intrigue. He was received courteously and given quarters in the Bala Hissar, about 250 yards from the Amir's palace. For a time all seemed to be well, although members of the mission met scowls on the streets of Kabul and visitors were few.

On September 2 an Afghan regiment, the Turkestani Ardal, paraded to receive its pay, which was eight months in arrears. Informed that they were to be given only one month's salary, the soldiers rioted, cursing their officers and calling for justice. They were soon joined by three other regiments, lately arrived from Herat and likewise unpaid.

After some confused milling about the soldiers headed toward the Amir's palace, where they were repulsed by the Kizzilbash guard. They then went to the British mission, to be met by gunfire from the sepoys; enraged, they returned to their barracks for their rifles, gathering a large crowd of Kabuli citizens on the way back. Meanwhile Yakub Khan did nothing but weep and wring his hands while the palace mullahs implored him to protect his guests. When he did finally send the Afghan commander in chief, Mohammed Daoud, and the eight-year-old heir apparent, Musa Jan, the soldiers were past persuasion. By three o'clock in the afternoon, after heroic resistance, Cavagnari and his escort were dead.

This melancholy event confirmed the old cliché of Afghan bloodthirstiness and treachery. But once again blind emotion, and total unawareness of the Afghans' side of the case, worked against an objective report of what had occurred. No evidence has ever been produced to indicate that the attack was anything but what it seemed—a spontaneous outbreak of mutinous soldiers. It is absurd to believe that Yakub Khan had plotted an event that would inevitably have cost him his throne.

Here again, just as when Burnes was murdered, the cause of

the outbreak had been the unwillingness of the Afghans to accept a situation that had been accepted in India. Burnes, Macnaghten, and Cavagnari were not "envoys," though the term was used to describe their status; they were "residents," whose assigned responsibility was to direct Afghan affairs rather than to promote a liaison between Afghanistan and Great Britain. Abdur Rahman, who knew the facts and had no reason to exculpate Yakub Khan, put the matter correctly when he said that "the British envoy looked upon himself as the ruler of Afghanistan and dictated to Yakub what he should do. This boasting was disliked by the Afghan people and they attacked him." [19]

When the report of Cavagnari's death reached India the army of General Roberts, which was only fifty miles from Kabul, was ordered to advance and occupy the city. On September 27 Yakub Khan rode to meet Roberts, and was coldly received, since the British were convinced of his role in the attack on Cavagnari. Nine days later, Roberts easily defeated the leaderless garrison of Kabul and entered the city.

The general who was now master of Kabul was a brilliant soldier but hardly a humanitarian; unable to identify any of the participants in the attack on Cavagnari, he summarily executed any Afghan who opposed the British advance on the specious grounds that all such were rebels against their sovereign—the same brand of legalism that had been used in 1839. Despite the protests of civilian advisers, this practice was continued until it was halted by specific orders from London.

Meanwhile the British government found itself in the position of the proverbial man with a tiger by the tail, for though the conquest of Afghanistan had been easy the Afghan people were reluctant to accept the fact that they had been conquered. Since British control was one of "sentry boxes," maintainable only through force, the occupation soon proved costly and brought loud outcries from the Indian taxpayers. The system of control by a British resident was obviously impractical, and it was also impossible to find a puppet for the Afghan throne. And then the tribes had begun to stir.

The first signs of trouble were attacks on foraging parties, to which Roberts promptly retaliated by reducing villages and driving their inhabitants out into the Afghan winter. But this only added to the resentment. At the same time, the Afghan intransigents found two leaders of ability in Din Mohammed, better known as Mushk-i-Alam ("fragrance of the universe"), the head mullah of Ghazni, and Mohammed Jan, khan of the Wardaks south of Kabul.

Early in December, Roberts learned from spies that the Afghans were planning an attack. On December 10 a tribal lashkar of Kohistanis was scattered by General Macpherson. On the following day a Wardak lashkar led by Mohammed Jan had an accidental encounter with Brigadier General Massy, who with four horse-artillery guns and 240 cavalrymen was crossing the plain of Chardeh near Kabul. Despite the cannon, the tribesmen advanced steadily until Roberts withdrew his troops into the shelter of the cantonment. This minor victory and the British withdrawal brought thousands of Afghans from neighboring villages streaming into Kabul, hoping to repeat the events of the winter of 1841. But this time the situation was different, for the British were well supplied, the morale of the soldiers was high, and Roberts was a far different man from the enfeebled Elphinstone.

After a few weeks of ineffectual sniping, the Afghans began to run short of provisions, and on December 23 they attempted to rush the cantonment, "coming on like capital fellows." [20] Their courage was useless; the British artillery mowed them down by hundreds. The following day another British army under Brigadier General Charles Gough arrived in a quiet city; the Afghans, carrying their dead and wounded, had returned to their villages.

This time, with their usual admiration for stout opponents, the British took few reprisals; in the words of a British officer, "They were fine men and showed the utmost contempt for death." [21] Three days later Roberts declared an amnesty to all who had participated in the fighting.

During the outbreak in Kabul the troops in Kandahar enjoyed quiet times. The British found a cooperative Afghan leader in Shir Ali Khan, son of one of the "dil" brothers, Mehrdil Khan, who had ruled Kandahar in the days of the Dost. This man, whose ambition exceeded his judgment, was made Wali or governor and carried on the civil administration, bolstered by the remembered authority of his father. The only spot of danger was Herat, where Ayub Khan, the younger brother of the deposed Yakub, was acting as governor.

In the interim the British government groped for a plan of settlement. The impossibility of controlling Afghanistan without a costly and perpetual military occupation was evident; the problem was what to do with the country. A solution appeared in the person of Abdur Rahman Khan, Amir Afzal Khan's capable and energetic son, who had been in exile at Tashkent for twelve years. His Russian hosts, who had been patient if niggardly, now suggested that he make a bid for the Afghan throne. Apparently they made no request for future favors; at any rate, they provided him with supplies for two hundred men and sent him across the border into Afghan Turkestan, where he was immediately joined by Sultan Murad Khan, the Afghan governor, and by Ghulam Hyder Khan, the commander of the Afghan northern army.

News of Abdur Rahman's appearance reached Lytton at an opportune time, since the wolves of the opposition were beginning to howl over a previously undisclosed deficit of 13,800,000 pounds in the cost of the war. With undiplomatic eagerness the Viceroy instructed Sir Lepel Griffin, the political officer in Kabul, to open negotiations with Abdur Rahman by asking him the reasons for his appearance in Afghanistan.

Abdur Rahman had not come to visit old friends; his reply was to submit his claim to the throne of Afghanistan and to ask the British to join with the Russians in guaranteeing the independence of the country. Griffin answered a few days later that Great Britain could not recognize any Russian interest in the matter, but that the British were agreeable to seeing Abdur Rahman accept the rule of Kabul.

Shortly after this letter was sent the Conservative government of Disraeli fell before the Liberals, and Lytton and his Afghan policy went with it. During the campaign Lytton's war had been a prime political issue; the Liberals had called it both immoral and impractical, thereby capitalizing upon similar sentiments among the British voters. Cranbrook was promptly replaced by the Marquess of Hartington, and Lord Ripon sailed for India as the new Viceroy. Lytton left India certain of his wisdom to the last, and rudely comparing the Liberals to "acorned hogs."

The new Viceroy was eager to end the expensive Afghan occupation, but he found that Abdur Rahman was reluctant to be known as a "British candidate." The Afghan leader in his turn was finding that the Ghilzai, never friendly toward him, obdurately refused to accept the clause in the proposed agreement calling for the separation of Kandahar from Kabul. But he succeeded at last in convincing the Ghilzai maliks that the terms offered by the British should be accepted in order to secure the latter's withdrawal from Afghanistan, and that later adjustments could be made. On July 17 he met with Griffin at Charikar, where he was formally accepted as the Amir of Kabul, and the money found in the Afghan treasury was turned over to him along with the antiquated cannon seized at Kabul.

At this moment ominous news arrived from Kandahar. Sir Donald Stewart who had left that city on March 27 on a march to Kabul, had defeated a lashkar of Ghilzai on the way. This left the force at Kandahar weakened and brought an attack by Ayub Khan, the governor of Herat, who had advanced toward Kandahar with a force of about eight thousand men. The British, although aware of this move, were not greatly concerned, since open battle with the Afghans had not been difficult. Brigadier General G. R. S. Burrows, with 2,734 soldiers, was sent to the Helmand where the Afghan Wali, Shir Ali, was waiting with two thousand Afghan soldiers. After twelve days in a broiling sun the British made contact with their ally, only to find that the Afghan troops had deserted and were trying to join Ayub.

On July 22 Ayub reached the Helmand, and a series of cavalry skirmishes took place between the two armies. Burrows was in a difficult position, since Ayub had the choice of two possible routes in advancing on Kandahar, and the heat was terrible. Messages from the cool comfort of headquarters, urging him to "strike a blow at Ayub," only added to his annoyance.[22]

On July 26 Burrows learned that Ayub was marching toward Kandahar by way of the village of Maiwand. The British army immediately moved to intercept. On July 27, at Mahmudabad —near Maiwand, where the Afghans were already in occupation—the British ran unexpectedly into the Afghan army, and the battle began. At first it consisted of an artillery duel in which, to their surprise, the British found themselves outclassed by the Afghan gunners from Kabul, who had been well trained and handled their cannon in exemplary fashion. After several hours a party of tribesmen who had infiltrated a ravine facing the British lines launched a spontaneous charge. It struck two companies of Jacob's Rifles, which broke and collapsed upon the Bombay Grenadiers. These crumbled in turn, and in panic the entire mass fell back upon the European Sixty-sixth Regiment.

Burrows tried desperately to re-form, but the cavalry refused to charge and matters were past mending. Most of the troops, who were now a mob, ran madly for distant Kandahar, but the Sixty-sixth Regiment held firm and fought to the last with splendid courage. Throughout the night the fugitives plodded toward Kandahar, tormented by thirst and fear. Fortunately for them the Afghans had paused to loot the baggage; but by the time the survivors reached safety 1,130 were missing and a thousand rifles, 250,000 rounds of ammunition, and all the transport were in Afghan hands.

This defeat, inaccurately known as the battle of Maiwand, was one of the few suffered by a nineteenth-century British army in Asia during open battle. General Burrows seems to have done everything possible; the Afghans owed their victory to the courage of irregulars who carried out their charge heedless of losses. Ayub's soldiers, with the exception of the artillerymen, had done little, and his cavalry had merely saved itself for the task of pillaging the captured camp.

This disaster provided the British public with a somewhat pleasurable horror at the thought of soldiers "wounded and left on Afghanistan's plains" as prey for the knives of bloodthirsty Afghan females. The many and luridly embellished fictions that were its literary aftermath had no more basis in fact than that the primary weapon of the tribesmen was a long knife. According to the report of one British officer who had been sent to oversee a burial detail, "Bodies had not been mutilated as reported nor was this done during the campaign; and though some of the dead were certainly found much cut about, I never heard of one authenticated instance of the perpetration of such loathsome barbarities as were related by some correspondents." [23]

After the disaster it was left to General Primrose at Kandahar, aided by a despondent Burrows, to revive the shattered morale. All Afghans were expelled from the city before the arrival of Ayub's army on July 29. The Afghans failed as usual to make any impression on the fortifications; but a British sortie met a bloody repulse, and the troops behind the walls settled down to wait for help.

Help was on the way. The first plan was to rush troops from India, but Roberts in Kabul pleaded for the opportunity, arguing persuasively that sepoys were no match for Afghans. On August 6 he left Kabul for Kandahar at the head of an army of about ten thousand men. Not a wheel turned; all supplies were on horse or muleback or the shoulders of eight thousand followers. Twenty-two days later the army had covered the 315 miles to Kandahar in a march that has rarely been equaled.

Ayub Khan, at the news of the British approach, raised his siege of Kandahar and took a defensive position in the hills north of the city. On October 1 Roberts launched a general attack, which found the Afghan irregulars resisting bravely if hopelessly while the soldiers of Ayub's army fled for Herat.

This battle drew the curtain on the second Anglo-Afghan war. In Britain both the government and the public were anxious to end what had proved a profitless affair. Only Kabul was under effective control, and its continued occupation could but weaken Abdur Rahman, who was already suspected by his subjects of pro-British leanings. On August 11 the evacuation of Kabul began, and in Whitehall the decision was taken to give up Kandahar, over the protests of Queen Victoria, who was convinced that the Kandaharis wished to retain "the benefits of Christian rule." But her opinion would hardly have impressed the British officers who walked the streets with their pistols in their hands, or the sentries who found it necessary to stand back to back. Fortunately the Cabinet was better informed when it instructed Ripon to order immediate retirement. Shir Ali, the Wali, prudently accepted a British pension and refuge in India; and on April 21, 1881, the city was handed over to Mohammed Hashim Khan, an officer of Abdur Rahman.

Anyone who studies the events of this war cannot but be struck by its similarity to Auckland's Afghan adventure. Each was motivated by fear of the Russian threat to India, and was set off by the appearance of a Russian mission at Kabul. It now seems clear that these fears by the British were unfounded. That the Russians could have invaded India across the passes and mountains of Afghanistan, coping with the logistic problems on the way, and arriving as a menace to the capable British Indian army, seems as unlikely as that the Afghans, who had resisted all other invaders, would welcome Cossacks. Without question, all that the British sought could have been gained by negotiation; but the temper of the nineteenth century had little of the requisite patience for negotiating with Asian rulers.

The war was costly for both sides. India lost twenty million pounds and three thousand soldiers; Afghanistan suffered still more heavily; for its dead were the best and bravest among those who had matched their stones and knives against foreign rifles. Once again, even greater harm was caused by the further check upon the economic and political progress that had been made following Shir Ali's establishment on the throne. And once again the Afghan's mistrust and hatred of the foreigner had been intensified, the power of fanatics and reactionaries had increased, and the authority of the government had been weakened.

Chroniclers in plenty have recorded the gallantry of the British soldiers and their sepoy comrades, the charges of the Lancers, and the march of Roberts and his men. Few, however, have written of the Afghan peasants, who as they met the British cannon "came on carrying their banners more proudly than ever." [24]

X

Abdur Rahman, the "Iron Amir"

Life is not a bed of roses.
—ABDUR RAHMAN

FEW kings so great have been more hated than Abdur Rahman. Only a few years have passed since his grim personality dominated Afghanistan, but in that time the visible traces of his rule have largely vanished. His deserted and crumbling palace frowns down on Kabul; his tomb goes unheeded in the midst of the city. A few faded and largely forgotten photographs show the swart face and the smoldering little eyes with their glint of sardonic humor. His people call him "the assassin"—which he was—and also the "friend of the English"—which he was not, though in the lands of the Hindu Kush it is the worse condemnation. Yet he was in many respects an outstanding monarch, a man of shrewdness, clear judgment, and iron will—a kind of Afghan Henry VIII.

Abdur Rahman mounted the throne of a country in chaos and left behind a nation. By the force of his personality he goaded his people out of the Middle Ages and into something resembling the eighteenth century. At the beginning of his rule Afghanistan was controlled by jealous and intransigent tribal leaders, who were committed to tribal feudalism. Western Afghanistan was held by his cousin and enemy Ayub Khan, a popular and dynamic leader, famed for his victory at Maiwand

and a favorite of the mullahs. At the center of Abdur Rahman's nominal domain were a snarl of independent tribes, addicted to feuds, tribal wars and banditry. Almost inaccessible in their rugged homeland were the Ghilzai, largest of tribes and resentful of Durrani hegemony. In the mountains of Kafiristan lived the infidel Kafirs, who counted up their manhood in Moslem heads. Clustered throughout the central mountains, the Mongol Hazaras waged frequent wars with their Pushtoon and Tadjik neighbors.[1]

Outside lay territory ruled by Persia, Russia, and Great Britain, its undemarcated boundaries hedged with perpetual threat, as the tide of imperialism still ran high. Within Afghanistan were a mutinous army, a chaotic government, an empty treasury, and an entrenched system of inefficiency and graft.

Twenty years of effort did not solve these problems; yet during his reign the Amir was able to consolidate and subdue his people as no ruler had done before him and to end for a time the cycle of internal war.

Abdur Rahman was born in or around the year 1844; Afghans view birth dates with indifference. After a boyhood in Kabul he went to join his father, Afzal Khan, the third son of Dost Mohammed, who was serving as governor of Afghan Turkestan. At the age of thirteen Abdur Rahman was made governor of Tashkurgan, a post he filled with precocious aplomb and generosity. On a tour of inspection two years later, his father found the townsfolk happy, and with good reason— taxes were not being collected—whereupon this experiment in juvenile nepotism came to an end.

Several years later Abdur Rahman again incurred his father's displeasure, this time from a report that he was "drinking wine and smoking Indian hemp." [2] For this, according to Abdur Rahman himself, he was sent to prison and kept in chains for a year (not a likely story). He was released and given command of the Afghan army in Turkestan, where he spent several years campaigning against the Uzbeg Mirs of Badakshan.

The struggle that broke out over the throne in 1863, when Dost Mohammed died, has been related in a previous chapter. Abdur Rahman was then about nineteen. Largely because of the young sirdar's ability, Afzal Khan and Azim Khan were able to rule as amirs for brief periods; but by 1869 the brothers were dead, and Abdur Rahman was a fugitive among the Russians. From here he emerged in the chaos of the British invasion to make his successful bid for power.

Thirty-six or so at the time of his accession, the new Amir was in the full vigor of robust manhood. A man of many contradictions, he could be either generous and grateful or cruel and suspicious; the polarity of his character may be seen in the fact that his two favorite foreigners were Gladstone and Bismarck. He had no trace of scruple in maintaining his kingship, and even today the mention of his tortures and executions brings a shudder in the Afghan bazaars. He professed a strong faith in Islam, but his fervor was always tailored to fit his policies. One of his most obvious traits was the sardonic humor that allowed him to mock in private at the dignity he insisted on maintaining in public.

Shortly after the British had evacuated Afghanistan and Abdur Rahman had occupied Kandahar, his cousin Ayub Khan marched on that city with an army of twelve thousand men. Near Girishk these troops met an army of the Amir's commanded by Ghulam Hyder. The battle was brisk, and at first swung toward the Amir, as the Herati cavalry followed its usual custom of prompt and rapid flight. Suddenly, however, a desperate charge by Ayub's general, Hussain Ali Khan, and eighty soldiers, gained a complete victory. Ayub then advanced and occupied Kahdahar.

This seeming disaster was turned into triumph by the Amir. Reasoning that Ayub had left Herat stripped of defenders, he ordered Quddus Khan, his commander in Turkestan, to attack that city. With a thousand Uzbeg horsemen, the latter galloped around the flank of the Hindu Kush and arrived at Herat before Ayub Khan realized that his base was threatened. The Amir's surmise had been right. Ayub had taken all his adherents on the march toward Kandahar, and Herat was in charge of a token garrison, which promptly surrendered.

At about the same time Abdur Rahman recruited a new army in Kabul and advanced toward Kandahar, to be joined by thousands of Ghilzai tribesmen on the way. Ayub at once evacuated Kandahar and took up a defensive position near the city, much as he had when faced by General Roberts. Abdur Rahman wrote of the battle that followed:

It was the usual custom for the whole of the trained soldiers before my reign began, that the moment they saw one party stronger than another, they left the weak and joined the strong. These four regiments, therefore, seeing that the battle was turning in my favor, at once turned their rifles from the top of the old city and fired at that body of Ayub's army which was fighting hard with my forces.[3]

Ayub Khan and his supporters fled toward Herat on a route that by now was thoroughly familiar. Finding the city held by the Amir, he continued into Persia. Eventually he went to India, where he accepted a British pension and visited Afghanistan no more.

As nominal master of Afghanistan, the Amir now attempted to extend the effective control of the government over the country by an impartial use of bribery, murder, torture, and treachery. His task was difficult; he declared with considerable truth, "Every priest, mullah and chief of every tribe and village considered himself an independent king and for about 200 years past the freedom and independence of many of these priests was never broken by their sovereign. . . . The tyranny and cruelty of these men were unbearable."[4]

One of the Amir's first moves was to strengthen the army. He instituted a kind of conscription to replace the forced levy hitherto used, and began to pay the soldiers with some regularity. Even this did not produce an efficient army, for the unhappy Tadjiks and Hazaras who were drafted into an unpopular duty showed little morale. Fortunately the Amir had a loyal and able subordinate in Ghulam Hyder Charkhi, the Red Chief of Kipling's "Ballad of the King's Jest."

During the twenty years of Abdur Rahman's reign his army and government were tested by three serious rebellions. The first of these broke out in 1886 among the Ghilzai, who never overcame their suspicion that in the war against the British the Amir had been something of a collaborator. In their opinion the two heroes of the war had been Mohammed Jan Wardaki

and Mushk-i-Alam, the latter of whom had died, and the
former, too famous to be arrested, had been murdered—
undoubtedly at the instigation of Abdur Rahman.

During the summer of 1886, the Ghilzai clans near Ghazni
began a revolt led by a mullah, Abdul Karim, a son of the dead
Mushk-i-Alam. (To the latter Abdur Rahman, who both hated
and feared him, had given the name Mush-i-Alam ("mouse of
the universe") because, he said, "his face was like that of a
mouse and his manner still more contemptible.") [5] Any
Ghilzai revolt in Afghanistan is a serious problem, because of
the size of this tribe and also because of its members' martial
abilities. The Amir used both gold and arms in an effort to halt
the rising. There is no question that if the Ghilzai had been
united in their opposition the Amir and his army would have
had little chance; but as usual they were torn by intertribal
hostilities. The Amir took few reprisals, an indication that he
realized the need to conciliate these troublesome people. Abdul
Karim escaped to India, but the grave of his father was opened
and its contents tossed into a ditch; and the Amir declared,
"More wars and murders have been caused in this world by
ignorant priests than by any other class of people." [6]

One reason for the Amir's success was that his troubles were
consecutive rather than concurrent. But the next revolt was not
long in coming. Governing Afghan Turkestan for the Amir was
his cousin, Ishak Khan, a son of the Amir Azim Khan and thus a
man with some claim to the throne. Abdur Rahman was aware
of the dangers of nepotism and was usually careful to keep his
relatives from positions of importance; but he had regarded
Ishak Khan as safe because of his extreme religious fervor as a
member of the dervish sect of Nakshaband, who were noted for
their asceticism.

Early in 1888, however, spies brought the Amir disturbing
reports of his cousin's activities. To test him, Abdur Rahman
went to a summer retreat at Laghman, where he arranged a
false report of his own death. Thereupon Ishak Khan immediately claimed the throne. His suspicions confirmed, Abdur
Rahman sent the Kabul army northward under the command
of his warhorse, Ghulam Hyder Charkhi, and ordered Ghulam

Hyder Tokhi, governor of Badakshan, to lead a force westward. The two armies made contact on September 23 and engaged the army of Ishak Khan six days later in a long and bloody battle near Tashkurgan. During this period of Afghan-Russian tension the northern troops were the best equipped in Afghanistan,[7] and only an accident won for the Amir. In the course of the battle some of his soldiers were captured by a band of Uzbeg horsemen. Jubilant, the Uzbegs decided to take their prisoners to Ishak Khan. But the latter, seeing these horsemen galloping toward him and recognizing Abdur Rahman's soldiers in their midst, came to the wrong conclusion. Leaping on his horse, he raced across the Amu Darya to safety, to the confusion of his followers, who fought on without their leader until sundown and then surrendered. Ishak Khan settled down as a guest of the Russians and devoted himself thereafter to religion.

This time the Amir meted savage punishment; rebellions were becoming too frequent and the Uzbegs, unlike the Ghilzai, were easy targets. Many of Ishak's officers were blown from cannons; hundreds of the soldiers were blinded and had their families sold into slavery. The severity of the reprisals became a matter of comment on the floor of the British parliament and the Viceroy of India wrote the Amir a letter of inquiry. The dour reply, "Neither do the English like rebellions," was an obvious reference to the sepoys blown from cannons after their revolt in 1857.

Three years later another outbreak occurred, this time among the Mongol Hazaras of the central highlands. As Shia Moslems and alien therefore in religion as well as in race, the Hazaras had always suffered at the hands of their neighbors and had retaliated whenever opportunity offered.[8] For a time they had accepted the rule of the Amir, but in the spring of 1891 they rebelled, declaring themselves, according to Abdur Rahman, a separate nation.[9] The Hazaras have written no histories and it is probable that their revolt was caused by the avarice of Afghan tax collectors. It is even possible that Abdur Rahman engineered the rebellion as a means of stimulating Pushtoon solidarity; at any rate this was the only occasion in which he sought aid from the Pushtoon tribes.

Aided by the harshness of the terrain and their own steady courage, the Hazaras held out for several years, but were crushed at last by an Afghan victory at Uruzghan, won as usual by Ghulam Hyder Charkhi. Thousands of the Hazaras were enslaved; their strength and endurance making them excellent laborers. Many others fled for refuge to India and Persia.

The fourth and last of the Amir's major internal conflicts was with the Kafirs of eastern Afghanistan, who for centuries had waged a war of extermination against their Moslem neighbors. Of the many Moslem leaders who had attempted to extirpate these "infidels," all, including Timur-i-Leng, had been defeated by the terrain of Kafiristan. Now Abdur Rahman attempted what had thwarted the mighty Timur, aware that the conquest of these pagans and their subsequent conversion to Islam would greatly increase his prestige—especially among the devout, to whom he was somewhat suspect. Also, the British had been showing an interest in the Kafirs, and an intrepid British official, Sir George Scott Robertson, had made a trip into the heart of Kafiristan.[10]

Thus four Afghan armies were secretly concentrated at Panjshir, Chitral, Laghman, and Badakshan on the borders of Kafiristan. In the winter of 1896 these columns converged, catching the Kafirs by surprise and winning an easy victory in a matter of forty days. The triumph is rendered less splendid, however, by the fact that most of the Kafirs were still armed with bows. After the Afghan conquest the region was renamed Nuristan ("land of light"), and many of the Kafirs converted to Islam. A number of them were settled in Laghman and Paghman, and landless Tadjiks were sent to take their place.

This proceeding brought repercussions in Great Britain, where the Kafirs had a certain fame thanks to the romances of Kipling and others. Since it was widely believed that the Kafirs were Christians, the missionary societies that were then at their zenith raised a wail of pious protest, whose substance was transmitted to the Amir by the Viceroy. Abdur Rahman, hiding his irritation at this meddling with his affairs, answered with candor that he "did not find any Christians among them." [11]

In the time left to him after dealing with rebellions and

internal pressures Abdur Rahman attempted to give Afghanistan an internal administrative structure. The army was reformed and staffed by a system known as *hasht nafri* ("eight men"), under which each village was ordered to select one man out of every eight to be sent for a two-year period of duty, and to pay for the cost of his uniform and upkeep. Nepotism was less frequent than in the past, with favorable effects on the officer corps. This was not because of any scruple on the part of the Amir but rather because most of his relatives had supported Shir Ali, Yakub Khan, Ayub Khan, and Ishak Khan, and were now living in exile.

Abdur Rahman also attempted to equip his soldiers with modern weapons. But since he was unable to pay for enough ammunition out of the limited resources of the country, his soldiers were seldom able to practice with their new rifles. And it was thought even less prudent to supply the soldiers with ammunition after one soldier fired point-blank at the Amir.

Civil government was also reorganized. The treasury was divided into two departments—state and royal—and both were moved into the palace, where trembling officials could be kept under the eye of the Amir. Most of the state revenue continued to be derived from export and import duties and the income from government land, although—like the Tudors, whom he resembled in many ways—Abdur Rahman did a brisk business in confiscation. The time-honored practices of graft and peculation were diminished by the frequency with which they proved fatal during the reign of Abdur Rahman.

Around his government, a complete autocracy, the Amir established a façade of popular representation, which of course fooled no one. A Supreme Council and a General Assembly were formed from among the chiefs whom the Amir preferred to keep in Kabul; but their function was purely advisory, and even advice was infrequently sought.

Law had a special interest for the Amir. Officially the legal code of the country was that of Islam as interpreted by Abu Hanifa—the most liberal of Moslem codes, as it happens. Judges known as Qazis were supposed to administer justice; but in practice the Amir often assumed this responsibility, and ruled by fiat rather than precedent. His criminal law was savage, since he was a firm believer in the preventive power of terror. Torture was both frequent and imaginative; luckless prisoners were expected to purchase their food and pay rent for their cells. Many of the Amir's judgments were observed by Europeans resident in Kabul and reported to India, where they were noted and preserved in print by Kipling. It was said that the boom of the cannon on the hill above Kabul might mean any of three things—the hour of noon, the death of the Amir, or the execution of some unlucky culprit; and according to reports, there were many days when it was heard every hour.

It should nevertheless be taken into account that Abdur Rahman deliberately fostered his reputation for savagery, and that many of the tales of his punishment were spread by the Amir himself. His decisions in fact often showed a crude sort of justice and a sympathy for the exploited. Kabul's *kotwal* or police chief, who used his power to satisfy a lust after the daughters of Kabul, was tied to a post on a sub-zero winter night and drenched with water, in order, as the Amir explained, to "cool his warm blood." A woman who sought divorce from an aged and toothless husband had her own teeth extracted at the Amir's orders; a baker who consistently short-changed his customers was baked in his own oven.[12]

The Amir had seen something of Western technology during his stay with the Russians, and appreciated its value. As a result, he hired various foreign specialists with a promise of lavish salaries and a guarantee of protection. Two European physicians were brought to Kabul, one to keep an eye on the Amir's gout, and the other—a woman—to safeguard the ladies of the zenana. An architect, an ordnance officer, a tannery specialist, and a dentist were imported, to form a small and anxious foreign colony.[13] The dentist justified his income by providing the Amir with a large and gleaming set of dentures, which Abdur Rahman used for political as well as masticatory effect: during a conversation with some powerful outlying chief, he would pause, remove them from his mouth, and polish them with his handkerchief. A report of this marvel to those unacquainted with the art of dentistry confirmed the Amir's reputation for supernatural powers which were commonly believed to be the gift of Satan.

These few foreigners could hardly have made much impression on the culture of the land, however, for Afghans were ordered on pain of dire consequences to keep their distance. This precaution was not really necessary; the Afghans were friendly, and no foreigner suffered offense or injury.

Very early in the Amir's reign, before he turned against the British and at a time when pressure from the Russians was causing him concern, he accepted an invitation from the Viceroy, Lord Dufferin, to visit India. The durbar held at Rawalpindi was carefully planned to impress the Amir with the might and majesty of Great Britain; the Indian army was mustered in full array, and the rajas of India were present in all the panoply of their wealth and ostentation.

The Amir was a hard man to impress. He viewed the thundering charge of the Bengal Lancers without emotion or comment, and the bejeweled rajas with the question, "Are they men or women?" At one of the many receptions he gave a speech during which some of the ladies in the audience tittered. The Amir paused and remarked to Lord Dufferin that there were women present. The Viceroy admitted that there were, and added that the British, unlike the Afghans, did not believe in keeping their women at home. The Amir, turning to examine the audience, granted that this must be true; but, he went on, from the looks of those present, he still believed they must keep the pretty ones at home.[14]

Any impression of British power that the Amir received on his Indian visit, was not reflected in his attitude which grew increasingly anti-British. He particularly resented the government of India, suspecting that his own statements and policies were not being accurately transmitted to London, and made persistent attempts to establish direct communication with the British government. This the British were unwilling to grant; but since they were anxious to retain the Amir's friendship and believed that London might accomplish more in that direction than Rawalpindi, in 1894 Abdur Rahman was sent an official invitation to visit England. At the time the Amir was ill, and it is doubtful whether he would have so jeopardized himself with his people in any event. On the other hand, the opportunity of going over the head of the Viceroy, who was now the hated Lansdowne, was too good to miss; so the Amir compromised by sending one of his sons.

The one chosen was the Amir's second, Nasrullah Khan, a devout and gloomy man who had taken two years from public life to learn the Koran by heart. Since he was known as a violent Anglophobe, it seemed doubtful that Nasrullah's reputation would be harmed by this journey to an infidel land; indeed it is possible that his father hoped the trip might liberalize his disposition.

The Afghan prince reached London in May 1895 and was swept into the tumult of an official reception. The British public, primed by a diet of Kipling and the Khyber Pass, was avid for a sight of an Afghan visitor of rank. To Queen Victoria, Nasrullah presented a letter from his father requesting the establishment of direct diplomatic communications between Kabul and London. Lord Salisbury replied for the Queen that such communications would necessitate ambassadors in the two capitals, and that past experiences of British ambassadors in Kabul had not been fortunate—a tribute of understatement to the experiences of Burnes, Macnaghten, and Cavagnari.

Nasrullah found nothing in England to change his views of the British, and returned more of an Anglophobe than ever. In globetrotter tradition, he set down his impressions in a book, which his father suppressed in the interests of international amity.

But Abdur Rahman was incensed by the British refusal of his request. He wrote:

"I do not wish to name any one Power in particular but . . . some resemble a leech that goes on sucking the blood till a man dies without feeling any pain. . . . Some Powers take new countries by the force of their strength and victories; others take them by fraud, treachery, and stirring up home quarrels between the chiefs of the country; themselves keeping behind the curtain." [15]

The Amir's disposition mellowed as time passed, possibly because he realized that death was approaching but more probably because he had eliminated all possible rivals. His chief desire was to outlive Queen Victoria, whom he regarded as the greatest sovereign of the age, next to himself. His wish was barely fulfilled. In May 1901 he fell seriously ill; a combination of Bright's disease and gout—a persistent enemy of his family—crippled his body but left his mind unimpaired. On September 20 a stroke paralyzed his right side. Eight days later, in open durbar, he handed control of Afghanistan to his oldest son, Habibullah Khan, along with a book of instructions on statecraft. He died on October 1, 1901, only about fifty-six years old but with several lifetimes' experience behind him.

There is no question about the influence of the "iron amir" on Afghanistan or the extent of his ability. He was one of the most capable rulers in the history of Asia, and Lord Curzon, who was by no means a friend, called Abdur Rahman the outstanding man of his time—an accolade Curzon did not readily bestow on anyone besides himself.

The instructions left by the Amir for his son are full of significance, for they are still the basis of Afghan foreign and domestic policy. "There is no question," Abdur Rahman wrote,

but that Afghanistan is a country that will either rise to be a strong, famous kingdom or will be swept altogether from the earth. In its present condition Afghanistan is of no use financially to any foreign government except for military service. In this last it can be of some use in helping a foreign government which may be crossing through Afghanistan to invade or attack another foreign country. But to keep possession of Afghanistan itself would not be a good investment for any foreign government for at least fifty or sixty years. . . . The policy of Afghanistan toward her two strong neighbors should be friendly toward the one which at the time is least aggressive and hostile to the country wishing to pass through her country or to interfere with her independence.[16]

Speaking of internal affairs, the Amir warned his successor to refrain from placing too much authority in the hands of the council of khans and maliks, until such time as its members were sufficiently educated; and when that time should come, the "people of Afghanistan will be governed for their safety by themselves." He cautioned against the installation of reforms until the people were ready for them, and concluded with a verse by Saadi, whom he was fond of quoting:

> That shrewd young boy will save the purse of money in his pocket
> Who looks upon every passerby as a pickpocket and a thief.

No other Afghan ruler has suffered so greatly at the hands of posterity as Abdur Rahman. Modern Afghans bitterly resent his signing of the Durand Agreement with the British, an act they regard as treason to the country. His cruelties are not long past, and the memory of relatives sacrificed to his rage or caution is still alive. Many Afghans point to the development of the spy and informer system he introduced as a hindrance to the nation's progress.

There is truth in these criticisms, but they disregard the condition of Afghanistan at the time of Abdur Rahman's rule. Constant internecine war, internal turmoil, confusion and chaos, and the steady pressure of rival imperialism all hampered the Amir's attempts to gain security, respect for law, and national independence. The Amir was a hard man; but as he observed, he "ruled a hard people."

After Abdur Rahman's death the bazaars hummed with tales of blue flames seen coming from his tomb as a sign that the soul of the occupant was in hell. And in fact three times the tomb was set on fire—an attempt by the mice to avenge themselves on the dead lion.

XI

The Zenith of Imperialism

> They put the nightingale in a golden
> cage, but still it sang, "My home. My
> home."—PUSHTO PROVERB

THE last years of the nineteenth century were filled with tension in Asia, and on several occasions war between Russia and Great Britain seemed inevitable. The rapid Russian expansion was halted only when it encountered the opposition of an emerging Japan; and the preoccupation of the British with India, "the brightest jewel in the Imperial Crown," became an obsession. These years marked the climax of the Great Game, whose players were the secret agents of Russia and Britain, whose playgrounds were the bazaars and alleys of ancient cities, and whose prize was a half a continent.

From the Sepoy Rebellion onward, British energies, stimulated by the concurrent forces of industrialism and imperialism, were concentrated on India. Bright young men escaped a life among the fogs and soot of Manchester and Birmingham by sailing for the shores of Ind, there to become pukka sahibs and to return malaria-wasted and choleric, with their tales of Poona. The millions that poured into British industrial coffers were in part due to the empire's political and economic control over dhoti-clad subjects. Prim lady missionaries set out to do battle against Buddha, Brahma, and Mohammed, while grimy factory workers read with satisfaction of the "thin red line of heroes" and of the exploits of gallant subalterns and sergeants major. For many Englishmen, India was a land of adventure, enchantment, and opportunity, where class lines could be hurdled and the drabness of Victorian England silvered by a brighter sun.

This national fixation accompanied, and to some extent produced, a fear of Czarist Russia as it widened its influence in central Asia and moved closer to India. The British leaders were uninterested in further Afghan adventures, since that country had proved an economic liability and a graveyard for not a few political reputations. But no less than the British people at large, they were gravely concerned with the seeming inexorability of the Russian advance, and with constructing the best possible defensive frontier.

Following Auckland's unhappy experience in 1839–1842 and the British annexation of the Punjab in 1846, most British officals leaned toward Lawrence's policy of "masterly inactivity," or "back to the Indus." But this program met strong opposition as the Russians continued their advance, and with the Conservative victory of 1874 and the arrival of the bellicose Lord Lytton as viceroy, it collapsed entirely. The displeasure of the British electorate with the second Anglo-Afghan war presently aided the return of the Liberals to power, and since their campaign had been largely waged on the issue, the Forward Policy was again discarded—although the House of Lords, a Conservative stronghold, held out to the end.

Soon the Liberals began to meet the same problem that had beset the policy of "masterly inactivity" in the past: the Russians, though fond of Gladstone and less than eager for the return of the Slavophobic Conservatives, were not inclined to miss an opportunity for territorial gain. Russia was bounded on the south by a territory inhabited by nomadic tribes, addicted to banditry and slave-dealing; and just as the East India Company had advanced into the chaos of post-Moghul India, so the expanding Russian state moved into the steppes of the Kirghiz, Kazakhs, and Turkomen.

The Russians were naturally aware of their favorable position at the gaming table of central Asian power politics. Instructions sent to Baron de Staal, the Czarist ambassador to St. James, put the Russian position clearly:

Great historical lessons have taught us that we cannot count on the friendship of Great Britain and that she can strike us by means of continental alliances while we cannot reach her anywhere. No great nation can accept such a position. In order to escape from it, the Emperor Alexander II of everlasting memory, ordered our expansion in central Asia, leading us to occupy today in Turkistan and the Turkistan steppes a military position strong enough to keep England in check by the threat of intervention in Afghanistan.[1]

Afghanistan, as a result of these Russian and British concerns, was faced with the problem of maintaining its independence in the face of pressure from its powerful neighbors. Abdur Rahman, the Afghan Amir, had no liking for either; he was an Afghan of the Afghans, with all the prejudices of his nation. At bottom, perhaps, he feared Russia more than Great Britain, for he saw that the Russian advance was one of accretion and incorporation—in the manner of an elephant, as he put it, "who examines a spot thoroughly before he places his foot down upon it, and when he once places his foot there, there is no going back."

Shortly after the British had evacuated Afghanistan in 1880, Russian activity in central Asia led to renewed tensions. The basis for British-Russian relations in the area was the vague Clarendon-Gortchakoff Agreement of 1872–1873, in which the Russians agreed that Afghanistan was outside their sphere of influence and that the territory to the north was the property of the independent Turkomen.[2] That this was a paper promise was soon evident from the Russians' advances and the gradual extension of their control over the Turkomen tribes. These actions were so successful that by 1881 only the oasis of Merv lay between the Russians and the Afghan city of Herat, in British eyes the "key to India." Merv itself was a level plain inhabited by about 200,000 Tekke Turkomen, whom the Russians viewed with considerable disapproval. "They are frightfully envious; they have no notions of decency or shame; and finally among all the Turcomans there is not a people so unattractive in every respect as the Tekkes of Merv,"[3] wrote a Russian observer, laying the foundation for future action. The British had no interest in the moral standards of the Tekkes; but their anxiety rose as they watched this Russian advance to a spot only two hundred miles from Herat, and it grew worse when the Russians announced that the khans of Merv had asked to be placed under Russian protection.

Gladstone and his government were in no position to risk war over a group of nomadic tribes most of whose members had never heard of Britain. Bismarck had just concluded a treaty with the Russians; France was hostile following the British takeover in Egypt; the madcap General Gordon in the Sudan was doing little to reassure a government dedicated to peace. Aware of all this, the Russians replied to British protests over Merv with the bland statement that in their opinion Panjdeh was the real problem, for its status was uncertain and it was inhabited by predatory tribes.

From Merv to Panjdeh was another jump of about one hundred miles, which obliged the British to inform the Russians that Panjdeh was inside the borders of Afghanistan. Such repeated extensions of Russian control seemed an ominous indication that Herat was an ultimate objective. As a result, the British suggested that a joint boundary commission be appointed, and when the proposal had been approved by St. Petersburg and Kabul, Sir Peter Lumsden was named the British representative.

Lumsden was soon on the scene. Arriving at Panjdeh November 9, 1884, with an escort of 1,600 men, he found that he was unable to begin work because of the absence of the Russian emissary, General Zelenoi, who had fallen ill and was enjoying a protracted convalescence. He reported to London that the Panjdeh oasis was securely under Afghan control—which was true only because the Afghan Amir had sent troops to the area since the Russians had made their claim. The inhabitants of Panjdeh were Sarik Turkomen, whose connections with Afghanistan were slight. Occasionally they paid a token tribute to the governor of Herat, but it was immediately recovered by neatly contrived robbery.

The Russian military officers in the area were far from concurring with either British beliefs or Afghan claims. They were headed by the sinister so-called Colonel Alikhanoff, whose real name was Maksud Ali, one of that faceless crowd of intriguers whose secret manipulations have done more for empires than the efforts of armies. Alikhanoff and his fellows had definite ideas of their own concerning the future of the area, and were as little affected by scruples as by the wishes of the foreign office in St. Petersburg.

Lumsden was anything but audacious; when rumors arrived of the approach of a Russian army, he became alarmed, and on February 20, 1885, he withdrew the British troops from Panjdeh, leaving behind Colonel West Ridgeway and fifty Lancers. On March 25 the Russian forces appeared and took up positions opposite the Afghan camp. Informed by Lumsden of this move the British government asked for an explanation from the Russians, and on March 28 received assurances that it was a peaceful one. Two days later the Russians attacked without warning.

The battle was short. The Afghans, numbering about two thousand under the command of a General Ghaus-ud-din, were miserably equipped; many of the soldiers had been issued cartridges that failed to fire. About four hundred Afghans were killed; Russian losses were negligible. The British took no part in the battle but fled forthwith—one luckless officer leaving his boots behind, to the discomfiture of his fellows in India and the glee of the Russians. Their flight, of course, was not the result of cowardice but the terror of underlings caught in a situation full of possibly grave implications.[4]

After the battle the telegraph line from Meshed mysteriously broke down, and a report did not reach London until April 9. The country was shocked and Gladstone was infuriated—partly as a matter of conscience, partly because the affair, coming on the heels of the British disaster at Khartoum, threatened to unseat his government. He promptly called for a vote of credit of eleven million pounds, called up the reserves, and mobilized the Indian army.

In reality Gladstone was anxious to avoid war, and the Russians—though they maintained stoutly that Alikhanoff and General Kumarof, the military commander at Panjdeh, were in the right—were embarrassed by the action of their field commanders. After a diplomatic interchange the Russian foreign office suggested that the matter be arbitrated by the king of Denmark. To this the British government agreed, and then attempted to convince its countrymen that it had won a major victory—a task beyond the forensic skill even of Gladstone.

At the time of the Panjdeh battle Abdur Rahman, the Afghan Amir, was meeting in India with the Viceroy, Lord Dufferin. He received the news calmly, and called for the British to honor their pledge to assist Afghanistan in the event of aggression. The Viceroy, considerably embarrassed, assured the Amir that any further aggression would be a cause for war; and after making it evident that Great Britain was willing to go no further, he informed Abdur Rahman that he was to be given 20,000 rifles, two batteries of cannon, and ten lacs of rupees.

The Amir's reaction was sardonic: "As the British government has declared that it will assist me in repelling any foreign enemy," he said, "so it is right and proper that Afghanistan should . . . stand side by side with the British government." [5]

What the Amir meant was that Afghanistan would be foolish to put any trust in the words of outside powers, and that any promises so made would be renounced the moment the situation changed. In 1895 Lord Curzon met with the Amir; when he explained that it was not his government that had been in power at the time of Panjdeh, but the Liberal government of Gladstone, the Amir laughed heartily. He was sorry, he said, that he was not a prophet so as to be able to tell what sort of British government might be in power next.

The European chancelleries, meanwhile, had been busy deciding that the northern border of Afghanistan should be delimited in Europe rather than on the spot—a decision that led the seething Lumsden to resign and to castigate his superiors in a most unmilitary manner. The smoothness with which the demarcation then continued is partly explained by the negotiators' unfamiliarity with the territory, about which they knew hardly more than they did of the other side of the moon. The border was to begin at Zulfikar Pass, about eight miles southwest of Panjdeh, move to Maruchak, and thence to the Amu Darya at a village called Khwaja Salar, which had been mentioned by Alexander Burnes in his travels of fifty years before.

After the agreement had been reached, the British border commission, now commanded by Colonel Ridgeway, was joined by a Russian group under Colonel Kuhlberg, and by an Afghan mission headed by Qazi Sad-ud-din, and began to survey the actual border. The Afghan, whose training was in theology rather than engineering, proved to be a hindrance, but demarcation was finally completed on January 18, 1888 after a fruitless search for Khwaja Salar, which is still missing.[6]

Time has since proved that what the Russian war office regarded as a successful steal was in fact a loss. The patience advocated by the foreign office would almost certainly have resulted in Russia's extending its territory to the mountains of the Hindu Kush and incorporating the Uzbeg and Turkic peoples of northern Afghanistan with their ethnic relatives to the north; instead of pausing at this stable boundary.

Although much of the Afghan-Russian border was demarcated by this agreement, the status of the districts of Shignan and Roshan to the east was still undetermined. This territory was of little interest to the Afghans, for it had almost no communication with Kabul and consisted of a mass of towering mountains inhabited by poverty-stricken Tadjiks and Kirghiz. But because it bordered both on Russian territory and on India, it was of interest to both Russia and Great Britain.

In 1891 a Russian officer, Colonel Yonoff, entered this area accompanied by a detail of soldiers, ostensibly in pursuit of Marco Polo sheep. But he took time out from hunting to establish a military post on the Sarez Pamir River, and to arrest another enterprising sportsman, Captain Younghusband of the Indian army, who was also wandering in the vicinity. When he returned in 1892 with a larger escort, Yonoff met an Afghan captain, Shams-ud-din, and a patrol of twelve soldiers. After heated words, the Russian slapped the Afghan's face; whereat Shams-ud-din fired at his assailant. The bullet was deflected by the Russian's belt buckle—perhaps unfortunately, since in the ensuing struggle all the Afghans were killed.[7]

Abdur Rahman was incensed at this recurrence of the Russian habit of killing Afghans in Afghan territory. He promptly protested to the British and announced that he was going to evacuate all Afghan soldiers from the Pamir region.

The British had other ideas. They were determined to keep a buffer area between Russia and India, and in the words of Colonel Holdich, were "not greatly concerned with the Amir's views on the subject." [8] Without much persuasion, Abdur Rahman agreed to accept the decision of a joint boundary commission and to remove all Afghan troops from the right bank of the Panja River. In July 1895 Major General Gerard and Colonel Holdich, representing Great Britain; General Pavolo Schverkovski, representing Russia; and Ghulam Mohiuddin, representing Afghanistan, met on the banks of Lake Victoria in the Pamirs. Two months later, after perilous surveying among the giant blue glaciers of those awesome mountains, the last boundary stone was laid.

Since that time the Afghan-Russian boundary has remained remarkably stable. Shortly after World War II, a Soviet-Afghan commission met to discuss adjustments necessary because of the shifting of the Amu Darya River. The Soviet negotiations were conciliatory, and the decision gave Afghanistan a patch of territory it had not owned before.

Regardless of the preoccupation of the Russians and the British with the Afghan northern frontier, the area of concern to the Afghans themselves was still the east. It should be remembered that Afghanistan began as a national state through the efforts of the Pushtoon people, who live almost exclusively in the south and east of Afghanistan and whose members spill over into the Indus Plain as far as the areas of southern Dir and Swat. Since the time of Dost Mohammed, the Afghans' interest in the eastern Pushtoons had been the basic factor underlying their foreign policy. True, the Kabul government had been able to exercise little control over these fierce and independent hillmen beyond that made possible by the Amir's prestige and pocket, but all the Amirs had considered the eastern Pushtoons to belong to the Afghan nation. The amirs Mohammed Afzal Khan and Mohammed Azim Khan were both sons of a Mohmand woman from this area, and Abdur Rahman's mother had been a Bangash tribeswoman from the Kurram Valley.

The weakness of Afghan authority in this region constituted an excuse as well as a reason for advances by the British into the frontier hills. For some time the British territory impinging upon the Pushtoon tribes was administered by the Punjab government, which followed a laissez-faire policy except when the raids became unbearable, whereupon a punitive expedition would be ordered. At first, such an expedition was a simple affair, for the nineteenth-century advance in weapons had not reached the Pushtoons, and the tribesmen were still armed with swords and matchlocks.

Beginning in 1884, with the appointment of Lord Dufferin as viceroy, British policy toward these predatory neighbors changed. The British pressure on tribal territory included an attempt to replace Pushtoon custom with British law. This development was caused partly by the fact that the Pushtoon tribes were uncomfortable neighbors, but the increasing power of the military at Simla and their unhappiness over the British inaction at Panjdeh were also involved.[9]

The responsibility for this policy in the south was assigned to an able political officer, Sir Robert Sandeman, who blended force, guile, and bribery in extending British control over the Baluchis of the Zhob and Bori valleys. The Pushtoons were another matter. As hillmen they were harder to reach and coerce than their desert neighbors, and unlike the Baluchis, they were not dominated by their chiefs.

One of the first moves of the forward policy in Pushtoon territory was to extend the Quetta railroad from Old Chaman to New Chaman, in violation of the Treaty of Gandamak. The British maintained that the old location was unfavorable for a railhead; but the strategic implications were obvious and brought angry protests from the Amir, which the British blandly ignored. Part of the difficulty between Afghanistan and Great Britain during this period, incidentally, arose from the condescending attitude of British officials toward Asians. For some reason the British, who had once judged Asians on the basis of merit, were now assuming that Indians and Afghans were basically inferior—a point of view that was irritating to the former and infuriating to the latter.

Personal feelings aside, the Afghans could not help but be alarmed as the forward policy unfolded. In 1889 and 1890 large-scale military operations were undertaken by the British against the Shiranis, Orakzais, and Isazais. Also, in 1889 Maharaja Protap Singh was stripped of his authority in Kashmir, and the country was placed under the control of a British resident. From Kashmir military expeditions were sent to Hunza and Nagar, two technically subordinate but actually independent principalities on its northwest border. Surrounded by their mountains, the Hunzas and Kanjutis of Nagar fancied themselves safe from attack and carried on a brisk business of looting caravans on the Leh-Yarkan route for booty and slaves. Neither the mountains nor a claim of descent from Alexander the Great proved effective, however; they were suppressed with ease and placed under the control of leaders who took their orders from the British.

Hunzas and Kanjutis are not Pushtoons, and Afghanistan had no claims on their isolated lands; but the pattern was disturbing. The Afghans became more alarmed in 1892, when the British annexed the Pushtoon Turis of the Kurram Valley. This move was partly brought on by the Turis themselves, since unlike nearly all other Pushtoons, they are members of the Shia sect of Islam. As a result of this doctrinal difference, added to the lure of the fertile Turi fields, they were frequently raided by the Orakzais to the north and their Jaji cousins to the west. No weaklings, the Turis were nevertheless handicapped by having no friends among the other Pushtoon tribes, and eventually asked to be placed under British control and protection.

Partly as a consequence of this steady pressure, partly because of a stream of visiting agents from Kabul, conditions in tribal territory grew increasingly serious. Many of the tribesmen were now acquiring rifles, stolen from the Indian army or smuggled through Afghanistan, and British military expeditions were turning from excursions into bloody affairs.[10]

After analyzing the situation, the Viceroy, Lord Lansdowne, concluded that the problem could only be solved by the demarcation of the frontier between Afghanistan and British India. In that event, he reasoned, the British would be able to disarm and control the tribes in their jurisdiction and to prevent Afghan agents and rifles from crossing the border. Accordingly, Abdur

Rahman was asked to receive a British envoy with plenary powers to conduct negotiations.

Abdur Rahman was alarmed at this proposal, for with the Forward Policy group now dominant at Simla he was fearful of the terms he would be offered. Therefore he coldly answered Lansdowne that he refused to receive such a mission. The Viceroy, furious, promptly put an embargo on all shipments of arms to Afghanistan, as well as on articles of iron, steel, or copper. The Amir retaliated by forbidding his subjects to ride on the Quetta railroad, by writing a letter to London in criticism of Lansdowne, and by repudiating his twelve-lac annual subsidy—the last a most painful reprisal.

Lansdowne reacted to the Amir's obduracy in the same manner as his predecessor, Lytton. Preparations were begun for possible war, and the Amir was informed that Lord Roberts with an escort of ten thousand men was being sent to Kabul. The message was couched in threatening terms, and closed by informing the Amir that the British did not intend to wait for indefinite promises but would draw their own conclusions from his actions.[11]

Faced with this ultimatum, Abdur Rahman informed the Viceroy, in a conciliatory note, that he was sending an emissary to discuss the British mission and to make plans for its coming. But he gave his envoy, a British engineer by the name of Pyne, instructions to travel slowly. As a result, Roberts, who had been recalled to England, left before Pyne arrived. Since Roberts was a leader of the Forward Policy group, and was also the Englishman most hated by the Afghans, his recall was a victory for the Amir.

In reply to the Amir's letter, Lansdowne sent a map showing the territory his government demanded. One glance confirmed the Amir's fears: all the lands occupied by the eastern Pushtoons, as well as Chitral, Asmar, and Mohmand were colored red. The Amir was now in a fearful predicament. He was aware that his refusal to accept the British demand would mean war; and unlike many of his subjects, he realized the extent of British military power and the impossibility of successful resistance. On the other hand, like all other Afghan amirs he considered the eastern Pushtoons to be one of the major bulwarks of Afghanistan. In his reply he put the Afghan position clearly:

As to these frontier tribes known by the name of Yaghistan (land of rebels), if they were included in my dominions I should be able to make them fight against any enemy of England and myself. . . . I will gradually make them peaceful subjects and good friends of Great Britain. But if you should cut them out of my dominions, they will neither be of any use to you or to me; you will always be engaged in fighting and troubles with them and they will always go on plundering. . . . In your cutting away from me these frontier people who are people of my nationality and religion, you will injure my prestige in the eyes of my subjects, and will make me weak, and my weakness is injurious for your government.[12]

Lansdowne was unimpressed by the Amir's logic. On September 19, 1893, he sent Sir Mortimer Durand, the Indian government's foreign secretary, to Kabul with instructions to insist that the Amir agree to the border set by the British. At the Afghan capital the party was received with courtesy and as negotiations began, Durand pressed each point with the confidence of a man backed by the strongest artillery. On November 12, 1893, what is known as the Durand Agreement was reached. In addition to accepting the previously specified changes in his northern border, the Amir gave up all claim to Swat, Bajaur, and Chitral, but was permitted to retain Asmar. The eastern frontier was to be demarcated by a joint commission on the basis of agreements reached at the conference, according to which many of the eastern tribes were detached from Afghanistan. The Yuzufzais were lost; it is true that only those in Bajaur had much contact with Afghanistan, although oddly enough these tribesmen are most emphatic in insisting on their Afghan identity. Part of the territory of the Afridis and Orakzais also went to the British, although some of it remained across the border; and the Waziris and Mohmands were similarly bifurcated.

Lansdowne was jubilant over the Durand Agreement, since it theoretically established a stable border and legalized British claims to territory hitherto disputed. In fact his elation turned out to have been premature, for the agreement brought more problems than it solved. Far from aiding in the pacification of the tribes, it placed barriers in the way of control from either

Kabul or Delhi, and it created an Afghan *irredenta* which remains a major threat to stability in the area.

More of the resentment among modern Afghans for the memory of Abdur Rahman can be traced to his signing of the Durand Agreement than to all his cruelties put together. It is difficult, however, to see what else he could have done, for the British were adamant and an invasion of Afghanistan would almost certainly have followed his refusal.

After the agreement had been signed, the tension grew as the British moved to extend effective control up to the Afghan border, and was intensified by the eloquence of Afghan agents who crossed the frontier and stirred the tribesmen with warnings of the loss of their cherished freedom. The rallying cry of "Islam in danger" was also used with effect, along with reports of the victories of the Mahdi in the Sudan and of the Turks over the Greeks.

The news of such events reached the tribesmen in highly distorted form, since the messengers were usually mullahs who freely exercised the privilege of ecclesiastical editing. Agents from Sultan Abdul Hamid II, who was attempting to shore up the collapsing Ottoman Empire, appeared in Kabul for long meetings with such frontier firebrands as the Mullah Powindah and Syed Akbar Akhundzada. Documents seized by the British in the house of the latter, a power among the Afridis, indicate the tone of the propaganda favored on the frontier: "You, Muhamadans, must take care lest you be deceived by the British, who are at present in distressed circumstances. . . . The Sultan, the Germans, the Russians, and the French are all in arms against the British at all seaports and fighting is going on in Egypt. England is disheartened nowadays." [13] Certainly the British would have had every reason for discouragement had this statement been true. That it was false was of little concern to the tribesmen, who had no opportunity to be apprised otherwise and for whom the priestly messengers had enormous prestige.

In the year 1897 the pressure of the British, the machinations of Abdur Rahman, and the love of freedom among the tribes combined to bring about the most serious revolt in the history of the frontier. The rising was begun in June by the pugnacious

Waziris in the Maizar Valley, and spread with startling rapidity all the way to the Malakand Pass, just south of Chitral.

Through the heat of the summer, perspiring British and Indian troops were hard put to keep the tribesmen in check. With their new rifles and their old skill in the hills, the tribal warriors were dangerous antagonists, following skirmishing and guerrilla tactics with skill and determination. Some of this tenacity was undoubtedly due to their leaders, a group of mullahs who beat the drums of religion with fanatical fervor. Among them were the Mullah Powindah, the Hadda Mullah, and Syed Akbar, but the most troublesome from the British point of view was the man known as the Bareheaded One or the Mad Mullah. His real name was Sadullah Khan and he came from Kabul accompanied, or so he claimed, by an army of invisible angels.

Nevertheless, such tribal fanaticism was exaggerated by British writers, who often confused nationalist opposition with religious frenzy. The tribesmen were Moslems to a man, and their leadership often came from among the articulate semi-educated priests; but without question the major cause of their resistance was a desire to preserve their old tribal independence.

Especially irritating to the British was the obvious fact that the Amir of Afghanistan was a prime mover of the revolt. In one attack at Shabkaddar, for example, the tribesmen were Safis, Shinwaris, and Khugianis, all from Afghanistan, and their leader was the Afghan Mullah of Hadda. Indeed, several Afghan soldiers in uniform were seen taking part in the fighting. But to British protests Abdur Rahman blandly replied:

No tribesman from my territories can do such an act in open manner. Some of them, however, have great faith in Mulla Hadda, and it is possible that they may have joined him during the night, traveling like thieves on unfrequented roads. How is it possible to keep watch on thieves during nights along such an extensive frontier. My kind friend, such an arrangement could only be possible by posting about ten thousand soldiers on all the mountain tops.[14]

Abdur Rahman's "kind friends" were aware of the Amir's duplicity, but their hands were tied as tribal fighting rose to unprecedented heights. In an attack on Tirah Bagh, the Afridi center, the British suffered nearly twelve hundred casualties, including a general; and though they gained their objective, their retreat proved costly.

The Afghan Amir cleverly used the risings to cover his negative reputation, a result of his habit of executing mullahs, with a cloak of sanctity. Even before the outbreak, a convention of priests met in Kabul, to which Abdur Rahman delivered a stirring speech on the glories of holy war and the duty of true believers to extirpate the infidel. At the same time, a book supposedly the work of the Amir, was distributed, calling in orotund style for Jehad. To British protests the Amir replied that he was speaking generally and in philosophic terms.

After a year of incessant and costly fighting, the tribes subsided into an uneasy quiet, while more than forty thousand British troops remained in tribal territory or on the border. Even this truce was illusory, for no British officer or soldier dared stray from the shelter of the cantonments, and British control was effective only where it was directly supported by force. Obviously the Forward Policy had proved to be an expensive failure; and the British policymakers now decided on a new approach.

The new program took effect in 1899 with the arrival of Lord Curzon as viceroy. Almost immediately Curzon withdrew the British forces to areas outside the tribal zone, and turned over the maintenance of order to tribal levies or to the tribes themselves. Two years later Curzon organized the North West Frontier Province. Politically the new province was divided into two zones: an "administered area" under direct British control, including the districts of Hazara, Peshawar, Kohat, Bannu, and Dera Ismail Khan; and a "free tribal zone" lying between the administered border and the Durand Line. The tribes in the latter were placed under five political agencies—Wana, Malakand, Khyber, Kurram, and Tochi—and dealt with through political officers. In fact, these tribes retained almost complete autonomy, and were paid heavy subsidies to keep the peace.

These events brought satisfaction to the Afghans although

Abdur Rahman did not live to see his intrigues bear fruit. The Afghan *irredenta* was left untouched, outside of British control, and to some extent the British had conceded its special status. But unfortunately a sword can be swung in more than one direction. From this time onward, the hills inhabited by the eastern Pushtoons were the haunts of secret agents, who were able to urge their case with gold—an activity that was, of course, highly acceptable to the tribesmen themselves.

XII

Amir Habibullah

If the water is over your head,
depth makes no difference.
—PUSHTO PROVERB

TRADITION in Afghanistan suffered when Habibullah Khan, oldest son of Abdur Rahman, mounted the throne in 1901 without opposition—a final tribute to his grim father. The new Amir was thirty-two and had been carefully coached in the art of Afghan kingship. Abdur Rahman's only other adult heir, Nasrullah Khan, besides being a whole brother of the Amir, was loyal chiefly to the Koran, and therefore no menace.

The new ruler was short and stout, with a marked facial resemblance to his father but with a pleasant and amiable manner. By nature he was a genial and tolerant man, fairly well educated and an excellent linguist. His greatest fault was excessive sensualism. Unlike Abdur Rahman, who had regarded sex as a pleasing but secondary aspect of life, Habibullah returned to the pattern of Timur Shah and found his chief satisfaction in the harem. By his many wives and concubines he fathered over one hundred children.

Habibullah's early foreign policy was dictated by the later policy of his father and was openly anti-British. This, as usual caused the British concern, particularly after the Amir had been sent a flattering message from General Kuropatkin, the Russian minister of war. Lord Curzon promptly countered by issuing

Habibullah an invitation for the Amir to visit India, which was politely declined. An attempt to apply pressure by withholding the Amir's annual subsidy proved unavailing; Habibullah simply made no attempt to collect it.

Some of the conflict stemmed from the personality of the Viceroy, Lord Curzon. Called the "last of the great proconsuls" —a phrase probably coined by himself—Curzon had an overwhelming egotism and was a proponent of the "white man's burden" school, thereby irritating some of his own countrymen as well as infuriating both Afghans and Indians.

In addition, the turn of the century led to a sharpening of British anxieties. The Russophobia that had been dormant for a time was revived with changes in Czarist foreign policy, and the Boer War demonstrated the precariousness of Britain's vaunted isolation. Certainly there were Russian activities during the years from 1900 to 1905 that from the British point of view could only be called provocative. Russian advances in central Asia continued, and the extension of the Russian railroad system from Tashkent to Khushk on the Afghan border was made in the expectation, according to a statement by the Czarist government, "of closer economic ties with Afghanistan." In Tibet, a Siberian named Dorjieff began to intrigue with the Dalai Lama, who contrary to custom had survived beyond childhood.[1] To counter Russian gold and promises, Curzon dispatched a diplomatic mission to Lhasa, headed by Younghusband (the same officer who had been arrested by Yonoff in the Pamirs). The mission reached the Tibetan capital after slaughtering some six hundred Tibetans on the way, and quickly persuaded the Lama not to make concessions or admit foreign emissaries without British approval.

Despite this triumph, Russian actions continued to be alarming. Even the debacle of the Russo-Japanese War failed to quiet the concern of the British over Afghanistan, for the humiliated Russians strove to check popular discontent at home by diverting antagonism toward an outside enemy. Lord Curzon was not a man to accept compromise or concession; and his commander in chief, the belligerent Kitchener, along with his excessive zeal had a paranoid fear of Russian intentions.

With Anglo-Afghan matters in a dangerous deadlock, Lord Curzon was recalled to England, leaving affairs in the hands of Lord Ampthill. Habibullah immediately announced that he was appointing twenty-four Afghans as emissaries to other countries, in violation of Abdur Rahman's promise to the British to deal with foreign nations only through their mediation. Curzon pressed for immediate invasion; but the British government had listened to viceroys before, and contented itself this time by asking the Amir to receive a British mission. Having compelled the mountain to come to Mohammed, Habibullah decided not to press his luck; he countered by a gracious acceptance of the British proposal, and a promise that his oldest son, Inayatullah Khan, would pay a visit to India. Since the prince was only sixteen at the time, this promise was not of much significance.

The British mission, headed by Sir Louis Dane, reached Kabul on December 12, 1904. Its members had been thoroughly briefed by Curzon, who was no believer in the delegation of powers. They were to demand an end of the Afghan boycott of the Quetta-Chaman railroad, as well as of Afghan intrigues among the tribes across the Durand Line; the demarcation of the frontier in the territory of the Mohammeds; and a new treaty on the same lines as the one they had concluded with Abdur Rahman.

Habibullah was gracious but obdurate. He said that he was perfectly satisfied with things as they were, for he had no fear of the Russians and considered himself as great a ruler as the Emperor of Japan. Then, with matters at a deadlock, he produced a treaty written in flowery Persian, with much hyperbole but no mention of the British demands. It merely restated the agreements made with Abdur Rahman and referred to Habibullah Khan as the "Independent King of the State of Afghanistan and its dependencies." This, the Amir said, was his final offer; the British would accept it or get nothing at all.[2]

The opposition on the part of the government of India was furious; Curzon, still in London, demanded an immediate suspension of negotiations. But again the Delhi warhawks were ignored by the Cabinet; Dane was instructed to ratify the treaty and did so on March 21, 1905. Immediately Habibullah's attitude became one of complete cordiality.[3]

Habibullah had cause for jubilation. The British gained nothing but the commitments made by Abdur Rahman, whose rejection by Habibullah would probably have led to an invasion. The Amir had obtained the renewal of the annual subsidy, 400,000 pounds for the arrears, and tacit agreement that he was an "Independent King." Habibullah continued to use the title of Amir, however, and it was not until the reign of his son, Amanullah Khan, that the title of Shah was resumed by Afghan rulers.

In June 1906 Habibullah received another invitation to visit India, which he accepted after stipulating that no political matters were to be discussed. One of the reasons for his change of mind was the departure of Lord Curzon from India, for the flamboyant Viceroy was much hated in Afghanistan. Habibullah reached India in January 1907, having left his brother, Nasrullah Khan, and his second son, Amanullah Khan, in Kabul as regents, and bringing with him an entourage of eleven hundred, most of whom he was afraid to leave behind. For two months he toured India, where he was shown everything that might impress him with British power, with special emphasis on military reviews. In typical Afghan fashion he made himself extremely popular with his hosts, gave gifts to the Sikh temple at Amritsar, became a Freemason of the Calcutta Lodge, and offered to marry several English ladies whom he met on his travels.

The trip was believed by the British to be an unqualified success, since according to their contention Habibullah was thereafter pro-British. But in this they were mistaken; he was as anti-British as his father, and no junket was likely to erase the prejudices of a lifetime. What the British mistook for friendship was the amiable and placid disposition of the Shah, who had little of the aggressiveness of his father and was mainly interested in enjoying the comforts of peace. So far as Habibullah was concerned, the experience was not worth the cost, since from this time on some of the Afghan leaders also expressed a muttering belief that the Shah had grown friendly with their traditional enemy.

Soon after Habibullah's trip the exceptional warmth of Anglo-Afghan relations returned to its customary coolness, this time as the result of some obtuse diplomacy at Whitehall. The defeat of Russia by Japan had reduced British Russophobia; the long-feared bear had become a paper tiger. The British defenses of India were bolstered by a clause of the Anglo-Japanese treaty of 1904 in which Japan agreed to cooperate in the protection of India's northwest frontier. And Germany now loomed as the chief rival of both the British and the Russians.

Under these conditions Great Britain and Russia settled their differences by signing the Anglo-Russian Convention of 1907. The British promised not to change the Afghan government, and the Russians agreed that Afghanistan was outside the Russian sphere of influence. That neither party had seen fit to inform the Afghans that their country was being discussed was a new blow to Afghan pride. The convention was not to come into effect until it had been ratified by Afghanistan, and this Habibullah refused to do. Growing hostility toward Austria-Hungary and Germany impelled the Russians to ignore this detail; they signed the agreement in 1908.

The conclusion of the agreement strengthened the belligerent anti-British party at the Kabul court. The entente between Great Britain and Russia also brought a temporary end to a practice that had become traditional in Afghan foreign policy—the exertion of pressure on one of Afghanistan's neighbors by the threat of dealing with the other. Habibullah still had influence with the frontier tribes, however, and he used this effectively to indicate his displeasure. The number of raids in the North West Frontier Province, a certain barometer of official Afghan attitudes, jumped from fifty-six in 1907 to ninety-nine in 1908, and to an uncomfortable total of one hundred fifty-nine in 1909.

Aside from the simmering antagonism toward the British, the quiet in Afghanistan of the years just before World War I was broken by a single notable exception. In 1913 some of the tribes of Khost, particularly the Mangals, broke out in a revolt whose pretext was the familiar one of taxation. The Afghan army was as inept as ever, and the government was driven to the dangerous expedient of asking aid from other tribes. Fourteen thousand Suleiman Khel, Shinwari, and Khugiani tribesmen who were eager for excitement, promptly volunteered—a force which, added to the army, was too much for the Mangals. After a defeat near Tindan the rebels asked for a truce and were granted easy terms by Nadir Khan, the Afghan commander.

One important internal development during these years was the growth of factions in the Afghan government and at the court. Abdur Rahman, a model totalitarian, had recognized the danger of such a process in a country like Afghanistan, and had suppressed such groups with ruthless thoroughness. Habibullah, on the other hand, was sentimental and lenient. After his accession many of those who had lived in exile during the reign of his father returned to Afghanistan, where they were greeted warmly by the new Amir and given positions of honor and responsibility. A number of these men were descendants of the twenty-one Barukzai brothers and were often further related as a result of the Afghan custom of marriages between cousins.

Within the immediate royal family were Nasrullah Khan, the king's whole brother, and his two oldest sons, Inayatullah Khan and Amanullah Khan. Nasrullah was loyal to his brother, but was hampered by a dour disposition and a religious fervor of unusual intensity. Inayatullah Khan was fat (a very unusual trait in Afghanistan) and, like his uncle, uncommonly devout; Amanullah Khan, his father's favorite, was able and energetic although somewhat erratic.

Outside this inner circle were three important groups. One, called the Musahiban ("equerry") or Yahya Khel, was made up of descendants of Sultan Mohammed Khan, the brother of Dost Mohammed who had ruled Peshawar as governor for the Sikhs. One of Sultan Mohammed's sons, Yahya Khan, had followed Yakub Khan into exile in India after the death of Cavagnari and the renewed British invasion in 1879. Here his son, Mohammed Yusuf Khan, had five children who were to play an important part in the development of modern Afghanistan. The five—Mohammed Aziz, Nadir Khan, Hashim Khan, Shah Wali, and Shah Mahmud—were all educated in India and returned to Afghanistan in 1901 after the death of Abdur Rahman. Having been well received by Habibullah Khan, the brothers soon rose to high positions in the Afghan government, where they showed much ability as well as a strong family loyalty. Nadir Khan, for example, was the general who ended the Mangal rebellion in 1913, and he was rewarded by the post of commander in chief of the Afghan army.

Another powerful group at the court was the Tarzi family, whose head, Mahmud Beg Tarzi, was descended from Rahimdil Khan, one of the "dil" brothers who had ruled Kandahar during the time of Dost Mohammed. Like the Musahibans, the Tarzis had lived in exile during the reign of Abdur Rahman and had settled in Damascus, where Mahmud Beg received a Western education and married a Syrian girl. Mahmud Beg had also been much impressed by the Young Turk movement, and upon his return to Afghanistan he struck out as a proponent of reform and published a newspaper, *Siraj-ul-Akbar Afghania*.

A third powerful family was the Charkhi, whose members were descended from Ghulam Hyder Charkhi, the commander in chief under Abdur Rahman, and one of the few men that grim amir ever trusted. The two sons of Ghulam Hyder, Ghulam Nabi and Ghulam Siddiq, were generals with influence among the tribes, particularly the Ghilzai.

Over these groups Habibullah Khan exercised a control that was mild but effective. He recognized the value of Western ways, but he also saw the danger of innovation in Afghanistan and was unwilling to jeopardize his own pleasant position for the sake of progress. When more foreign technicians appeared in the country, they received little aid from the king beyond the payment of extremely lucrative salaries. Some of these men were unscrupulous adventurers, who took advantage of Afghan hospitality to mulct the Afghan treasury of fantastic amounts before departing safe from extradition.

Perhaps the greatest of Habibullah's contributions to his country was his founding of Habibia College, Afghanistan's first public school—although the cynical assertion was made that it was built merely to house his offspring. Actually, the establishment of Habibia ("college" here meant a school with grades from first through twelfth) marked an important step forward; it was organized on the pattern of a French *lycée* and introduced Western education to the country. Among its graduates have been some of the most distinguished men in Afghanistan, including many of the present Afghan leaders.

The outbreak of World War I at first caused little stir in Afghanistan, for to most Afghans Germany was only a name and events in Europe were of little consequence. This indifference was abruptly ended, however, by the entry of Turkey into the war; from that time on the border hills became the setting for continual intrigues and deadly operations of the cloak-and-dagger variety.

Although the Afghans did not dislike the Turks as did many of Turkey's Moslem neighbors, neither had they any great affection for them.[4] But Turkey still retained some prestige from the past, and along with Afghanistan it had been almost the only Moslem land to avoid foreign control. Moreover, the revered title of Caliph had been claimed by the Turkish sultans since the time of Selim the Grim. Most Moslems had given little credence to this claim from the beginning, and later Turkish rulers, occupied as they were with the seraglio, had allowed it to lapse. The astute sultan Abdul Hamid, "the Damned," had revived it, however, in his struggle with the Young Turks, hoping to gain support from the conservative and priestly classes in his battle against these reformers. Thus the Turkish sultan claimed to speak in the name of Islam.

Oddly enough, the only places where the claim of the Turkish ruler to the spiritual leadership of Islam received much support were in India and Afghanistan. The Shia Moslems of Persia were merely contemptuous, and those of the Near East who had experienced the reality of Turkish rule were more inclined to believe that if the Turks had received supernatural assistance, it must have come from Satan.

The support for Turkish claims in Afghanistan and India probably sprang from a developing nationalism that looked to the Ottoman Empire as a bulwark of Moslem power in a Christian world. For years the khutba had been read in Indian mosques in the name of the Turkish sultan, and as early as 1878 Lord Lytton had informed his government that "Indian Moslems were by no means indifferent to the fate of Turkey." [5]

German planners had spotted this potential chink in the British imperial armor, and had entered the world of Islam with customary thoroughness. German businessmen, secret agents, and archaeologists were all at work, and German gold passed into receptive Asian pockets. The Kaiser continually stressed his support for militant Islam, and a group of Indian opponents of British rule, who had banded together under the name of the "Indian Provisional Government," had support from Berlin.

This group was a mixture of sincere patriots, opportunists, perpetual dissenters, and crackpots, whose leader, Mahendra Pratap, was still active as late as 1945, when he appeared in Japan as the head of an "Aryan Army." Many of its members had lived in the United States; they had little real influence, but they provided a convenient lever for manipulation by the Germans.

Both Turkish and German planners were aware that the sincerity of "Haji" Wilhelm would be questioned in Moslem quarters. The Turkish leader, Enver Pasha, accordingly developed plans for having the Sultan in his role of Caliph issue the call for holy war from the cities of Istanbul, Kerbela, and Nejaf. The summons was then transmitted through a network of mullahs, assisted by Turkish, German, and Indian agents.

The British took prompt action to counter this threat. Allowances paid to the tribes on the Afghan border were raised —those given to the Afridis were more than doubled—and strenuous attempts were made to bribe influential mullahs. Fortunately for the British, their old enemy the Mullah Powindah had died in 1913; but the Haji of Turungzai was still active, and his exhortations kept the Mohmands in ferment. Another trouble spot was a colony known to the British as the Hindustani Fanatics, and to its friends as the Mujahidin or "warriors for the faith." This band of zealots, with headquarters at Charmarkand in Bajaur and at Samasta on the right bank of the Indus, had been founded by Syed Ahmed Shah of Bareilly early in the nineteenth century, and had been a haven for refugees from India, including many of the sepoys after their rebellion. The fame of its members for their devotion to Islam and their fierce opposition to all other faiths had much influence with the powerful Yuzufzais among whom they lived.

Another contributor to the uneasiness in the Pushtoon hills was a group of Moslem students from India, principally from Deoband College in the Punjab. These men maintained close connections with the Indian independence movement that had been developing in the United States and were deeply concerned over the future of Turkey. Though they had been observed and infiltrated by the efficient British secret police in 1915, some managed to escape across the border to take refuge in Kabul or among the Mujahidin, where they continued their intrigues.

All these factors strengthened the militant anti-British faction at the court of Habibullah, which already had the support not only of Nasrullah Khan, the king's brother, but also of Amanullah Khan, the king's second and favorite son, and of the influential Mahmud Beg Tarzi. Only the king and a few of his older advisers opposed the plan of the warhawks for stirring up the tribes and eventually for an all-out attack on India.

Habibullah was too astute to be open in this opposition, however, for feeling now ran high and even his close relatives were beginning to regard his inactivity with suspicion. To counter it, he professed devotion to the Turkish cause, at the same time pointing out that the call to holy war was not valid since it had not been made in Afghanistan. He cautioned his eager courtiers to postpone any action until the British had been weakened by the war in Europe. He gave limited subsidies and limitless compliments to the Indian revolutionaries, and permitted a Kabul newspaper, *Siraj-ul-Akbar,* to carry a stream of violent attacks on the British. At the same time, in a correspondence with the British maintained through secret and trusted messengers, he suggested that they be influenced by his actions rather than his words.

Behind this duplicity were three considerations. First, the king's growing indolence left him with no stomach for war. Also, he had a much more realistic understanding of the relative strength of Afghan and British military power than his courtiers, who remembered their country's past successes and forgot the reverses. Finally, he believed that the Allies would win the war and show their gratitude to Afghanistan for its neutrality.

In August 1915 Habibullah's uneasy position was complicated by the arrival at Kabul of a Turkish-German mission, consisting of about eighty men and headed by Captain Oskar von Niedermayer and Kazim Bey. Among its members were the all but legendary Wasmuss, a German secret agent in Persia, and two leading Indian revolutionaries, Mohendra Pratap and Barkatullah. They had started from Baghdad, dodging their way among British patrols in Persia, and their purpose was to persuade Habibullah Khan to attack India.[6] For these men of courage and ability there had been difficulties from the outset. The Sultan's call for Jehad had been made before Turkey entered the war, and had caused only a few minor riots. Persia had been a disappointment, for the Shia Persians were at first lukewarm, and became hostile after a few Turkish expeditions had developed into orgies of rape and looting. Afghanistan and Habibullah Khan were the mission's last hopes for success.

In Kabul its members were given hospitality and rest, both of which they sorely needed after two thousand miles of constant danger. The degree of welcome varied, however, all the way from the enthusiasm of the militant anti-British group to the correct cordiality of the Shah. The members of the mission were assigned quarters at the Bagh-i-Baber, near Kabul, whence they began a series of interviews with Habibullah and intrigues with his subjects.

It soon became evident to Niedermayer that there was little to be gained from the Shah, even though Habibullah listened to the arguments attentively and professed complete sympathy with the cause of the Central Powers. He asserted that he was willing to lead an attack on India but that he preferred to wait for the German or Turkish army, which Niedermayer assured him would soon be on the way. Finally, after several months of negotiations, the Afghan ruler signed a preposterous draft treaty in which he pledged Afghan assistance in return for no less than 50,000 cannon and twenty million pounds in gold. Niedermayer knew he had failed, but carried out the farce of signing the document, and then on May 22, 1916, left Kabul, reaching safety after many dangers and winning the admiration of his enemies.

Although the Nierdermayer mission was technically a failure, its other, secret purpose was successful. While Niedermayer and Kazim Bey negotiated with the Shah, other members of the mission were dealing with his subjects and with agents from India. The Indian revolutionaries with the mission had soon been in touch with the Moslem students on the frontier, and through them with the tribes and dissident groups in India itself. The formidable if unrealistic plan in which this activity was to culminate was scheduled for completion in late 1916, when a general rising of Indian Moslems was to be coordinated with a similar revolt in Russian Asia. An army was to be raised from among German prisoners in Tashkent; Afghanistan was to be the center of the campaign, and in the event of success Habibullah Khan was to become king of India.

Habibullah smiled at the enthusiasm of his court for this improbable scheme, and did nothing. Indeed, it is now the general belief in Afghanistan that he kept the British constantly informed of developments—an activity that is probable if unprovable. At any rate, the British secret service worked with quiet efficiency to halt the plan by means of mass arrests in India, while rival agents carried out a deadly game of assassination in the hills of the frontier. That the tribes meanwhile remained peaceful though uneasy is almost certain evidence that Habibullah Khan was not supporting the Indian revolutionists. There were some outbreaks—the Mohmands, led by Abdul Wahid, the Haji of Turungzai, attacked Peshawar in 1915 and 1917—but these were not supported by other tribes and collapsed under the combined impact of heavy subsidies and of the airplane, a new weapon on the border.

Although the wisdom of Habibullah's inaction became evident with the collapse of the Central Powers, the victory of the Allies only increased the indignation of his subjects with their lethargic king. Many powerful courtiers, including some of his closest relatives, believed both that the Shah had let slip a golden opportunity to regain Afghan greatness and that he had been a traitor to Islam in not coming to the aid of the Turks.

Habibullah, though indolent, did not fail to discern the forces of hatred and anger rising around him. Only some striking gain for Afghanistan would mollify the disgruntled nationalists, and he thought he knew how to secure it. On February 2,1919, he wrote the Viceroy of India a letter pointing out the benefit to Great Britain of Afghan neutrality in World War I and his own part in maintaining it. In return, he asked complete sovereignty for Afghanistan, including unhampered permission to carry on negotiations with foreign powers.

What Habibullah had unfortunately failed to realize was what his father had understood—namely that gratitude has small place in the dynamics of power politics. The war-weary British, already concerned with the threat from the north of Communists at once more subtle and more deadly than the Cossacks, were in no mood to listen to Afghan importunities. Curtly they replied that they would continue to look after Afghanistan's external affairs.

At this time the practice of maintaining a winter capital, discarded after the loss of Peshawar, had been revived to satisfy Habibullah's habitual concern with comfort. At the new winter capital in the eastern city of Jalalabad while snow and biting winds prevailed in Kabul, cypress and deodar were green and flowers bloomed in the gardens. In December 1918 Habibullah Khan, accompanied by his brother Nasrullah and his oldest son, Inayatullah Khan, went as usual to Jalalabad, leaving his son Amanullah Khan in charge of the treasury and the garrison at Kabul. With most of his court, the Shah devoted himself to his usual pastimes, and in particular to hunting, of which like most Afghans he was passionately fond. Early in February he crossed the Kabul River into the district of Laghman, where on February 19 his hunting party camped at the foot of Khula Ghos Pass.

At three in the morning the camp was awakened by a pistol shot. Hurrying to the royal pavilion, the courtiers found in his bed the lifeless body of the king; he had been shot through the ear with the bullet penetrating the brain.

The assassin has never been identified. The Russians identified him as one Mustafa Saghir, an agent in the pay of Great

Britain; and the accusation was seconded, officially at least, by the Afghan government. The British in their turn placed the blame on the Afghan "war party," and specifically on Amanullah Khan, Nasrullah, Mahmud Beg Tarzi, and Nadir Khan. A romantic theory proposed that the assassination was the work of a survivor of a minor revolt that had taken place in Laghman years before, at the time Habibullah had become a Freemason.

The real mystery of Habibullah's death is how he had managed to avoid it for so long. His preoccupation with the harem and his failure to take a militant stand against the British had lost him the confidence of his subjects and the support of his relatives, and it is most probable that the deed was the work of those relatives, or of others close to the throne. As suspects the British may be eliminated because they had so much to lose and so little to gain from the murder; the Communists would have had a motive but not the opportunity. There is some evidence of a widespread plot in the making: shortly before Habibullah left Kabul for the last time an attempt had been made on his life, and two writers for *Siraj-ul-Akbar,* the paper published by Mahmud Beg Tarzi, had been arrested. Among the Afghans a rumor circulated that Tarzi, whose daughter had married Amanullah Khan, Habibullah's successor, was at the head of the conspiracy.

Habibullah died at the age of fifty, and had reigned nineteen years. Even though his memory is not revered in Afghanistan, he was not a bad ruler. He gave Afghanistan a generation of unaccustomed peace, and his geniality healed some of the wounds left by his father's repressive policy. Slowly but steadily, he had continued the introduction of Western technology to his country. He brought back to Afghanistan some of the country's outstanding leaders, whom he not only granted political amnesties but also placed in positions of responsibility. And by his founding of Habibia College he laid the foundation for his country's future development.

XIII

The War of Independence

> The death of the donkey is the feast
> of the dog.—AFGHAN PROVERB

HABIBULLAH'S sudden death without having named a successor, and the absence of primogeniture in Afghanistan, meant a renewal of the once customary scramble for the throne. The Shah was survived by scores of children, but only two were adult, legitimate, and influential: the eldest, Inayatullah Khan, a fat and placid man, deeply religious and with few qualities of leadership; and Amanullah Khan, the second eldest of those born to wives rather than concubines, who was twenty-nine at the time of his father's death. Habibullah's favorite, he had a strong if erratic personality, and the added advantage that his mother was the Ulya Hazrat or "first queen." He evidently inherited some of the traits of this lady, who was known and feared for her temper, and there is no doubt of her influence as the daughter of Mohammed Sarwar, leading chief of the Barukzai Durranis and the most powerful tribal leader in the country.[1]

Inayatullah Khan and his father's brother Nasrullah Khan had been with the Shah at the time of the murder, while Amanullah Khan was in charge of the garrison and the royal treasury at Kabul. With the king's body the royal party returned to Jalalabad, where at a meeting with the courtiers and tribal leaders Inayatullah and Nasrullah both put forth claims to the throne.

These claims lost out before Amanullah's energy, combined with possession of the treasury and the influence of his mother. On February 18, 1919, at a public meeting in the grounds of the palace, Amanullah delivered a stirring speech, vowing to bring the murderers of his father to justice, and at the same time doubling the salaries of the soldiers.[2] The populace received his oratory with approval (he had shrewdly suggested that the assassin was a British agent), and the army hailed his generosity, while in Jalalabad his mother devoted her efforts to securing the allegiance of the tribal leaders.

Although Nasrullah and Inayatullah promptly withdrew their claims in favor of Amanullah, they were arrested, along with the members of the Musahiban family, and brought to Kabul. Here Inayatullah and the Musahibans were soon released and restored to favor, and Nasrullah died, apparently of natural causes, while he was still in prison.

The new king, Amanullah Khan, had been born at Paghmam in 1890. Like his father and grandfather, he was short and stocky, an excellent horseman, a good shot, and a devotee of hunting. He was more active and energetic, and less libidinous than his father, but he had the latter's affability and cultivated an extremely democratic manner. He had been privately educated and was well informed about the outside world and impressed by Western culture. His weaknesses were stubbornness and an emotional instability which in his later years (he died in 1959) approached psychosis.

His first wife had died, and he was married again only once, this time to Souriya, the half-Syrian daughter of Mahmud Beg Tarzi. The queen was an attractive, well-educated, and intelligent woman, and had much influence over her husband. In fact, many of Amanullah's later problems grew out of his tendency to place faith in particular individuals, who were unfortunately not always those of sound judgment.

Since the beginning of World War I, Amanullah had been a leader of the Mashruta, the reform group at the court. In addition to being strongly anti-British, the Mashruta had a zeal for economic and social reform, which had earned Amanullah the dislike of the priestly and conservative faction headed by his uncle Nasrullah. On the other hand, most of the members of the Mohammedzai clan, including Inayatullah, were fond of the new king.

Amanullah lost no time in indicating that changes were in store for the lands of the Hindu Kush. At his coronation on March 1, 1919, he announced three goals: complete Afghan independence, the punishment of his father's murderers, and the abolition of the system of *beeger* (literally "seize"), a kind of forced labor resembling the medieval *corvée* and much practiced by landlords in territories not inhabited by Pushtoons.

On March 3 the new Shah wrote to apprise the British of his accession. Since the latter had already been informed by agents of Amanullah's coronation speech, they read his letter with interest. The message was friendly and informal, but it contained no suggestion that the new Afghan king considered himself bound by the agreements made by his father or grandfather. On the contrary, it spoke of the willingness of the "independent and free" government of Afghanistan to conclude agreements of a commercial nature.

At this time a series of unprecedentedly rapid changes had followed the Bolshevik revolution, the ensuing civil war, and the dislocations of World War I. In Europe the equilibrium of power and politics achieved by a century of tension and negotiation had been destroyed. In Asia the hard-pressed Communists had already begun to strike back against Allied intervention by decrying the evils of imperialism to its listening peoples.

And already the British position in Asia had deteriorated. The war-weary British people were undergoing the emotional letdown that followed their heroic efforts of the war years, and the tragic depletion of their national energy. Of the political and military men who had devoted their lives to Indian service, who spoke Pushto, Urdu, Bengali, and others of the myriad tongues of the subcontinent, who knew and were known by northern hillmen and naked Nagas, many had been lost in the mud of Mons and Ypres. Their replacements, who too often were beardless lieutenants eager to return to the fleshpots of Blighty, or debilitated veterans who drowned their resentments in alcohol, were faced by problems that would have taxed a Lawrence or an Elphinstone.[3]

With peace the cooperation between India and the British Raj that had marked the early years of the war had withered. India had contributed greatly to the war effort, and the expected rewards were not forthcoming. Of 943,000 Indians who had served overseas, 106,000 had been casualties. They had fought to make the world safe for democracy, but they had not brought that democracy home.

One of the causes of discontent in India was anger at the harsh terms the victors had imposed upon Turkey. Many Moslems from the Punjab had served in the British army, and their sense of guilt was great as they witnessed what seemed to be the end of Islamic greatness. Moreover, the Allied leaders were definite in asserting that no areas inhabited by non-Turks were to be left in Turkish hands; and since those areas included the city of Mecca, it was greatly feared that the holy city of Islam might be placed under infidel control.[4]

Another reason for unrest in India was the country's economic distress. The monsoon rains of 1918 were light, and the harvest of 1919 was a dismal failure. The ensuing famine left the Indian peasantry in no condition to resist the influenza epidemic, which in 1919 caused at least five million deaths.

The Afghan government's own stake in the growing disorder in India led to an exaggeration of the difficulties facing the British—which though serious enough, especially in the Punjab, were by no means beyond their control. Most of the reports that came to Amanullah about conditions in India were by way of the Indian revolutionaries at the Kabul court, who not only were victims of the habitual optimism of conspirators but were also anxious to prove their influence to their hosts. They heard the tocsin of revolution in the complaint of every Indian peasant, and worked hard to convince Amanullah that an uprising might occur at any moment.

Amanullah was willing to believe these forecasts, although some of his advisers had doubts. The new Afghan king was nothing if not self-confident, and cherished thoughts of ruling India as Afghans had done in the past, or at least of recovering the territory they had once held in the south and east.[5] He realized, of course, that any such plan would depend for success upon Hindu support, and that few Hindus had pleasant memories of Afghan hegemony. And as a Moslem he was so far from being a fanatic that he began to issue statements extolling Indian virtues, as well as to order Afghan agents in India to work for Hindu-Moslem cooperation.[6]

As reports came to Kabul of serious rioting in the Punjab the Afghan government took increasingly provocative steps. On April 13, 1919, Amanullah invited a number of influential frontier chiefs to Kabul and told them that holy war was imminent. At the same time he ordered a concentration of the Afghan army on the eastern border, where one section under General Sawleh Mohammed Khan proceeded to Dakka at the Afghan entrance to the Khyber Pass, and another under Nadir Khan to Matun in the province of Khost. A third, commanded by Abdul Quddus, was posted at Kandahar.

The British soon learned of these moves, but were less well prepared for them than in the past. Although their army in India numbered 334,000, in quality and morale it was a travesty of the disciplined professionals who had fought there in the name of Victoria. The British conscripts were anxious to go home; the sepoys were tainted by sedition, and among the Moslems by dismay over the weakened position of Islam.

Poor as they were, the British soldiers were still models of efficiency compared to the Afghan regulars, who as before were ill equipped, untrained, and poorly led. The Afghan conscripts supposedly received a monthly wage of twenty Kabuli rupees, a sum equal to one dollar, but usually this was in arrears or had been stolen by the officers. There was no staff, and except in Kabul there was little attempt at organizing even the brigades. Many of the soldiers were armed with Snyders or Martinis, whose romantic nineteenth-century heyday was now past; some of their ammunition was over twenty years old and as dangerous to the marksman as to his target.[7]

As in the past the real military strength of Afghanistan lay in its fighting tribes, whose members were well armed, skilled in the use of weapons, and so adept at irregular warfare as to have been regarded by their British opponents as the best guerrilla fighters in the world. Of this, and also the weakness of the Afghan regulars, the Afghan planners—who looked for a full-scale insurrection in the Punjab to trigger a concerted tribal rising—were well aware.

Unfortunately for Afghan expectations, the British leaders were no less well informed. They knew that a delay of at least two months would be necessary to allow the tribesmen to finish the spring harvest, and they were also aware of the growing sedition in the Punjab. Their conviction that prompt action was necessary to prevent its spread in India was given confirmation by events at Dakka where Sawleh Mohammed, the Afghan general, found himself unable to control tribal allies or even to coordinate the movements of his own troops. On May 3, 1919, a squad of Khyber Rifles escorting a caravan through the pass were turned back by tribesmen led by a notorious Shinwari outlaw, Zar Shah. Later in the day this same band killed five coolies who were at work on a water project at Landi Kotal. Finally, just before dusk, a party of about 150 Shinwari and Mohmand tribesmen crossed the border and occupied the village of Bagh, south of the Khyber Pass. It should be noted that the border in this area had never been demarcated; thus the Afghans held that Bagh was in Afghanistan, and the British that it was two hundred yards inside British territory.

These acts brought a declaration of war by the British three days later. Their claim that the action was defensive made the conflict more palatable to the electorate at home, but was of dubious validity. There was no question that the Afghan raids had been provocative, but there was a question whether the misdeeds of a few outlaws and the movements of a band of Afghan irregulars constituted an attack on India. The Afghans had simply moved into strategic positions while they waited for news of developments in the Punjab. Had the Afghans seriously intended invasion they would have moved more aggressively; and they would have met some success on the frontier, for the British levies in the area—the Khyber Rifles, Tochi and Wana Scouts—were all thoroughly disaffected.

Once they were at war, the British acted swiftly. Major General Climo, with a cavalry regiment and two infantry battalions, surrounded Peshawar and conducted a house-to-house search of this "city of a thousand sins." The Afghan postmaster and thirty-three others were arrested, and a mass of seditious material was seized.[8] On May 9, Brigadier General G. F. Crocker, commanding the British army in the Khyber, marched against the Afghan army, which had joined the irregulars at Bagh. The action was hastened by the loss of the water supply at Bagh and by ominous desertions from the Khyber Rifles.

The battle began at 4:45 A.M., as the first rays of the sun began to tint the bleak walls of the pass. Only a few shots at long range were fired; then the Afghans withdrew to a new position on Khargali Nala Hill. The next day the British received reinforcements led by Major General Fowler, who assumed command.

On May 11 another attack was launched, again early in the morning so as to avoid the heat, which was terrible, reaching over 120 degrees in the sun. The Afghans' resistance was weak; their artillery was no match for that of the British, and their soldiers consistently overshot the advancing British infantry—a common fault of inexperienced marksmen shooting downhill. When the British reached the ridge they found the Afghans gone, leaving sixty-six dead behind. Their own insignificant losses amounted to eight dead and twenty-nine wounded; in fact, sunstroke and heat exhaustion had accounted for more casualties than the Afghan bullets.

On May 13 the British army moved out of the Khyber and occupied the large Afghan village of Dakka, which they found deserted. On the open plains south of the dismal town they found a well-watered, spacious site where they bivouacked, within rifle range of neighboring hills. Four days later a more formidable enemy appeared: a large Afghan lashkar of Mohmands, Safis, Khugianis, and Shinwaris, all well armed and trained in the use of rifles since boyhood. Following their usual tactics they clambered to the top of the hills, took cover, and began to fire at the British camp.

The next morning, when the British advanced to eliminate this nuisance, they met a fire so intense that the advancing infantry was pinned about one hundred yards from the crest, and one regiment, the Thirty-fifth Sikhs, retreated in disorder. At this critical moment the British were rescued by the arrival of two sections of howitzers, which promptly began shelling the heights. After a heavy barrage the infantry advanced unmolested, and found that the artilleryless tribesmen had vanished.

This battle ended military operations in the north. It was decided that further advance toward Kabul was too risky, for the Afridis were up, the Khyber Rifles had been disbanded, and supplies could only move slowly and under heavy guard through the pass. As a result the British army remained at Dakka, where heat and boredom were enlivened by the visit of an occasional sniper.

On the central front the Afghans were more successful. At the head of the Afghan army stationed at Matun was Mohammed Nadir Khan of the Musahiban family, a capable and energetic leader who had instilled some of his spirit into his troops. Without waiting for action by the British, Nadir moved forward and captured their advanced post at Spinwan. He then executed a surprise march of twenty miles to the key British fort of Thal, bringing his cannon on the backs of elephants along a route that had been considered impossible for an army. Taking up position about five thousand yards from the fort, he began a heavy bombardment while swarms of tribesmen who had joined him added the fire of their rifles to the attack.

This successful sortie brought out the tribes and alerted the border from Thal to Baluchistan. When the Zhob Militia proved as untrustworthy as the Khyber Rifles—a final vindication of the critics of the Curzon Plan—the advanced British posts were left in desperate straits. All were evacuated; their retreating defenders suffered heavy casualties, especially among the officers, as they fought their way to safety. That the belligerent Mahsuds and Darwesh Khel Waziris had joined the fighting was to be expected; but for the British the participation of the peaceful Shiranis and Kakars was an unexpected blow.

For some reason—probably because he knew the weakness of tribesmen in attacking fortifications—Nadir Khan made no attempt to storm Thal but contented himself with bombarding it. This attack was sporadic and ineffective, and the British garrison was able to hold out. Meanwhile, all available help was on the way through the deadly heat. On June 1 a relieving army under General R. H. F. Dyer reached Thal; an attempt was made to attack the Afghans on the following day, but during the night the Afghans withdrew in good order.

On the southern front the Afghan army under General Abdul Quddus remained at Kandahar. The only hostilities took place when the British, under Lieutenant General Wapshare, captured the Afghan frontier fort of Spin Baldak. This, and a small skirmish in Chitral, ended the military actions of the third Anglo-Afghan War. That it is usually described as an overwhelming British victory is at least partly because outside observers have not heard the Afghans' side of the story. Their forces, with the exception of the Khyber army, were intact at the conclusion of hostilities; Nadir Khan had gained considerable glory, and the southern Afghan army had seen no action at all. Now that the tribes were roused at last, the British would have met far more serious opposition if the war had continued. In fact two more years were needed to quiet the Darwesh Khel Waziri alone, and the British suffered more casualties during that campaign than they had in the Afghan War. Moreover, an epidemic of cholera broke out in the British army, with heavy mortality.

While the soldiers rested, the diplomats had been active. On May 28, while the army of Nadir Khan was investing Thal, the Viceroy received a message from Amanullah Khan, who wrote that the actions of Sawleh Khan had been misinterpreted, and that the Afghans had not contemplated attacking India. He also requested an armistice. In the British reply, the conditions under which an armistice would be granted were "that the Afghans were to withdraw all troops from the border . . . that the British troops should remain where they now are in Afghan territory. . . . British troops will not bomb or machine gun Afghan localities or troops[;] further that you will undertake that your people will not fire upon or molest British aircraft." [9]

Amanullah's response was a blend of explanation, defiance,

and philosophy. He pointed out that the civil and military forces of Afghanistan were identical; that it was impossible to move the tribes from the border; and that he could not prevent Afghans from firing at planes, "for the feelings of our nations who do not have aeroplanes are bitterly excited by seeing your aeroplanes." And he observed in conclusion: "The spirit of freedom . . . has caused the withered hearts of the depressed classes of humanity to expand and blossom in every part of the world and has by an extraordinary force brought into being, loving peace and equality and has nearly brought to its death agony, oppression and domination among the various nations." [10]

Whether they were chiefly impressed by circumstances or by the Shah's philosophy, the British now agreed to a peace conference, which was held at Rawalpindi. The Afghan delegation was led by Ali Ahmed Khan, one of Amanullah's cousins, and the British by Sir Hamilton Grant. The discussions lasted a month, and were acrimonious in the extreme. To the astonishment and anger of the British, the Afghans did not behave in the least like emissaries from a vanquished nation. They put forth claims to all of Waziristan, to a much larger subsidy, and to their own independence and sovereignty; and in their spare time they made inflammatory speeches for the benefit of an admiring audience of Indians.

On August 8 a treaty was concluded. Its five articles called for the withdrawal of British troops and the cessation of British subsidies, and a stop to the flow of Afghan war materials through India. No mention was made of Afghan sovereignty, but at the request of the Afghan delegation a rider to the effect that it had been implied was attached to the treaty.[11]

Publication of the terms brought a torrent of abuse upon the harried British delegates. The British public found it difficult to understand how a war so costly in lives and money, fought over the issue of Afghan sovereignty, could have ended by conceding that very point after its victorious conclusion. Critics demanded to know why, when the reward for Habibullah's loyalty had been the bullet of an assassin, the enmity of Amanullah should be rewarded by granting his demands. And "old India hands" grumbled that British prestige in India had suffered a fatal blow.

What these critics failed to understand or appreciate were factors much in the minds of the British policy makers. India was seriously disaffected, and a continuation of the Afghan war might have led to wide-scale trouble; for the Ali brothers, leaders of the Indian Moslem movement, were openly supporting Amanullah, and Mohandas Gandhi had expressed his approval of the Afghans' objectives. And the British leaders were further harassed by the appearance to the north of an old bogey in a new guise—for the Bolsheviks, who were winning the struggle for Russia, were active in Afghanistan, and Amanullah was lending their agents a receptive ear. Two letters had been intercepted by British intelligence, one to Lenin from Amanullah Khan, the other from Mahmud Beg Tarzi to the Bolshevik foreign minister, and both of them cordial. In a third and still more alarming message (obtained in a manner undisclosed but undoubtedly interesting) a former Czarist diplomat, Michael Bravine, who was now a Communist agent, had written the Eastern Propaganda Department of the Bolshevik government that he was having much success with the Indian revolutionaries in Kabul.

That British control over Afghan external affairs was useless against this kind of activity—that it was in fact a hindrance—since it kept British representatives outside—was now obvious. The old policy of keeping a native agent in Kabul had been effective only so long as the threat was of a Russian military attack. But now the danger consisted of ideas rather than weapons, and of activities directed at the restless people of India.

The Afghans maintained and still maintain that they won their complete independence on the field of battle. An impressive monument built at Kabul shows a marble lion crouching in chains at its base—to the chagrin of the British—and the month of August was selected for the celebration of Istiqlal, or "freedom." Nadir Khan's campaign against Thal made him the popular hero of the war, and Amanullah Khan emerged from it with a popularity rarely possessed by an Afghan ruler.

XIV

Afghanistan Emerges

Allah is great but He sends no rain
from a clear sky.—Pushto proverb

FREED at last from restraint in foreign affairs, Afghanistan
began to coquette with all possible admirers. Mohammed Wali
Khan, a shrewd and capable Tadjik who had risen high in
Amanullah's estimation, was chosen to head a mission to the
West and to treat with whomever he could. Russia, Germany,
Italy, and the United States were the major powers to be visited,
and the first three promptly signified their willingness to welcome this newcomer to international society. In the United
States the Harding administration was frozen in an attitude of
isolation and very possibly was uncertain about Afghanistan's
precise location. Its vague reply was that the question of diplomatic interchange must be reserved for future consideration.[1]

As in the past, Afghan foreign policy was based upon the
actions of its powerful neighbors. At this time the threat from
the north had faded as the Bolshevik regime struggled against
civil war and Allied intervention; in fact, the capture of Orel by
Denikin in October 1919 marked the high tide of the counter-
revolution. This weakness increased the cordiality of the Afghans, whose traditional policy was to support the neighbor
who posed the least immediate threat.

Many Afghan leaders, although ignorant of the essential
nature of Marxism, in fact found much to admire in the propa-

ganda that Communist agents had brought to Kabul, particularly the attack on "bourgeois imperialism" and the call to the people of Asia to rise against their European masters. A letter from Lenin to Amanullah, which owed more to Machiavelli than to Marx, put the Bolshevik position this way:

In the name of the Workers and Peasants Government we express our sincere desire to enter into diplomatic negotiations with the Afghan people. . . . The Soviet Government from the first day that they received power have heralded to the whole world their desire not merely to recognize the right of self-determination of all people both great and small, but to render assistance to those people who are struggling for their independence.[2]

This message was followed by the arrival of an envoy, the aforementioned Michael Bravine, at Kabul on September 12, 1919; the first official foreign diplomat to enter the Afghan capital,—unless one includes Burnes, Macnaghten, and Cavagnari in the same category—Bravine was an excellent linguist and a skilled subversive, although an erratic personality.

Bravine's activities were duly reported to the British by agents in Kabul, and were held to be the cause of the continuing trouble on the frontier. In truth, the Afghans did not take Bravine or the promises that he made seriously, and though the Afghans continued their meddling with tribes across the Durand Line, they were motivated by nationalist aspirations rather than by Communist propaganda. So long as sedition continued to flourish in India, however, the British saw the hammer and sickle in every border raid. Undoubtedly much of the tension in India, and particularly in the Punjab, was caused by the Indian Moslem's resentment of the peace terms forced on Turkey, and by the added complication of the Turko-Greek War. Without question the Afghan government helped to stimulate this resentment, especially after Amanullah Khan had increased his prestige by the claim of having won independence for his country on the field of battle. In fact, during the summer of 1920 nearly twenty thousand Punjabi Moslems migrated to Afghanistan as a Dar-ul-Islam (land of Islam). Here they were soon dismayed by the cold winters, and the Afghans, though friendly, were dismayed in their turn at the size of the influx. Disillusioned, most of the migrants wandered back to the Punjab, only to find their homes taken by less religious neighbors.

This affair hurt Amanullah's prestige in India, but it added to the concern of the British who were now convinced that Amanullah had fallen under Communist influence.[3] In an effort to seek closer relations with Afghanistan, they invited Amanullah to send emissaries to India for discussions of a new treaty.

Always happy to discuss new treaties, the Afghans sent a delegation headed by Mahmud Tarzi to the hills of Mussoorie, where British negotiators were led by Henry Dobbs. The meetings were unfriendly; the Afghans refused to budge from their demands, and often offended their hosts by comments more true than tactful. When Tarzi was asked whether he did not agree that India was remarkably fertile, he said it was, but added that he was surprised to see the Indian people looking half starved. On exchanges like this the conference finally foundered.

In October 1920 the Afghans reciprocated by inviting a British delegation to Kabul. In January 1921 a group once again headed by Dobbs reached the Afghan capital, where conversations began with Tarzi and Nadir Khan, the two Afghan negotiators. The talks continued for eleven months, with the Afghans holding to demands the British considered impossible, while the latter held to the attitude of Lord Curzon, who was foreign minister. He had been anti-Afghan since the diplomatic victory of Habibullah Khan in 1906, and blamed his government's difficulties in India on unwarranted pampering of the Afghans. He had given the touring Afghan delegation of 1919 a chilly reception in London, and asserted that Afghanistan must continue to deal with the government of India.

Meanwhile the alarm of the British over the cordiality between Afghans and Soviets was increased by a treaty between the two in August 1921, which was extremely favorable to the Afghans—or rather would have been if it had been carried out. In addition to establishing diplomatic relations between the two countries, it called for the cession of Panjdeh to Afghanistan, for the institution of Bolshevik consulates at Herat, Maimana, Mazar-i-Sharif, Ghazni, and Kandahar, and for a yearly subsidy of one million gold or silver rubles to Afghanistan. Where the bankrupt Bolsheviks were to get the rubles was not discussed.

On November 15, 1921, much to the surprise of the patient Dobbs, the Afghans announced their readiness to sign a treaty with the British. This agreement, which remained the base for Afghan-British relations until the departure of the British from India in 1947, contained fourteen articles. The first five concerned the exchange of diplomatic missions and personnel; the sixth article gave the Afghans the right of unlimited transit across India, and the seventh stated that Afghan shipments should be duty free. There was no mention of the sovereignty over the Pushtoon tribes on the east of the Durand Line; but the parties each agreed to inform the other if military operations against tribes near the border were contemplated.[4]

This treaty would not have been possible except for a change in the attitude of the Afghans toward their neighbors across the Amu Darya, where the tumult of the Bolshevik revolution, of the counter revolution, and of Allied intervention was rising to its peak. In order to understand how this change came about, some understanding of the situation in the area is necessary.

The lands of central Asia north of the Amu Darya had been under Russian control for some time, even though the Russian administrators and soldiers in the territory were vastly outnumbered by Tadjiks, Uzbegs, and Turkomen. Only Khiva and Bokhara were even nominally independent, and in fact both of them took orders from the Russian government.

In these regions, with their crumbling ruins of once splendid capitals, revolutionary sentiment had flourished among backward peoples under the corrupt rule of Russian puppets. In Tashkent the Soviets had already seized power even before the Bolshevik coup in Petrograd in November 1917. In Bokhara the ruler since 1911 had been the Amir Said Alim Khan of the Uzbeg tribe of Manguit, whose family had dominated the country since 1783. Although Said Alim was under Russian direction and lacked the absolute power of his ancestors, he retained enough authority to satisfy his personal whims, including a fondness for boys. These predilections gave further impetus to a revolutionary group, the Djadid or "new" party, whose members had been inspired by the program of the Young Turks in the west. They were incensed when the short-lived Kerensky government granted Bokhara complete independence, and when Said Alim made it clear that he planned to return to the despotism of the past. An uprising by the Djadid in 1919, supported by central Asian units of the Red Guard, ended in failure and was followed by increased oppression. But even though the railroad tracks to Russia were destroyed, once the Bolsheviks began to prosper in other areas, they returned to Bokhara. Here for a time they were blocked by a force of Indian sepoys led by a Colonel Malleson—a phase of Allied intervention that remains all but unknown, and that came to an end when the British force was withdrawn to Meshed in Persia.

This event took place at a time when relations between the Afghans and Communists were still cordial. At the Bokharan court, where Afghan influence was strong, the Amir was counseled to make peace with the Russian revolutionaries. Said Alim, reluctantly agreeing, predicted mournfully that "as soon as the Bolshevists had gained control, they would undoubtedly take revenge by attacking the Holy State of Noble Bokhara." [5]

The Amir was right. On August 25, 1920, Frunze, commanding the Red Army in Turkestan, ordered his troops to aid the Djadids and to attack Bokhara. This time the conquest was complete; the capital fell on September 1, 1920. The Bokharan troops offered only token resistance, although a group of Afghan mercenaries in the Amir's service fought with enthusiasm.

It was very quickly evident to the Bokharan reformers that the hit-or-miss despotism of the Amir had simply been replaced by a more thorough oppression. The Red Guard, encouraged by hundreds of political commissars, was determined to establish a new society founded on revolutionary atheism—which both to the conservatives and to the Moslems of the population could only be anathema.

Reports of their resistance and of the tactics of the Communists sped to Kabul with the refugees from Bokhara. All this was disturbing to Amanullah Khan and the Afghan leaders, not so much because of the Uzbegs and Turkomen in themselves as because Bokhara had once been a seat of Moslem splendor. As the Communist repressions continued, many thousands of Turkomen crossed the Amu Darya into Afghanistan. That some of these fugitives brought with them their flocks of karakul sheep was to be of considerable importance to the future economy of the country. They were hospitably met and assigned lands in northwestern Afghanistan. But the accounts of the infidel domination of their country and of the rigors of Communist control over its Moslem population aroused increasing indignation as swarms of refugees continued to flee southward with tales of rape and desecration.

Amanullah Khan, always a dreamer, now had a new vision of greatness. This time it was based upon the concept of Pan-Turanism, the goal of the Young Turks, which after fading with Turkey's defeat in World War I had revived as the conquered Turkish lands slipped from Russian control. In fact, though the Uzbegs, Turkomen, Kirghiz, and some of the Chahar Aimak of Afghanistan were Turkish, the Afghan leaders were not, nor did they have much feeling of common identity. But since Afghanistan was the only independent Moslem state in the area, it seemed to Amanullah that his country might serve as a rallying point for what he envisioned as a Pan-Islamic rather than a Pan-Turanian movement.[6]

This grandiose aspiration was strengthened by the arrival in Kabul of the fugitive Amir of Bokhara and by a revolt that erupted in Russian Turkestan in the spring of 1921, at least partly as the result of Afghan intrigues among the Uzbegs north of the border. The name applied to this rising by the Russians—*Basmachi,* Turkish for "bandit"—was eventually used to characterize all anti-Communist activities in central Asia. Although there were brigands among the participants (the Turkomen, in particular, having long held robbery to be an honorable profession), most of the rebels were either Moslems angered by the Communist attack on religion or Uzbeg nationalists anxious to avoid Russian control.

The outbreak began among the Uzbegs of the Lokai Valley, and had soon almost overwhelmed the Communists and their ally the Young Bokharan Party. At the head of the rebels was a guerrilla chieftain and former horse thief, Ibrahim Beg, whom the absent Amir, Said Alim, promptly appointed commander in chief and, appropriately, master of the royal stables.

Many Afghans took part in the revolt, and a steady supply of arms and ammunition crossed the border. Nadir Khan was appointed Afghan commander in the north and instructed to assist the Basmachi without directly involving his own country. He was aided by the appearance of a new Basmachi leader in the person of Enver Pasha, one of the triumvirate that had ruled Turkey during World War I. The able and ruthless Enver, son of an Istanbul corpse-washer, in the course of his rise to prominence married a princess and annihilated the Armenians in Turkey. The Turkish defeat and the rise to power of his rival and enemy, Mustafa Kemal, had obliged Enver to flee for his life. Arriving in Moscow, he had convinced the Bolshevik leaders that it was his destiny to reconcile Marx with Mohammed; and indeed his name was still a great one in the lands of Islam. Having been sent to Baku for what the Communists had called the Congress of the Oppressed Peoples of the East, he promptly eluded his hosts on a hunting trip. He next appeared in Bokhara, where he called for holy war and Pan-Turanism.[7]

The ability of Ibrahim Beg and the prestige of Enver were of value to the Basmachi cause; but the future belonged to the machine gun, high explosives, and organization. On June 12, 1922, the Uzbeg riders led by Enver were crushingly defeated near Barsun, and on August 4 Enver himself was cut down by the saber of an unknown Red cavalryman in a skirmish near the Afghan border.

The news reached Amanullah Khan while he was on the northern border conferring with Nadir Khan. For some time he had been disturbed by the obvious growth of Communist power north of the Amu Darya, and he now decided to abandon all thought of expansion in the north and to concentrate as before on the east and south. Without Afghan aid the Basmachi movement collapsed into a brave but futile series of bandit raids, which Ibrahim Beg continued to lead for several years. The exiled Amir Said Alim settled down to a prosaic existence as a karakul trader in Kabul, with a subsidy from the Afghan government but no opportunity for his former pleasures.

It was now, while relations between Afghans and Russians deteriorated, that the British came into unusual favor. Amanullah, acceding to the latter's demands, asked the Indian revolutionaries to leave Afghanistan—no difficult decision, since even Afghanistan hospitality had been strained by these perpetual guests. Most of them made their way to Russia, where they were coolly received.

Meanwhile, the ancient city of Kabul was acquiring a faintly cosmopolitan flavor, as a Soviet legation was established in 1921, to be followed by British, French, German, Italian and Turkish missions. Most of these foreigners spent much of their time in attempting to bribe Afghans to act as agents, with occasional success but frequent failure. The somewhat exaggerated reports of this activity that reached the Afghan government did little to reduce its mistrust of foreigners.

By 1922 the Afghans' temporary friendliness toward the British was already fading with the decline of their own hopes in the north and the renewal of British activity on the frontier. Although the machinations of Communist agents also played its part, the most important reason for the cooling of relations was the concern of the British over the Pushtoon tribes on their side of the Durand Line, where since the Anglo-Afghan War the old Curzon system had broken down. Even though full-scale tribal revolts had been suppressed, not without difficulty, isolated raids and attacks not only had continued but were growing worse. To add to the alarm of the British, the tribesmen had become sufficiently infected with the virus of civilization that there were now occasional attacks on the wives and daughters of British officials, who had hitherto gone unmolested.[8]

In 1922, as a check upon incidents that were making frontier duty increasingly unpopular, the British adopted a compromise between the static Curzon system and the old, costly aggressiveness. The tribal levies, whose unreliability had been demonstrated in the Afghan war were replaced by Khassadars, scouts who were drawn from the tribes and who served under their own maliks. These men had as their only uniform a special turban; they furnished their own rifles, and were expected to keep a semblance of law and order in tribal territory.

Another innovation was to construct roads deep in tribal lands, and to station regular troops in advanced positions, in the hope that they would be able to move swiftly enough to stop any tribal outbreaks before they had a chance to spread. But when, as at Wana, the soldiers were forced to retire behind wire barricades at nightfall, this neither promised nor proved to be effective.

Finally, an expansion of the Curzon plan called for subsidies to tribes that were able to keep the peace, and for punitive expeditions against those who still found raiding more attractive. This, the notorious "scuttle, burn and bolt" program, was to be strengthened by the use of aerial bombardment.

There was immediate resentment on the part of the Afghans, particularly against the decision to station regular units in advanced positions. In this the Afghans saw a threat to their cherished *irredenta* and a sign that the British planned to extend their control over the independent tribes. Thus late in 1922, when the British began to implement the program, the Afghans retaliated by stepping up the agitation of tribal firebrands in their pay and by sending new agents across the border. Sizable allowances or subsidies were issued to a number of Waziri, Mahsud, Mohmand, and Afridi maliks and mullahs, men who were not only anti-British but naturally belligerent. In addition, Afghan border officials were to offer refuge to tribal outlaws who already had the habit of swooping down upon villages in the administered zone, raiding, plundering, and kidnaping, and then scurrying back to safety across the Durand Line. The undemarcated or illogical boundaries made the frontier ideal for this kind of thing. Both the Waziris and Mohmands had relatives on each side of the border, and the equally energetic Afridis had a back door to Afghanistan. As a result, at least a thousand men "wanted" by the British police were inside Afghanistan, and by 1923 the situation had become intolerable. When Amanullah Khan invited a group of trans-border chiefs to Kabul, gave them presents, and promised them his support the British announced their intention to break off diplomatic relations and hinted at possible military action.

This sobered the ebullient Amanullah, who was less confident of his ability to deal with a British attack than his speeches suggested. In addition, Afghanistan was now facing tribal troubles of its own, which the Afghan leaders believed to be due at least in part to spying and bribery by the British.

In March 1924 there was a revolt by the Mangals and Jajis of Khost. Since tribal flareups were common in Afghanistan and could usually be suppressed by a few discreet bribes, it was at first not considered serious. Moreover, although the Mangals and Jajis were both large tribes and noted as fighters, they had no connections with other tribes but were in fact continually at odds with the more powerful Ghilzai and Waziris who bordered their territory.

The original outbreak is believed to have been triggered by some of Amanullah's social reforms, since it was led by mullahs, in particular by the frenetic Mullah Abdullah, known also as the Lame Mullah. Soon, however, a new leader appeared in Abdul Karim Khan, a son of the exiled Amir Yakub Khan; though born to a concubine, he now made a claim to the throne. When the Afghan troops sent to handle the rising proved ineffective, the Afghan government was forced to take the dangerous step of calling for assistance from other tribes. A number of Mohmands, Shinwaris, Waziris, and Afridis responded; but even with their help the situation was grave, and at one time the rebel lashkar was only a few miles from Kabul. If the powerful Ghilzai had entered the fighting on the Mangal side, the capital would certainly have fallen; but ancient animosities were stronger than the prospect of loot, and the Ghilzai remained aloof. Finally a government victory at Charasiah, brought about in part by the use of two airplanes loaned by the British, ended the rebellion. The Lame Mullah was brought to Kabul and executed, while Abdul Karim returned to his refuge in India. Amanullah, the Afghan Asoka, promptly erected a new pillar of victory, this one dedicated to the "triumph of knowledge over ignorance." [9]

The Mangal revolt contained lessons that were clear to some observers but that were lost on the confident Amanullah. The continued weakness of the Afghan army was obvious, and it was apparent that the Afghan government did not have the power to halt a revolt carried out by several powerful tribes. The added stimulus that Abdul Karim had given to the rebels demonstrated that a leader of stature who was not directly connected with any of the participating tribes could minimize the effects of jealousy and foster cooperation among them.

The Afghans still maintain that this revolt was instigated by the British to counteract Amanullah's venturesome border policy, and that Abdul Karim's trip to Khost was arranged by British intelligence agents. As is usual in such cloak-and-dagger operations, there is no proof of this charge; but neither does its melodramatic character, or the proneness of the Afghans to such accusations, constitute proof that it is unfounded. Few places on earth have witnessed more consistent and successful undercover activity than the Afghan frontier.

Whatever the inciting cause may have been, there is no doubt that the revolt was fueled by tribal resentment toward Amanullah's social reforms. Among the tribes the mullahs were a potent force, less because of any real faith in their spiritual authority than as a result of their oratory. Most tribal mullahs knew little of the religion they professed, but they were usually vocal and capable of arousing the emotions of the tribesmen. They also had a conservative fear of change, less because of the threat to Islam than because of what it might do to their own positions of privilege, which they owed largely to the ignorance of their followers.

The growing opposition was lost upon Amanullah, who had the impracticality of many a sincere and idealistic reformer. His intense national pride, along with that of many Afghans who had knowledge of the rapid changes that were sweeping the world, was wounded by the backwardness of his own country. Unfortunately, like so many reformers in Asia and Africa, he failed to realize that Western progress was the result less of social patterns than of economic development. His attempts at reform were largely social and cultural, or aimed merely at concealing Afghan backwardness with a thin veneer of Western practices.

Some of his program did show wisdom. In 1922 he granted permission to the Oriental Institute of France to begin archaeological work in Afghanistan, where the only previous investigators had been enthusiastic amateurs in the British armies of invasion or an occasional early visitor like Masson, and where, consequently, a rich mine of information about the human past lay virtually untapped. Some useful excavations have been made by the Oriental Institute and by such able representatives as Foucher and Godard, but a great deal remains to be done—a task that is being undertaken by the present Afghan government.

Another of Amanullah's projects was in education. In 1922 the pioneer work of Habibia was supplemented by a second school, Istiqlal, staffed by a few French teachers. To these Ghazi, staffed by British-educated Indians, and Nijat, staffed by Germans were later added. This was a feeble beginning in a country where at least 90 per cent of the population was illiterate; but it was difficult to break down the prejudices of Afghan parents whose fears that education might turn their children into infidels were kept alive by the mullahs. Amanullah's educational program also continued the error made by the British in India, of confining its curricula to academic and nontechnical subjects.

Amanullah was little interested in the army, and the Turkish instructors whom he hired showed more interest in enjoying their handsome salaries than in improving the morale or efficiency of the soldiers. On the other hand, Amanullah had great interest in construction, and devoted himself to a foolish program of building. His major success was at the summer resort of Paghman, about eighteen miles from Kabul, where he built several residences in florid German style, as well as a cinema and a racetrack. Still more ambitious was his attempt to create a new city, Dar-ul-Aman ("abode of peace"), about five miles from Kabul, in the Turkish style of Ankara. Since crowded Kabul, hemmed in by its rocky hills, had no room for expansion, the idea was a good one; but like others of the king's enterprises, it was subject to his vacillating enthusiasm and was never completed.

As Amanullah went from plan to plan he won the approval of the increasing number of young Afghans educated in the Western manner, and with it the hostility of the mullahs and of the more conservative members of the population. A more serious handicap was his erratic personality, with its tendency to place complete trust in certain favorites. This led to enmities among other highly placed individuals, many of them related to the king by blood or marriage. For all his friendly and democratic behavior—he liked to walk through the bazaars unattended, shaking hands with his subjects—Amanullah was extremely stubborn, and inclined to equate opposition to his ideas with personal antagonism. On the other hand he was easily impressed by sycophants.

The coolness toward the king as a result of these failings was particularly marked in the Musahiban or Yahya Khel family, consisting of five able brothers and headed by Nadir Khan, the hero of the Anglo-Afghan War. All of the Musahibans were members of the Mohammedzai clan, and although they were descended not from Dost Mohammed but from his brother Sultan Mohammed, three were married to sisters of the king. Since their return from exile they had risen to high positions in the Afghan government; Nadir Khan, Shah Wali, and Shah Mahmud all three held the rank of general in the Afghan army.

The original rift between Amanullah and the Musahibans stemmed from a personal quarrel between the king and Hashim Khan. This grew more intense during and after the Mangal revolt, when Amanullah ignored the advice of Nadir Khan, a man of intense personal pride. Angered to find that he had less influence with the king than civilian advisers, Nadir Khan resigned his command of the army and accepted a position as Afghan minister to France. This too he soon resigned on a plea of ill health, to settle on the French Riviera, where he was joined by his brother Hashim.

These defections did not trouble Amanullah, since he considered himself the architect of Afghanistan's independence and the man destined to lead it to national glory. He found no lack of courtiers who were willing to flatter his vanity, and for advice he relied upon his queen Souriya, his father-in-law, Mahmud Tarzi, and Mohammed Wali Khan.

During the 1920's Amanullah found plenty of foreign capital to finance his plans, and used it freely to coax a large number of foreigners to work for Afghanistan. These included not only engineers, technicians, and teachers but also eleven Russian pilots who were brought in to man the embryonic Afghan air force.

For the most part the Afghans accepted this influx of infidels with good nature and hospitality, thus setting to rest the traditional tales of Afghan intransigence and fanaticism. Such incidents as did occur were in fact brought on by the visitors rather than by any malice on the part of the Afghans themselves.

In 1924 the Afghan police attempted to arrest an Italian engineer named Piparno, who had broken some minor law, and who was apparently unbalanced, for he fired through the door of his house and killed one of the policemen. After being tried and convicted, he secured a release from the claim upon his life which, according to Afghan law, belonged to the dead man's relatives, but was sentenced to one year in prison for the debt he owed the state. He escaped, probably by means of bribery, and made his way to the border, where for some unknown reason he surrendered himself to the Afghan border guards. This time he was summarily executed.

The incident caused excitement abroad, for in those days extraterritoriality was considered a European prerogative— although, of course, Afghanistan had never entered into any agreement concerning it. The Italian government lodged a protest, moved to close its diplomatic mission, and seized all Afghan assets in Italy. This move brought from Amanullah an apology and a payment of twenty-four thousand dollars to Piparno's survivors, which closed the matter. Piparno's execution had in fact been the unauthorized action of the Kabul kotwal or chief of police, who was promptly relieved of his post.

Another incident involved an erratic German globetrotter who came to Afghanistan on a motorcycle. The strange machine bumping along a country road frightened a horse, and an argument with the animal's owner ensued. The argument became a scuffle, whereupon the German drew a revolver and killed his opponent. This needless homicide drew a four-year prison term for the German, who was then immediately given a royal pardon.[10]

During these years Afghanistan's relations with its powerful neighbors shifted in their usual fashion. From 1924 to 1926, the Mangal revolt and the Soviets' formation of the states of Uzbekistan and Tadjikistan inclined the Afghans to a more friendly attitude toward Great Britain. After the tribal revolt, the possibility that other uprisings might be instigated tended to decrease Afghan activities among the tribes across the border; and the establishment of the two Soviet "republics" seemed an omen of pressures to come among the Uzbegs and Tadjiks of northern Afghanistan. The tension between Afghans and Soviets reached a peak in December 1925, with a brief skirmish over possession of the island of Urtatagai in the Amu Darya River. But since the Soviet Union was about to launch a new foreign policy, its soldiers were promptly withdrawn to the accompaniment of profuse apologies.

Afghan-Soviet relations now improved rapidly. The Soviets, eager to break down a wall of opposition of which Great Britain was the cornerstone, and correctly assessing the weakness of their enemies in the face of rising Asian nationalism, had decided to launch a campaign to increase their own prestige. They did not suppose that countries like India were ready for a Marxian revolution; rather, their aim was to put pressure on the imperial powers.

The reaction in Europe to this move was not quite what the Soviets expected. It brought, particularly in Great Britain, a fear of Russian Communism similar to the Russophobia of the nineteenth century, although this time it had more basis in fact. Faced by such troubles as a general strike at home and unrest in the Empire, the government headed by Stanley Baldwin was only too ready to ascribe them all to the malignant efforts of Communist agents—an attitude that led to a raid on the offices of the Soviet trade delegation in London and finally to the breaking of diplomatic relations between the United Kingdom and the U.S.S.R.

The British leaders also blamed the growing unrest in India upon the Communists, although it would now appear that they played a minor part in the nationalist movement there. The real force behind the steady growth of Indian nationalism was the leadership of Mohandas Gandhi, with his call for Moslem-Hindu unity—the possibility of which, despite repeated official disclaimers, had long been disturbing to the British.

Oddly enough, the drive for unity gained its greatest strength in the reputedly fanatical Moslems of the North West Frontier Province, whose Pushtoon tribesmen had been notorious haters of the infidel for a century. This development was largely brought about by one man, Abdul Ghaffar Khan, sometimes known as the Frontier Gandhi, the son of a Mohammedzai khan (but not one of the Durrani Mohammedzais) from the village of Utmanzai near Peshawar. A great bear of a man, Abdul Ghaffar was a fervent Pushtoon nationalist, whose personality and sincerity made him famous among the tribesmen.

In 1927 Abdul Ghaffar formed an organization which was first known as the Pushtoon or Afghan Jirga, but which in 1929 became the Khudai Khitmatgaran ("servants of God"). Its professed goal was independence through the Gandhian method of nonviolence, and its members wore uniforms dyed red with brick dust, which was plentiful and cheap—an unfortunate choice, since it encouraged the insinuation that they were motivated by Moscow and brought them the nickname of Surkhposhtan ("red shirts"). In reality, though some of the leaders had socialistic leanings, few members had ever heard of Marx.[11]

Although the Khudai Khitmatgaran was dedicated to the attainment of Swaraj (independence), it was of primary importance because it united the Pushtoon tribes. Its influence over the Mohmands and Afridis was particularly strong, although it must be admitted that they interpreted the doctrine of nonviolence in a strange fashion. The Mohmands, for example, led by the Haji of Turunzai, who had married a sister of Abdul Ghaffar, carried out a series of raids one of which actually threatened the city of Peshawar.

Trouble on the border and growing sedition in India were ascribed by the British rulers to Communist agitators. The Viceroy, Lord Irwin, told the Legislative Assembly in 1929, "The disquieting spread of the methods of communism has been for some time causing my Government anxiety. . . . All classes alike are threatened by the spread of these doctrines and no government can afford to ignore this insidious danger." [12] Many of the British leaders were also convinced that Afghanistan and its "radical" king were in the hands of the Soviet, and that the country was to be used "as a lever to overthrow the British Empire." [13] Without question the U.S.S.R. had increased its influence in Kabul and had purchased the support of some Afghan officials. But to regard Afghanistan as a military threat to India was nonsense, and can only be explained as a renewal of the Russophobia of the nineteenth century. The statement in Parliament that the twelve rickety biplanes of the Afghan air force were a menace may be excused as political bombast. But it is difficult to understand how Sir Thomas Holdich, who was regarded as a leading expert on Afghanistan, could solemnly maintain that the Afghans were peculiarly susceptible to "Jewish" communism because of their descent from the Ten Lost Tribes of Israel.

In this atmosphere of tension the exuberant Amanullah Khan startled his subjects by announcing that he planned to make a royal visit to Europe.

XV

The Afghan Revolution

A frog stood on a clod and said, "I can
see Kashmir."—PUSHTO PROVERB

AMANULLAH'S decision to visit Europe, following an invitation from the king of Italy, set a precedent—before him no
other Afghan monarch had left Asia—and was an indication of
his self-confidence. In large part the trip was motivated by
Amanullah's zeal for reform, which had been further strengthened by the examples of Mustafa Kemal of Turkey and Reza
Shah of Iran.

On December 7, 1927, Amanullah and Queen Souriya,
accompanied by a number of courtiers and a mountain of
baggage, departed for India, leaving Afghanistan in the charge
of the Wazir, Mohammed Wali Khan. The trip through India
was in keeping with the strained relations between the government of India and Afghanistan. When Lord Irwin, the Viceroy,
developed a timely bout of malaria and was unable to act as
official host, the slight was not lost upon the sensitive Afghans.
Amanullah was further incensed by the refusal of the British to
allow him to visit the imprisoned Gandhi and in retaliation he
delivered frequent speeches calling for Hindu-Moslem unity
and leaving no doubt in the minds of his Indian audiences as to
where he stood on the question of Swaraj. It was a relief to both
parties when on December 26 the Afghans sailed for Europe.

The first stop, a ten-day visit to Egypt was again hardly a success, since Amanullah outspokenly criticized the Egyptians for their complaisance under British control. He also kept King Fuad waiting for thirty minutes at a military review; such tardiness was not unusual in Afghanistan but was regarded in Egypt as a serious breach of protocol.

Next came Europe and a parade of triumphs. The year 1928 was a prosaic time of peace; editors were short of newsworthy items, and a royal party from a little known country made excellent headline material, the more since Amanullah was both affable and mildly eccentric, and since Queen Souriya had not only charm but a beauty that lent itself to favorable comparison with the royal pulchritude of Europe. In Italy Amanullah received from the king the Collar of the Annunciation (which made the two men cousins) and from the Pope the Order of the Golden Spur. Presidents Doumergue of France and Hindenburg of Germany followed with lavish presents and decorations. In England the Afghan party was met at Victoria Station by King George and Queen Mary, and was treated to a twenty-three-day whirl of activity that included demonstrations of British military power as well as the Oxford-Cambridge boat race.[1]

After leaving England Amanullah went to Moscow—once more evoking worried headlines in the British press—for the first visit of royalty to the capital of revolution. The reception offered the party by President Kalinin may well have fluttered whatever ghosts of the Old Bolsheviks still hovered about the domes of the Kremlin.

From the U.S.S.R. the Afghan party went to Turkey, where Amanullah was impressed by the progress made under the program of Mustafa Kemal, and then to Iran, where the affable personality of the Afghan king made a favorable contrast to the dour arrogance of Reza Shah Pahlevi. From Teheran the royal party motored to Kabul, a remarkable feat in view of the condition of the roads, arriving on July 1 with Amanullah at the wheel of a Rolls Royce.[2]

Foreign observers have criticized this junket, particularly in view of the condition of the Afghan treasury. But in fact the tour not only brought needed favorable publicity for Afghanistan but was more than paid for by the value of the presents

Amanullah had received. Furthermore, its diplomatic results included treaties with Finland, Latvia, Liberia, Poland, Switzerland, Egypt, and Japan. Some of these, for example the one with Liberia, were merely the expression of diplomatic exuberance, but others led to an increase in trade.

The most significant result of the trip was its effect on Amanullah Khan himself. Since boyhood the Afghan king had been avid for reform, but his zeal had been hampered by a lack of firsthand knowledge of the outside world. The sight of Europe profoundly disturbed him as he compared it with his own nation's backwardness. Shortly after his return, at the festival of Istiqlal, the celebration of Afghan independence, Amanullah summoned a Loe Jirga ("great council") of Afghan maliks and chiefs, such as was called only in times of national emergency. To these notables, many of whom were uneasy in the Western dress they had been asked to don for the occasion, the king delivered a long speech outlining his program of political and social reform. A legislative assembly of 150 members was to be elected by the vote of all literate male Afghan adults; hereditary rank was to be abolished; and military service was to be extended to three years. These proposals met with general approval; but when Amanullah announced that he intended to eliminate the veil, establish compulsory female education, and require that all government employees content themselves with one wife, the delegates sat silent.

Nevertheless, for a time these startling changes went unchallenged; indeed, many of the young urban Afghans greeted them with approval. When Queen Souriya, who as an ardent feminist must have been largely responsible for her husband's attention to the status of women, dramatically threw off her veil at a public meeting in Kabul, her example was quickly followed by many of the ladies of the city; and even those of more conservative tendencies discarded the tentlike birqa for a half veil.

Then suddenly this parade of progress was halted by a roadblock which indicated that the old Afghanistan had not quite forsaken its ways. Apparently (the evidence is contradictory and scanty) in November 1928 a caravan of Suleiman Khel Ghilzai on their winter migration to India met a band of Shinwaris whom they mistook for (or perhaps recognized as) bandits. The Suleiman Khal resisted, and several of the Shinwaris were killed before a company of soldiers arrived and arrested the Ghilzai nomads. They were able, however, either to convince the local commandant of their innocence or to satisfy his avarice, and were released.

Soon afterward the Sangu Khel clan of the Shinwaris, to which the dead men had belonged, rose in revolt and captured the military posts of Achin and Kai. These successes brought out other Shinwari clans, and the rebels seized the forts of Torkham and Dakka, capturing large stores of military equipment and meeting little resistance. The Khugianis and Safia, who had been watching with interest, now joined in the rising, and a lashkar containing several thousand tribesmen moved against the city of Jalalabad.

The Afghan government showed little concern at the news, since tribal risings were nothing new, and since the Shinwaris were not on friendly terms with their more powerful Afridi and Mohmand neighbors. The only action taken was to dispatch five hundred soldiers from the Kabul garrison under the command of a Colonel Mahmud Khan Yarwar. The arrival of these troops and negotiations by Shir Ahmed Khan, the governor of Jalalabad, left the Shinwaris still unimpressed, and still encamped outside of the city. The Afghan government now realized belatedly that this was a serious revolt, and sent most of the Kabul garrison to the east along with Amanullah's cousin Ali Ahmed Jan, who had influence with the eastern tribesmen. At the same time the government issued a call for tribal assistance—the same dangerous procedure that had been used in the Mangal revolt.

Unfortunately, the cold Afghan winter had set in, and the tribesmen showed no eagerness to collect the rifles and ammunition they had been offered for service against the Shinwaris in a campaign that promised little booty and considerable bloodshed. Gaus-ud-din Khan, a chief of the Ahmedzai Ghilzai near Gardez, did appear to collect the rifles, whereupon instead of proceeding to Jalalabad he went back home. The only other applicant was an improbable figure who was to prove Amanullah's nemesis.

The mountainous district of Kohistan, directly north of Kabul, was the home of the Kohistani Tadjiks, whose belligerence is a marked exception to the usually placid Tadjik temperament. Here, in the little village of Kala Khan, about twenty miles north of Kabul, lived the notorious bandit Habibullah, popularly known as Bacha-i-Saqao ("child of the water carrier") from the occupation of his father. While serving in the Afghan army the Bacha had been sentenced to jail for striking an officer, but had escaped to Peshawar, where he operated a teahouse as a front for smuggling, disposing of stolen property, and a variety of other, equally illegal activities. Returning to Afghanistan in 1928, he gathered a band of followers who were impressed by his enormous strength, his skill with a rifle, and the cruelty of his disposition, and became the scourge of the caravan routes across the Hindu Kush.[3]

Upon hearing of Amanullah's call for tribal aid and the promise of free pardon that accompanied it, the bandit came to Kabul, where he was given rifles and a general's commission in the Afghan army. After noting the defenseless condition of the Afghan capital, he returned to Kohistan, gathered his robber band and a number of new adherents, and launched a surprise attack on the city. Although his total force numbered only three hundred men, the audacity of the move was such that only swift action by Abdul Aziz, the minister of war, and a determined stand by the cadets of the military school, kept it from succeeding. After twelve days of fighting, the Bacha, slightly wounded by shrapnel, withdrew his men to Kohistan.

During the growing confusion the government of India managed the evacuation of the foreign colony from Kabul, in which a total of 586 persons were flown to safety—a remarkable demonstration of skill considering the altitude, the season, and the nature of the aircraft. Only one life was lost, that of a Polish woman who stepped into a propeller in the haste of departure.[4]

But now the defenders of Kabul, in the overconfidence of victory, made the mistake of pursuing the Bacha into his snow-covered homeland. Here they found thousands of Kohistanis flocking to join the local hero, and after a week of fighting they were surrounded by overwhelming numbers and were forced to surrender. This left Kabul undefended; and on January 14,

1929, the Bacha and his men were back. This time the capital was captured almost without resistance while Amanullah and the remnants of the royal guard barricaded themselves in the royal palace.

At this juncture all Amanullah's customary optimism deserted him. After a family meeting he abdicated in favor of his older brother Inayatullah Khan, and fled the city in the Rolls Royce he had brought from Europe, hotly pursued by the Bacha's horsemen. He had a close call when his car stalled in a snowdrift, but he worked it free just in time to arrive ahead of his pursuers in Kandahar, to which Queen Souriya had been evacuated earlier in a British airplane.

Inayatullah was not the one to save the situation, if indeed it could have been saved at all. After three days of negotiations with the Bacha he followed his brother in flight, and the bandit leader made a triumphant entry into the royal palace. Here on January 27 he assumed the crown as Amir Habibullah Ghazi and began to organize a government—a difficult task since the royal treasury had departed with Amanullah and Souriya. But his bandit background had given the Bacha practice in the use of threats and torture, and by such means he was able to wring a considerable sum from the unhappy citizens of Kabul.[5]

Difficult though it is to understand how such a transfer of authority could have taken place, it should be remembered that the Afghanistan of the time was almost entirely an agricultural and pastoral country with a subsistence economy. Many of the provincial and local officials simply continued to carry out instructions from Kabul, without regard to who issued them. Some of Amanullah's aides, especially those in what remained of the Afghan army, consented to serve the Bacha in return for lavish financial rewards and the promise of future favors. But the civil government was so depleted that only two of the Bacha's cabinet were able to read; the bandit Amir himself was totally illiterate.

Meanwhile Amanullah had been received with little cordiality by the people of Kandahar. But irritation at the thought of a Tadjik on the Afghan throne, together with the influence of Amanullah's mother began to gain him support from the

Durranis, and he encouraged it still further by taking the cloak of Mohammed from its shrine and showing it to the populace. At last, with a lashkar of five thousand Durrani tribesmen, Amanullah moved north on the road toward Kabul.

This attempt had every possibility of success. Only a small garrison at Ghazni barred the road to Kabul; the Hazaras and Wardaks had joined the fight against the Bacha; moreover, Ghulam Nabi Charkhi, the son of Ghulam Hyder Charkhi, Abdur Rahman's commander in chief, had raised the standard of Amanullah in the north, and with an army largely recruited in the Soviet Union had occupied Mazar-i-Sharif. But at this moment, on April 26, for reasons that have never been adequately explained, Amanullah Khan abandoned his advance and ordered a retreat to Kandahar. There were rumors that Amanullah had been informed that some of his associates were plotting his assassination, or that the powerful Ghilzai—through whose territory the lashkar was passing—were preparing to join the Bacha. At any rate, instead of re-entering Kandahar, where his Durrani kinsmen were thoroughly disgusted, Amanullah halted outside the city, collected his family and the remnants of the royal treasury, and left Afghanistan forever.

The king's flight made it much easier for the Bacha to extend his control over the country. In the north, Ghulam Nabi heard the news and withdrew into the Soviet Union. In Kabul the bandit raised a motley army of ten thousand men, mostly from Kohistan, whom he paid with money extorted from Kabul merchants and equipped with the stores in the government arsenal. All possible rivals were eliminated through execution, including Hayatullah Khan and Abdul Majid Khan, half brothers of Amanullah; and Amanullah's cousin Ali Ahmed Jan, who while attempting to organize resistance in Kandahar was captured and murdered with extreme cruelty.

But the authority of the bandit Amir was mostly an illusion. It was only because the region was so decentralized, and the cities were so few and scattered, that an individual even with the Bacha's drive and courage was able to seize control of Kabul and Kandahar, and by the use of extorted funds to recruit an army of assorted malefactors eager for loot and excitement.

There was little to enable the Bacha to consolidate his rule. He had no standing whatsoever among the Pushtoon tribes, which up to this time had taken no part in the fighting but waited aloof for the inevitable agents of the Bacha's downfall to do their work. And indeed that work had already begun.

From their self-imposed exile in France the three Musahiban brothers, Nadir Khan, Hashim Khan, and Shah Wali Khan, heard the news, and immediately left for Asia. After arriving at the city of Peshawar on February 25, 1929, they crossed the frontier and went to the Afghan fort of Matun in Khost province, the scene of Nadir Khan's triumph in the Anglo-Afghan War. Here Colonel Nur Mohammed, the Afghan commander, placed himself and his soldiers at the disposal of Nadir Khan. The colonel had been the Bacha's commanding officer during the bandit's brief military service and had been offered the post of commander in chief in the Bacha's army—to which Nur Mohammed replied that he would give the Bacha his old rank of private if he would rejoin his outfit.

About this nucleus Nadir Khan gathered a lashkar made up of Mangals, with whom he had been popular since his intervention in their behalf during their revolt in 1924. He was also aided by his brother, Shah Mahmud, who had remained in Afghanistan and who as governor of Khost province had made many friends among the tribesmen. With his lashkar Nadir Khan advanced toward Kabul, only to be forced to retreat when fighting broke out among hostile clans in his forces. The tribesmen's usual difficulty in forgetting ancient enmities was exploited by agents of the Bacha. Another advance by Nadir Khan broke down for the same reason.

Fortunately for Afghanistan, Nadir Khan was a man of iron will. Again he gathered a lashkar of Mangals, Jajis, and Jadrans, along with sections of Ahmedzai and Tota Khel Waziris. To these a welcome addition was a contingent of about one thousand Darwesh Khel Waziris from across the Durand Line, who were probably the most skillful warriors of all the Pushtoons.

This time the advance was successful. After defeating the troops of the Bacha in several battles, the tribesmen reached Kabul on October 9, with the Warziris, under their chief, Allah

Nawaz Khan, leading the van. For a short time the Bacha and a few of his adherents held out in the palace, but then, seeing his dream of kingship vanish in the smoke of the burning city, the outlaw galloped off to the hills of Kohistan.

For five days Kabul remained in the hands of the tribesmen, who collected everything the Bacha had overlooked. The Waziris had been promised "golden shoes" for their part in the affair, and in default of the promised footwear they took whatever else was of value. The citizens of Kabul, numbed by catastrophe, did not resist the plundering, and there was little rape or bloodshed.

On October 16 Nadir Khan entered the city to the cheers of tribesmen and townsmen, the former satiated and the latter ruined by anarchy. At a great Jirga on the following day the tribesmen and such notables as remained in Kabul offered the throne to Nadir Khan, who accepted. A few days later the Bacha surrendered himself on the promise of a pardon. The promise was broken, and the bandit was publicly executed—through no fault of the new king, who was unable to restrain the tribesmen or to resist their demands for the death of the bandit.

Thus the Afghan revolution ended—with the bandit Amir dead, Amanullah Khan a refugee in Italy, and the throne once more in the possession of the Durrani Mohammedzais, albeit a different branch of the clan. The revolution left a deep imprint on the country and brought problems that are only now ceasing to be felt. To some extent it had been a triumph of reaction; and the new rulers, although personally favoring social and political reform, had learned a lesson and were determined to maintain a cautious pace in their country's journey toward progress. Moreover, the coronation of Nadir Shah was by no means popular with many Afghans. There were a number of others in Afghanistan who according to the principles of royal succession had far better claims to the throne, including both sons of the prolific Amir Habibullah and direct descendants of Dost Mohammed. Many of the young urban populace believed that Nadir Shah had "put his beard in the hands of the mullahs," and chafed at the reversal of the reforms of Amanullah. Still others believed that the Yahya Khel had been tools of the British in an attempt to oust the Anglophobe Amanullah.

As a result the new rulers moved with care. Gone were the days of Amanullah's unattended strolls through the bazaars; the informers and secret police of Abdur Rahman were back again. But although progress had received a serious check, not all of the gains of the past were lost. Foreign visitors and workers soon returned to the Afghan capital, the schools closed by the Bacha were reopened, and bright students were sent abroad for advanced training. The new rulers, indeed, were as eager as Amanullah had been to develop the country; but since their position was precarious, stability came first.

The revolt had captured the attention of many Western observers, most of whom placed the blame on the turbaned heads of the mullahs. No less an authority than Arnold Toynbee, for example, considered Amanullah's attempt to impose Western garb on Afghans the "crowning folly that cost him the throne." [6] The Afghans themselves scorn this point of view, still maintaining stoutly that the revolution was set on foot by the British secret service for the purpose of overthrowing a king who was too friendly with the Soviet Union for their comfort. They agree that such leading mullahs as the Hazrat Sahib of Shore-Bazaar and Shir Agha of Jalalabad were important contributors to Amanullah's defeat, through the influence they exerted in preventing powerful tribes like the Ghilzai from coming to his assistance; but they scoff at the suggestion that these men were the prime movers of the affair.

It must not be forgotten that the Afghans still cherish their Anglophobia, and are fond of blaming past and present ills upon the British. On the other hand, this bias does not eliminate the possibility that the British did have a hand in the matter; indeed, a considerable amount of circumstantial evidence exists to support the Afghan charge. There is no question that the British leaders, particularly those in India, were concerned about Amanullah's support of the Red Shirts on the frontier and his cooperation with the U.S.S.R., or that they disliked him personally for his role in the Anglo-Afghan War and for his activities in India on his way to Europe.

Officially the government of India maintained strict neutrality throughout the revolution, permitting no aid to either side. On the frontier, British officials were "taxed to the utmost to keep the tribes from headstrong action" [7]—boon to the Bacha, since Amanullah was more popular among the tribes on the British side of the Durand Line, particularly the Afridis and Orakzais, than he was with those in Afghanistan; what the British referred to as "headstrong action" was the readiness of the tribes to come to Amanullah's aid. Indeed, the Afridis and Orakzais had already decided to ignore British orders and enter Afghanistan, when their plans were disrupted by the outbreak of fighting between Shia and Sunni Orakzais; and the Turis helped their coreligionists. Some of the Afridis maintain that this intertribal fighting was stimulated by the British to prevent aid from reaching Amanullah, pointing out that a leading instigator, Mullah Mahmund Akhundzada, was generally considered a British agent on the border.[8]

Whatever the truth of the matter, there is no doubt that the British action in preventing aid from reaching Amanullah was disastrous for the Afghan king. Within India there was considerable agitation as the result of this decision—mass meetings in many cities, "Amanullah days" in Bombay and Lahore, and a number of petitions asking the government for permission to take part. On January 7, 1929, the government finally invoked its police powers to prevent any accusations of complicity from appearing in the Indian papers.

Foreign correspondents were less hampered. On January 14 *Pravda* and *Izvestia* accused the British, as might have been expected; on the same day the *Deutsche Tagezeitung* also carried the charge, and the *Journal des Débats* did so on the day following. Part of this exceptional unanimity was caused by the discovery that Colonel T. E. Lawrence was just then stationed at the fort of Wana in Waziristan. The official insistence that this most famous of British agents was serving as a "typist in the office" was hard to swallow, since although Lawrence was then posing as "Aircraftsman Shaw," British officials were aware of his true identity.

The Afghans had no doubt of his mission. They still assert that he wandered throughout Afghanistan disguised as a holy man mounted on a white mule, to organize opposition to Amanullah Khan. The same report was also current in India, where one unfortunate mullah, Syed Pir Karam Shah, was mobbed in Lahore by a crowd convinced that he was Lawrence in disguise. On January 2, 1929, Amanullah's tottering government gave official credence to this rumor by offering a reward for the capture of the "arch spy of the universe, Colonel T. E. Lawrence." [9]

The truth will probably remain unknown. The publication of *Revolt in the Desert* had made Lawrence famous, and his eccentric behavior added to that fame. Fantasy thrives in Asia, and the story of Lawrence's purported activity has long since passed irretrievably into legend. Years after his death he was solemnly reported to have intrigued in Urumchi; and still later, during the Donetz sabotage trial in the Soviet Union, the accused testified that they had been working for Colonel Lawrence—a statement such as abounded during the Stalinist purges. [10]

But the Afghans' accusations against the British rest on more solid foundations than the presence of Lawrence, who was hostile toward the Conservative government of Great Britain and who, moreover, had little knowledge of Persian or Pushto. The revolt is often described as a widespread tribal rising; but in fact only the Shinwaris rose in strength, although they were later joined by the Khugiani, by some of the Ghilzai, and by outlaws from all areas. The revolt began with the Sangu Khel, the most easterly section of the Shinwari tribe, and one that would have been in direct contact with British frontier officials. These Shinwaris declared their action to have been caused by the social reforms of Amanullah, particularly his attempt to abolish the veil—an odd rationalization, since Shinwari women, along with those of most of the tribes, are usually unveiled.

One development that stirred up resentment among the tribes was the circulation on the frontier of thousands of pictures with the face of Queen Souriya adroitly superimposed upon the body of a naked woman surrounded by men in foreign clothes. There is no evidence to connect these pictures with the British secret service, except that the technical means for producing them were probably beyond the ability of any Afghan at the time, and that forgeries of this sort have been commonly used among the credulous and uneducated tribesmen. Not many years later thousands of pamphlets were scattered from British planes in an attempt to discredit the Red Shirt movement. These messages from above contained the statement that departed saints had appeared to the signatories—a group of fictitious mullahs—to report that the Red Shirts were looked on with disfavor by Allah and should be shunned by true believers.[11]

There can also be no question that the Bacha had spent much time in British territory, some of it in a British jail. He had returned to Afghanistan from Parachinar shortly before the Shinwari outbreak, and he came well equipped; the .303 rifles with which his followers were armed were far better than the weapons of the Afghan troops. During the Bacha's attack on Kabul, in which most of the fighting took place around the grounds of the British Embassy, the bandit, despite his assumed title of "Ghazi" was most circumspect with the infidel. The Embassy, which was hit by hundreds of bullets, found itself in more danger from the royal troops than from the bandits.

The Afghans do not deny that part of the success of the revolt must be ascribed to influential mullahs who feared the threat of reform to their own positions. Rumors swept Afghanistan at the time that Afghan girls sent to Turkey supposedly to be educated had in fact been given to lustful Germans; these, no less than the assertion that the Afghan schools were producing infidels, and that Amanullah secretly worshiped an idol, were no doubt spread by the mullahs and believed by those of a piously salacious turn of mind. It should be noted, however, that the people of Kabul took no part in the rising, that the schools were promptly reopened by Nadir Shah, and that Amanullah's dress reforms, which are given such priority by Toynbee and others, only applied to the royal gardens at Paghman. Indeed, Afghans are far from wedded to their turbans or native dress; influential, educated, and well-to-do Afghans preferred karakul or Western hats and Western tailoring long before Amanullah, and continue to do so to this day.

XVI

Between the World Wars

> A bag of wool will make a rope for a
> donkey or a robe for a mullah.
> —PUSHTO PROVERB

NADIR SHAH, the new ruler of Afghanistan, was a man of much ability, a strong leader with will and determination even though he was physically frail. At the age of forty-five he was slender and wiry, with a beard tinged with grey, and an air of unbending authority due in part to his military background. Unlike the liberal Amanullah Khan, he was a devout though not fanatical Moslem, and his thinking was basically conservative. His major flaws were a tendency toward severe and arbitrary action and a conviction that anyone who opposed him was *ipso facto* an enemy of the nation.

One of the first acts of the new dynasty was to conciliate the mullahs whose power was at zenith after their part in the downfall of Amanullah.* A *firman* or ukase was issued to the effect that the institution of purdah, the seclusion of women, would remain mandatory in Afghanistan. This of course pleased the zealots among the priestly class, who were aware that their au-

---

* The dynasty was once called the Musahiban or Yahya Khel to distinguish it from the family of Amanullah, but is now generally referred to as the Mohammedzai. Amanullah, after years of bitterness, finally accepted the situation in 1950, when peace was made in what was essentially a family quarrel.

thority rested in great part upon the ignorance of Afghan wives and mothers. In addition, prominent mullahs received special favors; Mohammed Siddiq, the Hazrat of Shore-Bazaar, was appointed ambassador to Egypt, and Shir Agha of Jalalabad obtained a sizable government pension.

Although popular with the priests, these actions were anathema to young and progressive Afghans. But Nadir Shah, despite his conservatism, was not himself in favor of the seclusion of women, and his brothers believed that it was a handicap to the country. The king's action was the result of necessity rather than piety, since he saw that the support of the conservative and reactionary elements was indispensable to a stable government.

For a time Nadir Shah governed by fiat, in the usual manner of Asian despotisms. His four brothers, all of whom were able and had a strong family loyalty, were given posts of importance; the government of Afghanistan became a family compact, in which vital decisions were made after conferences of the immediate family, with Nadir Shah providing the energy and Hashim Khan the subtlety and guile. But although the brothers differed among themselves with true Afghan individuality, they generally presented a united front once a decision had been reached.

The next move by Nadir Shah was an attempt to revitalize the Afghan army. Equipped with a gift of ten thousand rifles from the government of India, the soldiers were regrouped under the command of Shah Mahmud, the most popular of the brothers. The pay of a private was raised to about two dollars a month, and *malakoot,* the system of deducting a soldier's provisions from his wages, was abolished. Though these changes brought a slight improvement in morale, they failed to make army life popular with the conscripts.

Nevertheless, the new government was soon troubled by revolts. In May 1930 the fractious Shinwaris, full of enthusiasm after their recent success, began hostilities, which according to their own account were prompted by zeal for the cause of the deposed Amanullah, but that owed more to cupidity than to principle. The revolt was thus ended by judicious bribery.

A second revolt began in July 1930 among the Tadjiks of Kohistan, led by an uncle of the Bacha. This was a more serious matter as not only had the Kohistanis tasted a moment of glory during the reign of their countryman; they had also been well armed as the backbone of the Bacha's strength. When the Afghan army proved unable to cope with this menace, the new government called for aid from the tribes. Many of the Pushtoon tribesmen responded to this summons, and the revolt was brutally suppressed. Nadir Shah then displayed his diplomatic ability in persuading the tribesmen to return home without looting Kabul, which indeed had little left to loot.

The same year, 1930, saw the Soviet Union violating the sovereignty of Afghanistan—the only such instance in the twentieth century. The units of the Red Army that crossed the border and advanced about forty miles into Afghanistan were theoretically in search of Ibrahim Beg, the old Basmachi, who was carrying on what amounted to a one-man war against the U.S.S.R., using Afghanistan as a base. No doubt the Russian move was also a reaction to the overthrow of Amanullah Khan, which the Soviets saw as a blow to their interests and a triumph for the British. After protests from Kabul and London the Russians withdrew, but they had made their point. During the next year units of the Afghan army under the command of Shah Mahmud forced Ibrahim Beg from Afghanistan into the U.S.S.R., where the old wolf was trapped at last.

With the country quiet if not controlled, Nadir Shah began the task of establishing a stable government based upon something more permanent than the support of the tribes. On October 31, 1931, he issued a constitution, copied after one promulgated in 1923 by Amanullah Khan—a document that is, with minor changes, still in effect.

The constitution provided for a cabinet, a senate, and a house of representatives, and the throne was made hereditary in the family of Nadir Shah. The cabinet, made up of eighteen departments, was assigned the practical work of governing; it consisted of the prime minister, the presidents of house and senate, the directors of mines and agriculture, and the ministers of war, state, foreign affairs, interior, justice, education, health, finance, commerce, and post.

The constitution placed the king at the head of the executive, legislative, and judicial departments, made him commander in chief of the armed forces, and proclaimed the inviolability of his person. He was given the power to declare war or proclaim peace, appoint the prime minister, approve the appointment of all officials, and make laws by fiat in times of emergency. These sweeping powers left the Afghan legislature with little but consultative responsibility. In essence, therefore, the Afghan government was a limited oligarchy, with the power elite concentrated in the inner circles of the Mohammedzai family.

Local administration was left unchanged by Nadir Shah. The country was divided into five major provinces or Wilayat, and four minor provinces, or Hakumat-i-Ala. Administering these were Walis or Hakumat Naibs, who had always been appointed by the central government and were always staunch supporters of the royal family. Police chiefs and military commanders shared power with the civilian heads; in some places, notably in the southern and eastern provinces, they held basic authority.

This structure remains virtually unchanged, with one exception: in 1949 the cabinet was reorganized and a new top-level council was set up. This group, composed of six members and headed by the prime minister, was given the authority to make any governmental decision with the approval of the king.

With the constitution established, Nadir Shah turned to the problems of the national economy, which after the turmoil of the civil war had been near collapse. Despite sporadic efforts by Amanullah, Afghanistan in 1930 was still overwhelmingly pastoral and agricultural; there was literally no industry, only fragmentary handcraft, and scanty trade. While the majority of Afghans tilled the soil or kept their flocks, nearly all the commerce of the country, with the exception of that carried on by the Kuchis or camel nomads, was in the hands of Sikh and Hindu merchants.

This primitive economy had been sufficient while Afghanistan remained isolated from the outside world, to supply the relatively small population with what their standard of living required—although that standard, at least when it came to food, was considerably higher than in many Asian countries. Now that the veil of isolation had been lifted, a growing urban population was beginning to demand products that could only be obtained through foreign trade.

Since the reign of Abdur Rahman and even to some extent that of his predecessor, Shir Ali Khan, the Afghan rulers had sought to introduce something of Western technology to the country. These attempts were sporadic and unplanned, and those of Amanullah especially were usually concerned with the more showy and less significant aspects of Western culture. Most of them had collapsed because of the lack of understanding of the Afghan government, combined with the apathy, inertia, and conservatism of the Afghan people.

Nadir Shah, a military man to the core, had a firm faith in organization and discipline; he was also aided by a broader knowledge of Western ways than had been possessed by any previous Afghan ruler. In addition, he had the services of Abdul Majid, an able merchant from Herat who had made a fortune in trade with the Soviet Union and who was to guide Afghan economic policy for the next twenty years.

One of the first steps of the new government was to establish a bank, the Shirjat-i-Ashami-i-Afghan (now the Bank-i-Milli) with a capital of 120 million afghanis—a new monetary unit replacing the old Kabuli rupee. A second move was to grant monopolies to Shirkats or holding companies in areas of production. These companies, apparently an imitation of Italian Fascism, were set up for two reasons. The first reason was that any attempt to develop production demanded the investment of private capital, which in Afghanistan was difficult to secure. Few Afghans, particularly among the Pushtoons, had any experience in trade or craftsmanship, and it had been the practice for generations to invest any available surplus in the safety of land. The possession of monopoly power by the Shirkats, plus the fact that the Afghan government, through holdings of members of the royal family, was often the majority stockholder, meant that investors took very little risk. In turn, the situation served to strengthen the control of the ruling groups over the country, since those who invested in the Shirkats had an obvious interest in a stable government.[1]

One of the most important steps taken by Nadir Shah was

toward improving transportation and communication. At the start of his reign only a few miles of anything resembling a road could be found in the entire country, and transport was almost entirely on the backs of camels and donkeys. Throughout half of the year large sections were completely isolated from Kabul as drifting snow closed the passes and floods swept away the primitive bridges. Although during the reign of Amanullah a start had been made toward improving transport, it had consisted as usual of poorly conceived and atrociously executed projects, such as the abortive construction of a railroad from Kabul to the resort of Paghman. Nadir Shah wisely decided that Afghanistan should hurdle the age of rails and concentrate on motor traffic. One of his first projects was the construction of a motor road from Kabul over the Hindu Kush to Mazar-i-Sharif, which involved great numbers of workers.[2]

The schools closed by the Bacha, who had seen no reason to develop in others a skill he had managed without, were now reopened. For a time foreign teachers were excluded, and all instruction was given in Persian and Pushto; but this linguistic purism was soon abandoned for lack of qualified Afghan instructors and of books. Habibia and Ghazi colleges returned to the use of English and again employed teachers from India; Istiqlal hired French instructors, and Nijat brought in a few Germans.[3]

Despite these constructive moves the position of the new dynasty remained unstable. To many Afghans it was annoyingly clear that the ruling family had a less valid claim to the throne than a number of others; though descended from the Barukzai brothers of the nineteenth century, it traced its ancestry not to Dost Mohammed but to his brother, Sultan Mohammed, by no means a hero in Afghan history. Moreover, Amanullah, despite his erratic tendencies, had been popular, especially with urban young people, who preferred his easy affability to the stern aloofness of Nadir Shah.

A major reason for the unpopularity of Nadir Shah was the rumor that he was a British puppet. This had scant basis in fact, but in the atmosphere of an Asian bazaar facts are often powerless against rumor. The British no doubt found Nadir Shah a more comfortable neighbor than either Amanullah or the fantastic Bacha-i-Saqao, and the instability of his rule meant that he might be more susceptible to outside pressure. But Nadir Shah and his brothers were Anglophobes born and bred; Nadir Shah had been a leader of the "war party," which the British held responsible for the Anglo-Afghan War of 1919, as well as the military hero of that struggle.

There were, however, circumstances that appeared suspicious to the Afghans. The new British Minister to Afghanistan, Richard Maconachie, had previously served as political officer in the Kurram Valley, and he had held a long conference with Nadir Shah before the latter entered Afghanistan for his successful campaign against the Bacha. The British, who had given nothing to the hard-pressed Amanullah, had donated 10,000 rifles and 180,000 pounds sterling to the new regime. What was still more important was the apparent change in the traditional Afghan policy toward the Pushtoon tribes on the British side of the Durand Line.

The years 1930–1933 in the tribal zone were turbulent ones even for a land with its tradition of violence. The Red Shirts, led by Abdul Ghaffer Khan and his brother Dr. Khan Sahib, gained many adherents, especially among the Mohmands and the Afridis. Raids became more frequent and harder to put down, and in the battles into which they sometimes developed the tribesmen proved increasingly efficient. In 1931 a tribal lashkar actually captured the city of Peshawar and had placed the cantonment under siege before reinforcements arrived. Units of the Indian army were displaying an ominous sullenness after half a century of unswerving devotion. And as the traditionally chivalric attitude of the tribesmen toward women declined, there had been assaults upon British women, an all but unheard of occurrence in the past. The punitive actions brought on by all this in turn caused the tribes to appeal to Kabul, but this time they were coldly advised to make their peace with the British.[4] Although to many Afghans this reversal of policy was evidence of Nadir Shah's perfidy, the real reason was his consciousness that the new dynasty was unstable, and that given provocation, the British could arrange its overthrow with relative ease.

In any event, Nadir Shah's noninvolvement with events on the other side of the Durand Line was much resented, particularly among the growing number of young and educated Afghan nationalists. In June 1933 this resentment took tangible form when Mohammed Aziz Khan, the oldest of the Mohammedzai brothers, who was serving as Afghan ambassador to Germany, was shot and killed at the Afghan Embassy in Berlin. The assassin was a young Afghan, Kemal Syed, a graduate of Nijat College who had gone to Germany for advanced study, and who gave as his reason the betrayal of the eastern tribes by the Mohammedzais. Despite his obvious neurotic tendencies, there seems no reason to doubt that what he said was true.

Not long afterward another student, also from Nijat, entered the British Ministry in Kabul for the purpose of killing the British minister. Although his wild attack failed of its purpose, it did result in the death of the ministry's chief clerk and two servants. For the government, the situation was an ominous reminder of the killings of Burnes, Macnaghten, and Cavagnari. The assassin was promptly executed, and thirty-two of his friends were sent to prison, where for fourteen years they were known to the other inmates as the "British prisoners."

The culmination of this surge of violence took place on November 8, 1933, during a celebration that included soccer games between the Kabul schools on the grounds of the royal palace. As Nadir Shah entered the grounds a participant, who again was a student at Nijat, sprang forward and fired at the king with a revolver. The shots struck Nadir Shah in the shoulder and the mouth. He was carried into the royal pavilion, where he died without regaining consciousness.

The murder is often said to have been part of an anti-Mohammedzai plot that had been laid at Nijat. But even though all three of the student assassins were from the German-staffed school, it appears more likely that the king's murderer was motivated by a personal grievance. One year to the day prior to his assassination, Nadir Shah had called General Ghulam Nabi Charkhi to an audience in the palace and accused him of complicity in a brief revolt of the Dari Khel Ghilzai, with whom he had much influence. Ghulam Nabi was one of the sons of Ghulam Hyder Charkhi, the Amir Abdur Rahman's commander in chief, and one of Amanullah Khan's most zealous supporters. He was also a man of touchy temper, and his reply to Nadir Shah's accusations was an abusive charge of infidelity to the previous king. This was too much for the equally quick temper of Nadir Shah, who ordered Ghulam Nabi's immediate execution—a serious error, since in removing the possibility of legal redress, he had placed the matter in the realm of personal vengeance.

Nadir Shah's assassin was a seventeen-year-old youth, Mohammed Khaliq, whose father was a servant of Ghulam Nabi and who, following a common Afghan custom, had himself been adopted by the general. He was not, as is often asserted, a natural son of Ghulam Nabi, and though he may have been influenced by the strong feeling against Nadir Shah at Nijat, his original motivation would seem to have been outrage over the execution of his adopted father.

At the time of the king's death Mohammed Hashim Khan, the oldest of the surviving brothers, was in Afghan Turkestan, and Shah Mahmud, the youngest, was in Kabul. Contrary to precedent, Shah Mahmud made no bid for personal power, but promptly proclaimed Mohammed Zahir Shah, the only son of Nadir Shah, as the new king. Here again the close family loyalty of the brothers worked to the benefit of the ruling family and the country.

As is true of so many Afghan rulers, the memory of Nadir Shah is not revered in Afghanistan, and attempts to install him in a national hagiology seem doomed to failure. The characteristic independence of the Afghan temperament is opposed to any authority, particularly when its exercise is harsh, arbitrary, or autocratic; and Nadir Shah, despite many outstanding attributes, was by nature stern and occasionally merciless. Yet from an objective point of view it is clear that Nadir Shah did much for his country, and that a ruler of his sort was necessary at the time. The anarchy lurking in the Afghan hills, the chaos following the revolution, and the reactionary priesthood, all needed a strong and sometimes ruthless hand to control them. This Nadir Shah provided, and the Afghanistan he left behind was once again on the road toward stability and progress.

The new monarch, Mohammed Zahir Shah had been born in Kabul on October 15, 1914, and was nineteen at the time of his coronation. He had attended both Habibia and Istiqlal colleges and had gone with his father into exile in France, where he studied at several lycées. Returning with his father, he had graduated from the military school in Kabul and had then been appointed minister of war and education at the precocious age of eighteen.

Unlike his father, Zahir Shah had, and has, a gracious and friendly though rather shy and retiring personality. Like many Afghans he is devoted to hunting and outdoor sports, but unlike his generally gregarious countrymen he prefers the company of a small group of intimates to crowds. It was not to be expected, in age-conscious Afghanistan, that he would be able to exercise effective leadership at his accession, but he had at his service three able uncles who were prepared to supply that lack. For the next twenty-two years the king remained in the background while Mohammed Hashim Khan, Shah Wali Khan, and Shah Mahmud exercised executive authority as a sort of fraternal college. Until 1946 the dominant member of this triumvirate was Mohammed Hashim Khan, the oldest surviving brother, who acted as prime minister. Although like the rest of his family and indeed like most upper-class Afghans, he was gracious, courteous, and affable, he was also introverted, quiet, and secretive; and he differed from his brother, Nadir Shah, in eschewing force and violence in favor of astute manipulation and devious planning.

For some time after the death of Nadir Shah the Afghan government halted all projects and anxiously awaited further developments. But as the country remained quiet—another indication that the king's death had not been part of a larger plot—the cautious program of economic development was resumed. Now, however, the new rulers were faced with a problem: on the one hand they were determined not to accept aid or technicians from the Soviet Union, and on the other, anti-British feeling was now so strong that it would have been impossible to protect British nationals. After serious consideration the Afghans approached Germany, just as it was entering the

Nazi era, and within a short time a number of German experts and technicians had arrived in Afghanistan.

From the Afghan point of view, Germans were desirable foreigners. Their country had no history of imperialism in the area, and was on unfriendly terms with both the Soviet Union and Great Britain. Moreover, many of the Germans who came to Afghanistan not only were capable workers, but were anxious to spread the influence of the Third Reich and careful to avoid offending Afghan sensibilities.

From 1935 to the beginning of World War II, the German influence in Afghanistan steadily increased. German engineers built dams and bridges throughout the country, and installed a hydroelectric plant at Chak-i-Wardak, south of Kabul, which added to the capital's meager supply of power. Finally, Lufthansa was allowed to install air service from Kabul to Berlin, and for the first time in history the Afghan capital, at least, became accessible to the outside world without the difficult journey through the Khyber or other passes.

That much of the German work was shoddy and ill-conceived, seems to have been due less to the inefficiency of the German engineers than to the dearth of native technicians. The frequent collapse of impressive-looking bridges, and the failure of imposing dams to hold water, brought no ill will toward the Germans who had engineered them.[5] Always admirers of strength, the Afghan leaders were impressed by German political and military gains. As they began to be courted by Nazi agents preparing for the Fuehrer's war, they were attracted even by Nazi racism, with its stress on "Aryan" superiority; after all, one of the homelands of the Aryans had been Afghanistan. The old legend that the Afghans were the lost tribes of Israel now gave way to an insistence on their Aryan ancestry.

Germany's Axis allies were also active in Afghanistan, but with less success. A Japanese trade mission visited Kabul in 1934 with a mass of shoddy merchandise, apparently on the theory that Afghans would buy anything. This proved such a mistake that a quarter of a century later much of it still lies gathering dust in Afghan bazaars. In their zeal the Japanese even persuaded the first secretary of their embassy to embrace Islam, an obvious gesture that gave rise to scornful resentment rather than approval.[6]

Abroad, Afghanistan's continued attempt to obtain prestige grew increasingly difficult in the face of the impending war. In 1934 Afghanistan joined the League of Nations under the sponsorship of Turkey, and Afghan representatives took part in the disarmament conferences. In 1937 Afghanistan signed the Treaty of Sa'adabad with Turkey and Iran, a harmless pledge of mutual nonaggression that nevertheless marked the first time that either the Turks or the Afghans had shown any friendship for their Persian neighbors.

During this period Afghanistan had its first taste of diplomatic relations with the United States. Although the latter had been one of the first countries approached by the Afghans after they gained their external independence, their overtures had been rejected by the Harding administration. In July 1934, after the election of Franklin Delano Roosevelt and the United States' recognition of the Soviet Union, a note went to the U.S. Department of State suggesting that it might be well "to strengthen the political and economic relations" which Afghanistan had and still has with the high government of the United States." President Roosevelt, somewhat puzzled as to just what these relations could be, responded with a friendly letter; but it was not until 1936 that the United States chargé d'affaires in Iran visited Afghanistan and concluded a treaty of friendship. No diplomatic mission was set up, however, and the United States continued to deal with Afghanistan through British offices. In the same year the Afghan government demonstrated its confidence in American altruism by granting a 75-year concession to the Inland Exploration Company of New York for the development of Afghanistan's presumed petroleum deposits— the first and only time that such a concession has been given.[7] But the threat of war made American investors reluctant, and in 1939, after a few preliminary soundings, the Inland Exploration Company gave up its concession.

Throughout these years the Afghan government's chief concern was with the Pushtoon tribes east of the Durand Line, whose territory was increasingly regarded as an *irredenta* as

nationalism began to replace the traditional ethnic or tribal
loyalties. The border areas continued to be turbulent. The
Afridis, after the Peshawar fighting of 1930–1931 and a few
subsequent punitive expeditions, lapsed into an uneasy quiet;
but their Mohmand neighbors continued their strenuous opposition to the British, encouraged by the fact that most of the
tribesmen lived in Afghanistan. In 1939 over a thousand men
whom the British classed as outlaws were living among the
Afghan Mohmands, including that inveterate Anglophobe the
Haji of Turungzai.

From the British point of view the most serious problem was
in Waziristan, whose people were as unyielding as the rocks that
covered the landscape. Aerial bombing, punitive expeditions,
bribes, fines, military posts and roads were tried with equal lack
of success, as those who had been defeated vowed revenge and
the rest remained belligerent, at least in intent. In 1936, when
an Indian court ruled that a Hindu girl who had been abducted
by her Moslem lover was to be returned to her parents, popular
indignation was set aflame; for the young woman had embraced
Islam, and the incurably romantic Waziris maintained that the
government had no right to interfere in any affair of the heart.
In truth, the Waziris and their relatives the Mahsuds, who carry
laissez-faire to its ultimate, seldom allow a government the right
to interfere in anything.

Using the name Islam Bibi ("child of Islam"—as the young
lady had chosen to be called) as a rallying cry, a group of
mullahs headed by Haji Mirza Ali Khan,the famed Fakir of Ipi,
stirred up rebellion among the Madda Khel and Tori Khel
sections of the Waziris. Three British divisions had to be sent
into action, and by the time an uneasy peace was made in 1937
they had suffered over a thousand casualties. Their own planes,
tanks and armored cars notwithstanding, the British found
tribal fighting increasingly difficult; not only were the tribesmen now armed with efficient long-range rifles, but they retained the advantage of greater mobility. The Fakir of Ipi was
never caught, but remained safe at Shawal near the Afghan
border. From this refuge he continued to be a thorn in the side
of Great Britain, and later of Pakistan, until his death in 1959.

Not all the trouble makers were local products. In 1939 a foreign firebrand appeared on the border. Syed Mohammed Sa'adi, known as the Shami Pir ("Syrian saint"), was a native of Iraq and belonged to a family of repute in Islam. The Shami Pir was related to Souriya, Amanullah's queen, and his avowed intent was to restore Amanullah to the throne. On June 15, 1939, he proclaimed Zahir Shah an usurper and called for the tribes to join in an attack on Kabul.

Even by proxy, it seemed Amanullah was still dangerous. The Waziris, ready for any pretext, began to gather; and sections of the Suleiman Khel Ghilzai crossed the border from their homeland east of the Durand Line to attack the Afghan fortress of Matun. This onslaught was successfully resisted, no other tribes rose, and British agents were able to persuade the Shami Pir to withdraw at a price of twenty thousand pounds and free transportation back to Baghdad.

It is maintained in Afghanistan that the appearance of the Shami Pir was another attempt by the British to put pressure on the Afghan government, prompted by their anxiety over the presence of the Germans in Afghanistan. No evidence is available, but it is probable that the Iraqi was merely acting on his own.

Several months later saw the beginning of World War II, in which the Afghan leaders prudently sought to remain neutral. Their sympathies were primarily with the Axis, especially after the German attack on the Soviet Union. But unlike Amanullah Khan, they were realistic enough to be aware of their dangerous position now that the great powers whose mutual rivalry and suspicion had helped to preserve Afghan independence were acting in concert. The government therefore announced a position of strict neutrality, which it reiterated in a royal proclamation on August 17, 1940.

That neutrality remained constant throughout the war, although it was strained by an Allied demand, made in the fall of 1941, for the expulsion of all Axis nationals. Not only was this ultimatum a blow to national pride, but it demanded the violation of one of Afghanistan's strongest traditions—the law of hospitality. Many of the Afghan leaders advocated resistance, but Hashim Khan saw the situation more clearly; the fate of Reza Shah Pahlevi in Iran was an object lesson while the largest British army in the history of the frontier was poised at the Afghan border. The upshot was that Axis nationals were asked to leave the country, although the Afghan government took the prudent step of calling a Loe Jirga ("great council") of Afghan chiefs to confirm this action.

After this there were only minor incidents involved with the war. A few daring German and Italian agents penetrated the frontier and approached the tribes. One of these was led into a lethal ambush by a counteragent; another was arrested after a clash with a unit of the Afghan army.

XVII

Afghanistan 1945-1953: "Pushtoonistan"

> You can coax an Afghan into Hell;
> you cannot drive him into Heaven.
> —AFGHAN PROVERB

THE end of World War II found the leaders of Afghanistan and the growing numbers of its educated elite anxious for change. Many of these men had long been dissatisfied with their country's slow progress, but they had been held back by their own uncertainty over the situation in the outside world as well as by the caution of Mohammed Hashim Khan, the prime minister. Nor had he been opposed to change; but having taken office during the chaos following the overthrow of Amanullah Khan, he had been primarily concerned with stability and internal peace.

But now the Afghan government had demonstrated its stability, and it seemed that the time had come for the Afghan leaders to take definite steps in the direction of progress. The move was to be hedged with dangers and uncertainty, for the world of 1945 was vastly different from the one with which the Afghans had been familiar. Germany was prostrate and dismembered; the remote United States of America had emerged as the world leader. The Soviet Union had survived the war, scarred but as inscrutable and as powerful as ever. Great Britain, on the other hand, had come to the close of an era of imperialism, and was quietly preparing to leave India forever.

The realization of what had long been a fervent Afghan hope, welcome as it was, brought a host of new problems. Despite the courage its people had shown in opposing aggression, to some degree Afghanistan obviously owed its independence to the presence of the British on its border. Without that counterbalance, it was uncertain whether the expansionism of Communist Russia could any longer be contained by the banks of the Amu Darya.

The Afghans quickly realized that the power of Great Britain as a barrier against Soviet expansion had been replaced by that of the United States of America—a situation that boded well, since at the time the Americans stood higher in the Afghans' esteem than any nation. Its effort in World War II had impressed them greatly; and the few students who had gone to America had returned full of enthusiasm for it. What was still important from the Afghan point of view, of course, was the reputation the United States then enjoyed in Asia for its position on imperialism.

Early in 1946 Mohammed Hashim Khan, whose health was poor, retired to private life after having directed Afghan affairs for thirteen years. He was replaced as prime minister by Shah Mahmud, the youngest of the Musahiban brothers; and for the first time Zahir Shah, who was now thirty-two, began to take an active part in Afghan political affairs. Shah Mahmud, an affable and handsome man, was undoubtedly the most popular of the royal brothers. Aware of the importance of the United States in the destinies of Asia, he sent his son, Zalmai Khan, to America for advanced education. This was a break with precedent; hitherto France had been the country to which most of the royal family had gone.

One reason for Shah Mahmud's popularity was his reputation for tolerance and his dislike of the arbitrary methods of Hashim Khan. Characteristically, his first official act was to issue an amnesty to a large number of political prisoners, including the members of the family of Ghulam Nabi Charkhi and the students who had been jailed after the attack on the British Embassy in 1933. Some of these men were promptly taken into government service; one became the king's private secretary and was later president of the Afghan senate.

The next action of the new government was to announce a plan for economic development that was more ambitious than any proposed by Amanullah Khan. Actually this plan had been in existence prior to the war, and a few preliminary steps had been taken before hostilities began. Now, it was to be resumed on an expanded scale.

It will be recalled that Afghanistan's economic dictator since 1932 had been Abdul Majid Khan, the minister of national economy and a firm believer in governmental action and control. Under him what then existed in the way of production had been grouped into Shirkats—holding companies which were given monopoly powers, and in which the government usually controlled a majority of the shares. This arrangement, he believed, strengthened the government, allowed a large degree of planning, and coaxed reluctant Afghan capital into needed investment.

One of these Shirkats controlled the production of Afghanistan's major export product, karakul, and had been particularly successful after karakul became fashionable in the United States. As a result, since its own imports had been small, Afghanistan built up a credit of around twenty million dollars. This credit was now allocated to a program of economic development, to be centered upon the construction of an irrigation and hydroelectric power complex in southern Afghanistan that would make use of the waters of the Helmand and Arghandeb rivers. Most probably this idea had originated with students who after returning from the United States with engineering degrees had been promptly assigned to high places in the Afghan government, and who had been impressed with the success of the Tennessee Valley Authority.[1]

On the surface the project seemed sensible. Each spring the snow-fed waters of the two rivers, unchecked by dams or other barriers, poured their spate into the southern deserts, leaving a far too meager summer flow. It was believed that the Helmand project would make arable a large amount of hitherto worthless land, whose sale, rental, and taxation would more than pay back the investment. It was also argued that these lands could be used to settle some of Afghanistan's nomads, who were meeting with increasing hostility from the sedentary agriculturists.

Before World War II, when the project was first formulated, as a small beginning a number of Japanese engineers had been employed by the Afghan government to superintend a multitude of Afghan laborers working with picks and shovels. Now the Afghans approached Morrison-Knudsen, Inc., a construction company with headquarters in Boise, Idaho, which agreed to carry out the program. Soon a number of American engineers and technicians began to appear; base camps were established in Kandahar and Girishk, and a subsidiary company, Morrison-Knudsen Afghanistan, Inc., was set up at San Francisco.

American aid was also sought in the field of education. Through the U.S. Department of State a number of teachers were recruited for service in Afghanistan, usually on three-year contracts. Most of these were assigned to Habibia, the oldest and largest of Afghan shools, although a few went to conservative Kandahar. Dr. Paul Bushnell, professor of education at Wooster College, Ohio, was chosen to direct Habibia College, which soon had fourteen American instructors, including four women. This last experiment, begun with some misgivings on the part of the Afghan government, proved a complete success.

It was in these halcyon days of Afghan-American cordiality that the diplomatic missions of the two countries were raised to the status of embassies, and a career officer, Eli Palmer, was appointed the first U.S. ambassador to Afghanistan. The Soviet Union, on the other hand, watched the influx of Americans with concern and filed frequent protests, all of which were ignored. This was to be expected; less so was the pique shown by British and French nationals over their replacement as diplomatic and cultural leaders.

This drive for social and economic improvement was checked by a new development—the events connected with the British withdrawal from India.

Many foreigners have expressed surprise at the dismay with which the Afghans greeted the appearance of Pakistan—a dismay that led Afghanistan to cast the sole vote against the admission of Pakistan to the United Nations. But such surprise was merely a new reflection of the old ignorance of outsiders concerning Afghanistan. Hindu India itself was hardly more alarmed or distressed by the successful campaign of Mohammed Ali Jinnah for a new Moslem nation than were the Afghans. To clarify their position, it may be well to review some facts of their history.

Afghanistan's beginning as a nation was simply the result of an attempt to unite the hitherto divided Pushtoon peoples. Although in the area empires had come and gone, their leaders often and their soldiers usually Pushtoons, no serious or successful attempt was made to unite the tribes until the time of Ahmed Shah. It is true that Ahmed Shah relied largely on his own tribe—the Durranis—and placed Durrani chiefs in positions of importance; but he also tried strenuously to gain the adherence of the other Pushtoon tribes, offering them complete equality with the Durranis. Thus Afghanistan began not as a typical nation-state with definite boundaries, but as the unification of a loose ethnic group with common customs, traditions, language, and ancestry. Other ethnic groups living either among the Pushtoons or in territory under their control were generally treated with some tolerance; some, notably the Kizzilbash, received opportunities nearly equal to those enjoyed by the Durranis. But throughout Afghan history there has been no doubt but that the nation had been founded by the Pushtoons. In fact a more correct name for it would have been Pushtoonistan, "land of the Pushtoons." Its actual name is due simply to the Durranis' contact with the Persians, and to the prestige of the Persian language from its association with the glories of the Saffawis and the Great Moghuls.

The early rulers of Afghanistan were unable to establish a nation in the modern sense of the word because the loyalties of their people were to the person, the clan, or the tribe rather than to a nation state. To some extent developments in nineteenth-century Afghanistan paralleled earlier developments in Europe; there was much the same struggle to erect a dynastic system in an essentially feudal society, in which the tribes, and to only a degree their individual khans and maliks, assumed the role taken by the European nobility.

Despite its weak nationalism, Afghanistan has always had one notable characteristic distinguishing it from similar "ethnic states." This is the ethnic pride of the Pushtoons, a trait so prominent that it has impressed whomever has encountered them since their first appearance in history. With "Pushtoonism" as a base the possibility of nationalism was obviously there, and it was this possibility that nineteenth-century Afghan rulers hoped to realize. That they failed was the result partly of internal weaknesses, but primarily of circumstances over which they had no control.

The "time of troubles" brought about by the conflict between the Saddozais and Mohammedzais weakened Afghanistan to an extent that permitted the Sikhs to extend their power over the Pushtoons who had spilled out from the hills as far east as the Indus River. The Sikhs' domination was tenuous as well as unnatural, however, and it was only through savage repression that they were able to maintain it.[2] Quite probably the success of Dost Mohammed in stabilizing Afghanistan would have resulted in the end of the Sikhs' dominance and their withdrawal across the Indus, had it not been for the British invasion of Afghanistan in 1839, which brought chaos and a resurgence of tribal feudalism. Once again, before Dost Mohammed was able to restore stability to the nation, the British simply took the place of the Sikhs as the masters of the Pushtoons who lived between the hills and the Indus.

From then on the cycle recurred with almost monotonous regularity. Just as the Amir Shir Ali Khan had overcome internal opposition and established the control of the central government, the second British invasion of Afghanistan took place. This time the war and occupation that again reduced Afghanistan to chaos did bring to the throne a man of ability and determination, the Amir Abdur Rahman. But his accomplishments were counterbalanced by the Forward Policy originated by the British in response to the real or imagined threat of Russian designs on India, which in 1878 forced the Amir Yakub Khan to sign the treaty of Gandamak, renouncing all claims to the Khyber and Michni passes and upon the Pushtoons living on their flanks. Still later, in 1893, the same British policy forced the Amir Abdur Rahman to accept the Durand Agreement.

So far as the Afghans were concerned, this agreement did not set up a final frontier, nor did it mean a renunciation of interest in the Pushtoons living east of the Durand Line. It must be admitted that many actions by the British with regard to this territory—for example, the Anglo-Afghan Treaty of 1921, a clause of which guaranteed reciprocal information on both sides of the Durand Line—suggest that at least some of the British themselves saw the agreement as establishing spheres of influence rather than a fixed border. At any rate, there is considerable truth in the contention of the Afghans that both the Treaty of Gandamak and the Durand Agreement were obtained through force or the threat of force and ought consequently to have been declared invalid.

Thus pressed by the British, the Afghans were able to do little more—apart from encouraging a good many tribal revolts—than to maintain friendly contact with the Pushtoons east of the Durand Line. But every Afghan ruler from the time of Dost Mohammed held as the cornerstone of his foreign policy the hope and expectation that the territory occupied by these eastern Pushtoons would some day be joined with that of their western brothers.

Before Pakistan, many British officials understood and sympathized with the Afghans' position. Sir William Barton, a frontier officer of long experience, wrote:

For more than a century [the Pushtoon lands east of the Durand Line] had formed part of the Afghan kingdom to which they were united by sentiment and loyalty as well as by race. Where the national spirit is as strong as with the Pathan the expectation that the British official hierarchy would wean them from a ruler who embodied Afghan or Pathan nationalism was based upon the flimsiest grounds.[3]

There were practical reasons, of course, for the Afghan government's interest in these detached Pushtoons. Their five or six million people comprise some of the most powerful Pushtoon tribes. Although much of the territory is marginal, there are many areas of high fertility. Then, too, the Durand Line itself was an ethnological monstrosity, drawn with bland and lofty disregard for the bifurcation of tribes, and even of particular villages, that would—and did—result from its creation. Basically, however, the Afghans' concern with these Pushtoons was a matter of nationalism, identical with the preoccupation of the Serbs with Bosnia before World War I, of Italy with the Italians under Austrian rule in the nineteenth century, and so on. Usually in the past such *irredenta* have eventually been united with their own people, and the feeling of confidence among the Afghans that this would eventually be true of the eastern Pushtoons was bolstered by the special treatment accorded them by the British and by the absence of any real effort to incorporate them into the framework of British India.

Until 1932 the Pushtoons under British jurisdiction were divided into the Settled Districts and the Tribal Agencies. Roughly, the Settled Districts comprised the land from the base of the hills to the Indus, including almost all the territory that had been under nominal control of the Sikhs. This area, originally under the authority of the Punjab government, was detached in 1901, under Lord Curzon, and became a separate North West Frontier Province, governed by a chief commissioner who was directly responsible to the central government at Delhi. In 1932 the status of the region became that of a governor's province; in 1937 the province was allowed to form an elected ministry under the terms of the Government of India Act of 1935.

The Tribal Agencies were another matter. They comprised the land between the beginning of the hills and the Durand Line, including the territory of almost all the powerful tribes that had never accepted outside domination. Under the five "agencies" of Malakand, Khyber, Kurran, North Waziristan, and South Waziristan (to which the government of Pakistan has since added a sixth agency, that of Mohmand), these tribesmen were dealt with through political officers, who with one hand allowed them almost complete autonomy while with the other they kept them in check by means of subsidies, aerial bombing, and punitive expeditions.

In short, the British did not attempt to incorporate the "free" or "independent" tribes (the words usually used by British officials to describe them) into India, but dealt with them as quasi-independent entities whose status depended on treaties or agreements between the government of India and the Jirgas of the tribes themselves. This fact encouraged the Afghans to believe that in the event of a withdrawal from India the British would certainly allow these people to return to their old allegiance. These hopes received some confirmation in private conversations with British officials of a time when their main preoccupation was with the Indian Congress Party and its relentless march toward independence. But the hopes were chilled by the meteoric rise of the Moslem League with its call for the division of the Indian subcontinent.

As early as 1937, the Afghans had been so alarmed by the success of the League's propaganda in the Frontier Province that they abandoned their chilly attitude toward the Khudai Khitmatgars—who, although nominal supporters of the Congress Party, were actually working for an independent Pushtoon state.[4]

Events after World War II moved with such rapidity that they caught the Afghans by surprise. On February 20, 1947, Prime Minister Clement Attlee announced that self-government would be given to India by June 1948, adding a recommendation by Lord Louis Mountbatten that the principle of partition be followed. On June 3, 1947, the proposal was adopted by Parliament, with the provision that a plebiscite in British India (but not the princely states) should give the population the choice of joining Hindu India or Moslem Pakistan. To this the Afghan government promptly protested, asking that two additional choices be offered in the North West Frontier Province—union with Afghanistan or the establishment of a separate Pushtoon nation. Their request brought a curt refusal; a second request was met with silence.

This summary dismissal is difficult to explain. Whether the Pushtoons of the North West Frontier Province would necessarily have voted for either of the Afghan alternatives, it is impossible to say. But the fact remains that these Pushtoons had been separated by force from the Pushtoons of Afghanistan and were now limited, willy-nilly, to a choice between two successor states, one of which had no previous existence and thus no possible claim to the territory.

Part of the reason for the decision of the British was no doubt the unhappiness of the "old India hands" over an expulsion which they blamed primarily on the Hindus and their leaders Nehru and Gandhi. Ever since the Sepoy Rebellion, the Moslems of India had been given special favors, and had reciprocated with a more constant loyalty than was shown by the Hindus. It is true that there had been Moslem agitation, notably after the defeat of Turkey in World War I, but the successful drive for Swaraj was primarily due to the Hindus. No doubt the British reasoned that their long-range interests would be better served if a strong Pakistan were set up to counterbalance a possibly hostile India.

This reasoning is to some extent confirmed by the number of British officials who rushed to their typewriters to defend the inclusion of the Pushtoons in Pakistan. For anyone of experience and intelligence, their arguments smack of rationalization more than of reason. Those arguments include the thesis that Pushtoons are somehow different from Pukhtoons and the statements that Persian rather than Pushto is the Afghan court language and that the Durranis do not speak Pushto. For more than a century, British officials—beginning with the brilliant Mountstuart Elphinstone—had maintained that Pushtoons, Pukhtoons, and Afghans were identical; and the point has never been questioned by any Indian or by the people themselves. The Durranis do of course speak Pushto (and often Persian as well). Persian has indeed been the court language of Afghanistan since the nation's beginning, as a result of the prestige of the language, its extensive literature, and its large vocabulary. Ahmed Shah, the founder of Afghanistan and one of its leading poets, wrote in Pushto; and many Afghan rulers, including Abdur Rahman and Shah Shuja, had been born to Pushtoon mothers from east of the Durand Line. But the very name

Pakistan is a refutation of the British argument, since the first *a* was designated to represent Afghania or the "Afghan province" —in other words, the North West Frontier Province.

At any rate, the plebiscite in the North West Frontier Province showed 289,244 votes for union with Pakistan and 2,074 for union with India. The Afghans, however, were unimpressed by the seeming one-sidedness of the result. They pointed out that only 55.5 per cent of the eligible voters cast ballots in the plebiscite, whereas 68 per cent had voted in the provincial elections of the previous year—an indication that a considerable number had boycotted the polls. The Afghans maintained, furthermore, that any other result would have been impossible in a land that was 98 per cent Moslem, and in view of the communal hatred that was sweeping India—especially since the Koran was used to designate the ballot boxes of Pakistan and the Sikh Granth those of India.

The Afghans noted further that the Pushtoons in the tribal agencies were not allowed to vote. Instead, a British official, Sir George Cunningham, went on a tour in which he "interviewed the Jirgas of all the big tribes from end to end of the frontier. Without exception they stated and confirmed in written statements that they were part of Pakistan and wished to preserve the same relations with Pakistan as they had with the British." [5] This statement is of course true as far as it goes, but it contains a number of fallacies obvious to the Afghans. For one thing it would have been unthinkable for the tribes, more conservative in religion and less well informed generally than their neighbors in the North West Frontier Province, to choose "kafir" India over Moslem Pakistan. But there is an even greater irony in the clause "they . . . wished to preserve the same relations with Pakistan as they had with the British"—which apparently meant one thing to Sir George Cunningham and quite another to the Afghans—and most probably still another to the tribesmen themselves. After all they were autonomous in their relations with Great Britain and received a lucrative yearly subsidy of 7,500,000 pounds from the British.

The Afghans realized that this situation was acceptable, if annoying, to the British, for whom the frontier lands were merely the fringe of empire and the subsidy a small item in an imperial budget. But to Pakistan, economically distressed from the outset, plagued by sectionalism, and locked in a continuing quarrel with India, it would have been intolerable. Obviously Pakistan would attempt to do what the British had been frustrated from doing, namely to incorporate the tribesmen within the state. And Pakistan in its adherence to Islam had a weapon stronger than all the armies of Great Britain.

The Afghans have also contended that the meetings with the tribal Jirgas were no less meaningless than the plebiscite itself in the light of conditions at the time. Since August 16, 1946, the day of "Direct Action," India had been swept by mass murder, looting, and rape from Calcutta to the Punjab. For a time, despite the pugnacity of the Pushtoons and their devotion to Islam, the North West Frontier Province remained quiet; but as refugees began to arrive with tales of terror, communal passions arose, and around the campfires and in the bazaars, stimulated by the exhortations of fanatical mullahs, the tribesmen soon turned to violence. On September 7, 1947, there were mass attacks on Sikhs and Hindus who had gathered for asylum at Peshawar and Nowshera. Within a few days all the Sikhs and Hindus in the province were dead or in flight.

The Afghan government took the courageous step (as did the leaders of the Khudai Khitmatgaran) of openly condemning the atrocities, in an opposition to the sanguinary mullahs unknown since the days of Amanullah Khan. The Sikhs and Hindus who were able to reach the Afghan border found refuge and protection and were later sent to India by way of Iran—a partial payment for debts incurred by Afghan raiders of the past. None were injured on Afghan soil. Such forbearance could not be attributed to a deficiency in Islamic zeal or to distance from the bloodbath in India, for there were many Afghans who perished in the massacres. Most of these were of the Suleiman Khel Ghilzai, whose distinctive appearance, arrogant behavior, and reputation as moneylenders made them obvious targets.

Following the flareup of communal violence, tension remained high in the North West Frontier Province and in the Tribal Agencies. On October 25, 1947, it found release in the tribal invasion of Kashmir. Once again the Afghan government did its utmost to prevent the tribesmen from joining the fighting, in direct opposition to the mullahs, who were calling for holy war. The attempt at restraint was partially successful, but since the invasion took place during the fall migration of the Ghilzai it was impossible to prevent some of these nomads from participating.[6]

There is no question that the communal hatreds and the Kashmir invasion both contributed to the establishment of Pakistan and at the same time prevented the consideration of Afghanistan's claims regarding the eastern Pushtoons. The meetings of the Jirgas with Sir George Cunningham took place in November 1947, immediately following the outbreak of communal violence and during the Kashmir fighting. It would have been almost impossible during this period for any tribesman to suggest any action that might be construed as anti-Pakistan and pro-infidel. Quite probably the support given by the Moslem League and Pakistani officials to the tribal invaders of Kashmir was partly motivated by a conviction that Kashmir, with its Moslem majority, should by right be part of Pakistan. But it is also likely (as both Afghans and Indians insist) that in part this support was intended at once to arouse Moslem enthusiasm, block Pushtoon separatism, bring discredit to the Khudai Khitmatgaran, and hinder action by Afghanistan. The Khudai Khitmatgaran, incidentally, had now ceased to call for a united India and were advocating instead a separate nation, "Pushtoonistan," to be formed out of the North West Frontier Province and the Tribal Agencies.

Toward the end of November 1947 the Afghan government sent a young official, Najibullah Khan, to Karachi for a series of conversations with Mohammed Ali Jinnah and Pakistan's foreign minister, Sir Zafrullah Khan. Najibullah stressed the Afghans' concern over the fate of the Pushtoons east of the Durand Line, and requested a declaration of Pakistan's intentions in this area. Neither of the Pakistani leaders put anything on paper, but they apparently convinced the Afghan envoy that Pushtoon autonomy would be respected; at least, this was the message the envoy brought to his government.

On June 16, 1948, it became apparent that the Afghan envoy either had been misled or had drawn unduly optimistic conclusions. On that date the Pakistan government invoked its police powers and arrested Abdul Ghaffar Khan, Dr. Khan Sahib, and other leaders of the Khudai Khitmatgaran, who were given rapid trials and sentenced to prison or house arrest for "conspiring with subversive forces active on the frontier." At about the same time the Pakistani military authorities, who had previously reduced the number of battalions stationed in the Tribal Agencies from the forty-eight maintained by the British to a meager five, began to reinforce these advance garrisons and to use their air force against remote dissidents. One of the primary targets of these raids was the headquarters of the Fakir of Ipi close to the Afghan border; for that formidable opponent had now transferred his lifelong hatred of Great Britain to Pakistan.

From this time on the Afghan government relinquished all hope of a compromise by Pakistan and campaigned openly for the creation of an independent nation, "Pushtoonistan," to be made up of the Pushtoons of the North West Frontier Province, the Tribal Agencies, and Baluchistan. In this campaign they made use of their many contacts among the tribes and all the resources of the Kabul radio and the Afghan press department. Pakistan, all the while stoutly maintaining that the matter was of no consequence, retaliated by increasing tribal subsidies, stepping up police activities in the frontier province, and releasing a barrage of attacks on Afghanistan from its own press and radio.

On August 12, 1949, a number of Afridi tribesmen met at Tirah Bagh, the center of their homeland, and after deliberation announced the establishment of a new nation, Pukhtunistan or Pushtoonistan, for which they adopted a flag with a red mountain fronting a rising sun. Their proclamation read in part:

We of the national assembly of Pukhtunistan having formed the first nucleus of a free and independent Moslem government amidst the lofty mountains of Tirah express the hope that with the help of Almighty God and the support of brave and freedom-loving Pukhtuns this young plant may in a short time grow into a sturdy tree which will not only benefit Pukhtunistan (from Chitral to Baluchistan and from Khyber and Bolan to the banks of the Indus) but will also fulfil its obligations to the cause of progress and world peace.[7]

In Afghanistan this action was greeted with great enthusiasm, and the government announced that it was extending immediate recognition and support. At about the same time another Jirga met at Razmak and elected the Fakir of Ipi president of southern Pushtoonistan. Soon thereafter the Afghan Loe Jirga met in Kabul and announced that all treaties between Afghanistan and Great Britain, and specifically the Durand Agreement, were null and void.

Pakistan, plagued by internal difficulties, officially dismissed these developments as figments of the Afghan imagination or the work of a few dissidents in Afghan pay. But in reality the Pakistani leaders were gravely concerned, and in December 1949 they attempted to exert pressure on Afghanistan by halting shipments of petroleum products, on the pretext that the Afghan tankers did not meet safety requirements. At the same time Afghan export and import traffic through Karachi, then Afghanistan's major shipping link with the outside world, slowed to a virtual halt. To the tribes Pakistan offered a mixture of threats and favors. Subsidies were continued; those to pro-Pakistani maliks and mullahs were increased, and a number of long overdue economic ventures were begun on the frontier. These included hydroelectric projects at Warsai, Dargai, and Malakand, sugar mills near Mardan, a wool factory at Quetta, and a cement plant at Peshawar. No attempt was made to reach the tribesmen at Tirah Bagh or Razmak, but units of the Pakistani army returned to the border and the air force was used to bomb the homes of leaders known to be in favor of Pushtoonistan.

The world reaction to this new crisis was varied. India from the beginning supported the Afghans' position and on January 1, 1950, signed a treaty of "eternal friendship" with Afghanistan. A number of "Pushtoonistan days" were held in Indian cities despite vigorous Pakistani protests, and Indian orators and editors upheld the Afghan claims.

The United States, caught in an unfamiliar role in unfamiliar territory, took the part of an anxious bystander, hoping for peace but uncertain how to bring it about. Both Afghanistan and Pakistan were friendly toward the United States and hostile toward the Soviet Union, and since it was obvious that the conflict was not in its own interest, the United States proposed on three occasions to help mediate the dispute, once offering to act as mediator, and subsequently suggesting the offices of Egypt and Turkey. Each time the proposal was accepted by Afghanistan and rejected by Pakistan, which contended that the matter was an internal one and not subject to mediation.

On the other hand, the Afghans were dismayed that the United States repeatedly refused to provide Afghanistan with arms—a decision motivated by the belief that such assistance was more likely to be used against Pakistan than against the U.S.S.R. The Afghans pointed out that such fears had not prevented Great Britain from providing arms to Pakistan and that the Spitfires of the Pakistani air force were in marked contrast to the twelve rickety pre-World War II biplanes with which Afghanistan was equipped. This discrepancy was particularly distressing to the Afghans when, in June 1949, Pakistani planes bombed the village of Mogholgai, almost two miles west of the Durand Line, and inflicted a number of casualties. The incident was admitted by Pakistan but was blamed on a pilot's error. The Afghans refused an offer of compensation, pointing out with some truth that the explanation was an interesting commentary on Pakistan's relations with its citizens.

XVIII

Afghanistan in the Cold War

If a mouse were as big as a bullock it
would still be the slave of the cat.
—PUSHTO PROVERB

PERHAPS no year in its history was more full of consequence
for Afghanistan than 1953. During that year, three unrelated
events took place that were to exert a profound influence on the
country and to lead Afghanistan along new paths of diplomacy
and internal development.

The first of these occurrences was the victory in the American
presidential election of General Eisenhower, and his placing of
the direction of American foreign policy in the hands of John
Foster Dulles. The Dulles program cannot yet entirely be
assessed, but the Afghans have never been in doubt about one of
its phases—the decision to block Soviet expansion into the
Middle East by a system of alliances supported by massive military assistance. To the Afghans this so-called "northern tier"
concept was and remains the pinnacle of folly. No amount of
American military aid to countries as weak as Iran, Pakistan, or
Iraq could, in their opinion, do more than annoy an advancing
Soviet army. And the Afghans were absolutely convinced that
the Soviet leaders had no such intentions.[1] On the other hand,
they believed American military aid to selected nations would
seriously disturb the balance of power in the area and force

neutralist countries to divert attention and funds from vital development projects in order to enter a foolish arms race.

Two months after the change of administration in Washington, Moscow announced the death of Joseph Stalin. From the promptness with which the policy of the U.S.S.R. changed in relation to its Asian neighbors, it seems obvious that Soviet planners had long chafed under the dour dictator. Apparently Stalin had been indifferent to the new or underdeveloped nations to the south of the U.S.S.R., and especially so after his government had suffered reverses in Iran and Turkey in 1945 and 1946. Consolidating Soviet gains in eastern Europe, rebuilding the Soviet industrial system, and preparing for the war with the capitalist world that he, with Marxian orthodoxy, believed inevitable were Stalin's preoccupations. He had so little concern with Asian attitudes that the U.S.S.R. refused to take part in the United Nations program of technical assistance or to become a member of UNESCO. This was not a policy to make for popularity in Asia. Even more irritating to Eastern nations was the directive from the COMINFORM, which at the time was under firm Soviet control, instructing Asian Communists to oppose and impede "bourgeois nationalism," in keeping with the traditional Leninist-Stalinist view that the success of their revolution could only be achieved by "armed struggle" waged by local Communist parties against the national bourgeois government. This could not but irritate the governments concerned, but what was even more damaging to Soviet interests was that it also tended to alienate the people of Asia. "Bourgeois nationalist" groups such as the Congress Party of India and the Moslem League of Pakistan had successfully led the fight for national independence and had gained wide popular support in the process. Afghanistan did not have a Communist party, but the Afghan leaders were close observers of their neighbors. There had been, besides, a number of unsavory incidents in Afghanistan which deepened Afghan distrust of the U.S.S.R. Most of these were in the murky field of espionage and infiltration. A Russian engineer seemingly defected to seek refuge in Afghanistan, where he became a Moslem, married an Afghan girl, and was employed by the Afghan government, only to return to a position in the Soviet Union as head of intelligence at the spy center of Tashkent. Although Afghanistan had been the scene of just such cloak-and-dagger operations for a century, incidents of this kind tended to increase a suspicion of the Russians that was already acute.

In September 1953 Radio Kabul startled its listeners by informing them that the prime minister, Shah Mahmud, had resigned his office "for reasons of health," and had been replaced by his forty-three-year-old nephew, Mohammed Daoud. At the time Shah Mahmud's health was reasonably good (although he died of a heart attack a few years later); behind the announcement was a basic change in Afghan leadership. Shah Mahmud, the last active member of the band of brothers who had rescued Afghanistan from the bandit Amir, restored its stability, and ruled it for a generation, was by nature liberal and progressive, but these qualities had been curbed by his caution. The group he headed was not made up of the medieval reactionaries often found in the Middle East. On the contrary, Shah Mahmud and his supporters were heartily in favor of progress, and as strongly nationalistic as Afghans generally are. But their policies were conditioned by their experiences, and in particular by the remembered chaos of 1929 and the many years of imperialistic probing and pressure to which Afghanistan had been subjected. They would have liked to move forward, but not at a pace that might jeopardize their positions of privilege.

Mohammed Daoud, supported both by his brother Mohammed Naim, the Afghan foreign minister, and by his cousin the king, led a group of younger men to whom this cautious approach had grown intolerable. These men not only chafed at the snail-like pace of Afghan economic development but were determined to devote their efforts to the Pushtoons east of the Durand Line, whatever the dangers and difficulties inherent in such a policy.

The shift in leadership from older conservatives to aggressive youth is a familiar pattern in contemporary Asia and Africa. In Afghanistan the transfer was peaceful; if Shah Mahmud and his supporters felt any rancor, they hid it and continued to work for the government. Nevertheless, what had occurred was a revolution, albeit a most unusual one. Even though the men concerned were few in number, closely related, and not personally unfriendly, their attitudes were poles apart.

The new prime minister, Mohammed Daoud Khan, was the oldest son of Mohammed Aziz Khan—the Mohammedzai brother who had been assassinated in Berlin in 1932—and thus a cousin of the king.[2] Educated at Habibia College and the Afghan Military School, Daoud had shown drive and determination in putting down a revolt by the Safi tribe in 1947, and prior to his new appointment had acted as minister of defense. This background, and his own dynamic and confident personality, equipped him to command, and he had as a further advantage the charm of manner usual among his family. As prime minister he had the support and admiration of the king and of his younger brother, Mohammed Naim, the country's foreign minister. These three, together with another relative, Ali Mohammed Khan, an elder statesman whose political career extended all the way back to the days of Amanullah Khan, now held control of Afghan affairs.

The foreign and domestic policies that were launched almost immediately by the new government were radically different from any of the past. For over a century Afghanistan's policies had been almost entirely dictated by the country's position between two aggressive and antagonistic powers, and the necessity of preserving its independence. Although concessions and favors had been sought from both Russia and Great Britain, Afghanistan had made every effort to prevent either country from gaining a foothold or from establishing contacts within its borders. Thus, for all the proximity of the Russians and of the British in India and the technical ability of Soviet and British nationals, no more than a few Britons and no Russians had ever been employed by the Afghan government. Both Great Britain and the U.S.S.R. maintained sizable embassies in Kabul, but these, and particularly the Soviet Embassy, were kept out of bounds for most Afghans as though they were nurseries of bubonic plague; and the diplomats and embassy personnel were kept under constant surveillance by the police.

This traditional policy was considered neither necessary nor wise by the new Afghan leaders. In their judgment the past danger to Afghanistan had been that one of their powerful neighbors might either invade and occupy the country or over-throw the Afghan government by intrigues with the powerful tribes. That these fears were justified had been amply demonstrated by Afghan history. The threat to Afghanistan was not the result, in the new leaders' opinion, of any desire by the U.S.S.R. or Great Britain to take over their country; rather, it was a consequence of the struggle between two world powers.

Great Britain was now gone from the Afghan borderlands; its place was taken by neutralist India and unstable Pakistan, neither of which was a threat to Soviet security. Of course, the British withdrawal had also removed a traditional check to Soviet aggression, but in the opinion of the Afghan leaders the move had made any Soviet attack so improbable as to rule it out of their own considerations. This does not mean that the Afghans had suddenly developed a belief in Soviet altruism; on the contrary, they were quite sure that Soviet actions were always motivated by their own interests and by those alone. But, they reasoned, assuming Soviet planners to be reasonable men, those interests could only be injured by an attack on Afghanistan. The country would be economic liability to the U.S.S.R.; to control it would be difficult and costly; and, most important, any such aggression would have disastrous repercussions among the neutralist nations in Asia and Africa.

Politically Afghans are anything but naive, and they were well aware of new patterns of aggression possible to the Soviet Union through its control of foreign Communist parties. As Prime Minister Mohammed Daoud said when questioned on this point, "Does anyone think we have not heard of Czechoslovakia?" [3] But the Prime Minister and the other Afghan leaders believed that the danger of infiltration and subversion was remote in Afghanistan, where there was no Communist party, but where there was a widespread police system, and where only a few thousand people could possibly be described as proletarian.

Moreover, Afghan leaders had watched the development of communism in Asian countries and had reached certain basic conclusions. It seemed to them that the leadership for Communist movements in Asia came primarily from frustrated intellectuals, from men unable to make satisfactory careers for themselves in business or government and outraged by the human misery they saw around them.

Afghanistan, the Afghan leaders felt, has few of the necessary ingredients of communism. Many Afghans are poor and the Afghan standard of living is low although the country has never known a famine. There have been differences in wealth, power, and social position but these were less marked than in other Asian countries. The ordinary citizen, whose standard of living would not differ markedly from his counterpart in India or Iran, for example, retains pride in his dignity and worth as an individual, a pride in the case of the Pushtoons that is extreme. The Afghans, in short, have little in common either with the miserable crowds that throng so many Asian cities or with the typical Asian peasant, who is oppressed by hopelessness and a sense of inferiority no less than by grasping feudal and medieval landowners.

Moreover, to a remarkable degree, Afghan members of the upper classes and the ruling group have avoided ostentation and snobbery. Members of this class have almost universally cultivated a democratic and egalitarian manner, and rarely does any barrier exist between them and the humblest of their countrymen. This egalitarianism in turn stimulates the social mobility that is so common in Afghanistan but so rare in most other Asian countries. Thus the Afghan government has for years sent students abroad for advanced study on the basis of ability rather than family background. As a result, Afghanistan has produced few frustrated intellectuals such as have provided Communist leadership in many Asian countries.

It was likewise improbable that any part of the Afghan power structure—the upper bureaucracy, officer corps, tribal leaders, or religious community (groups that are often interrelated)—would have found Marxian theory appealing. Quite aside from the implicit threat communism presents to their own status, its philosophy runs directly counter to their intense dislike of authority.

If there had been any attempt at subversion, the Afghan leaders, and particularly Mohammed Daoud, were confident that the government's political police would soon uncover it. To a degree unknown in most countries, Afghans almost without exception—whether in the nomad camps, the tribal villages, or the cities—are members of some specific and well-defined group among whom every individual action is common knowledge. Since an Afghan's fundamental loyalty is still to such a group, any attempt to infiltrate it would be virtually certain of failure. Thus, for example, an Afghan nomad does not identify himself with other Afghan nomads, nor an Afghan mechanic with other Afghan mechanics. In both instances the identification is with the extended family, or perhaps with the clan or tribe.

To sum up, the new Afghan leaders concluded that the traditional aloofness toward the Soviet Union was no longer necessary. There was also a growing irritation toward the United States, which in their estimation had not lived up to what had been expected of it. Part of this reaction was the result of familiarity. Hundreds of Americans, employed by Morrison-Knudsen, or the Embassy, or directly by the Afghan government, had lived in Afghanistan since World War II. Some of these had earned affection and respect; others had aroused indignation. Obviously, the arrival of a number of foreigners in a country whose people had met relatively few outsiders and were inordinately sensitive, could not but lead to problems, the more so since Americans had scant knowledge of Afghan customs and little inclination to observe them. The years following World War II were difficult ones in which to recruit technically capable and emotionally stable Americans to work in a country as devoid of Western conveniences as Afghanistan.

Unfortunately, little care was exercised by the Department of State or Morrison-Knudsen in screening prospective employees, or in providing those selected with information about Afghan folkways. Morrison-Knudsen had little experience in Asia and failed to follow the example of American oil companies, whose political officers do so much to adjust the meeting of American and Asian cultures. The Department of State had no experts in the area, and made only limited attempts to develop any. In general, it followed its policy of rotation, even shortening assignments in Afghanistan, as a "hardship post," to eighteen months. Thus members of the American diplomatic mission arrived with no knowledge of the language or problems of Afghanistan, only to be replaced as they began to acquire them. From 1947 to 1953, moreover, United States ambassadors to Afghanistan were, without exception, senior career officers serving their last term prior to retirement. These men were often capable and certainly experienced, but it was hardly to be expected that they should exhibit outstanding energy or enthusiasm in the last stage of their careers.

Some of these circumstances were unavoidable in the light of America's recent entry into central Asia. Far less excusable was the appearance of an occasional maladjusted individual in government service. One such was an American ambassador who succeeded in making himself the most disliked diplomat in the country—a considerable feat, since it meant outstripping the built-in lead with which any British ambassador to Afghanistan begins his term of office.

On the whole, the Afghans accepted these occasional American stupidities with good humor; and some Americans, generally those who attempted to understand and appreciate Afghan customs and problems, were extremely popular. And the Americans themselves were attracted by the many admirable qualities of the Afghans—an almost universal reaction. Although generalizations are dubious, it is probable that among their supposedly inveterate enemies, the British, Afghans are the favored Asians, and it is interesting to note that Britishers who took Afghan wives during the snobbish nineteenth century did not receive the social censure usually bestowed on a man who married a "native." Sir Robert Warburton, the noted British officer who for many years was in charge of the Khyber Pass, was the child of such a marriage.

Contributing more to the increasing irritation of Afghans toward the United States were two things: resentment toward its policy in Asia, and dissatisfaction with the Helmand Valley project. For about four years the Afghan government had sought military aid from the United States in the hope of modernizing the Afghan army, whose equipment was almost ludicrously antiquated. The infantry still carried rifles of Snyder and Lee Enfield type, dating from the nineteenth century, and ammunition was so scarce and unreliable that few soldiers were even able to fire their weapons. The twelve biplanes of which the Afghan air force consisted dated from World War I, and the artillery was equally antiquated. That some of the Pushtoon tribes were better armed hardly contributed to the stability of the government.

The consistent refusal of the United States to provide weapons left Afghanistan the only non-Communist nation on the Sino-Soviet periphery that had been so neglected. To the argument that such arms would be used against Pakistan rather than the Soviet Union, the Afghans insisted that they had no intention of attacking Pakistan. And, without queston, however much the hostility between themselves and Pakistan played a part in their desire for a larger and better equipped army, the real reason behind the request was a desire to establish control over the tribes. Obviously, the existence of large semi-independent groups of well-armed men in the country remained a constant threat to the central government. The mischief of which many of the tribal leaders, particularly the unalterably reactionary mullahs, were capable had been amply demonstrated in 1947, when a revolt of the Safi tribe was barely put down by the Afghan army. This was an ominous portent, since the Safis were not one of the larger tribes, nor did they have the support of their Mohmand and Afridi neighbors.[4]

In addition, the Afghan leaders feared that the tribes east of the Durand Line might once again be bribed or induced to invade Afghanistan, as had happened in the past. In 1949 Mohammed Amin, one of the numerous half brothers of Amanullah Khan, appeared in Waziristan plentifully equipped with cash and began recruiting for an attack on Afghanistan. Mohammed Amin was not ideally suited for this task, since he was known to have married an Englishwoman, and the plan collapsed under the opposition of the Fakir of Ipi; but the pattern was disturbingly plain to the Afghans, who of course believed that Pakistan was behind it.

The Afghans were willing to accept the American refusal of

arms, however, so long as no such aid went to Pakistan. Britain, it is true, had done this already, and for a time the Pakistani army had been commanded by a Britisher, General Gracey. But the inauguration of the Baghdad Pact, and later of the Central Treaty Organization, which brought massive American military aid to both Pakistan and Iran, ended for the Afghans any confidence in the profession of the United States to be a friend of all parties. The Afghans realized, furthermore, that despite an ostensible aloofness from such regional defense alignments, the United States had actually been a prime mover in their formation.

It was also irritating to the Afghans that aid to their country under the Point Four Program, and later under the International Cooperation Administration, was far less than that given to Iran or Pakistan. By 1956 Afghanistan had received the equivalent of about six million dollars in technical assistance, whereas Iran and Pakistan had been given over one hundred million dollars each. The latter nations were both larger than Afghanistan, but the discrepancy struck the Afghans as unfair in view of the income to Iran from its oil and of the developments left behind in Pakistan by the British; and in any event, although Afghanistan had about one-half the population of Iran, it had received only one-twentieth as much aid. What galled the pride of the Afghans was not the amount in itself so much as the implication that their country was considered of little importance.

The second major cause of irritation, the Helmand Valley project, was technically the operation of a private American company; but in Afghanistan, as elsewhere in Asia, it is difficult to dissociate American private enterprise from the American government and its foreign policy. And in fact the United States government had been involved in the program from the beginning as well as during its later stages, when financing by the Export-Import Bank brought the Department of State into the picture.

Some of the dissatisfaction with the project stemmed from unduly optimistic expectations. But this was not all. The original cost estimates had been absurdly low, and the seventeen million dollars with which Afghanistan had launched the program were soon largely spent for American salaries, equipment, and supplies. Meanwhile, fashions had changed, karakul had gone out of favor, and Afghan fur producers found themselves in competition with South Africa and the Soviet Union. With the Afghan dollar balance exhausted and the project far from complete, the Afghans were forced to approach the Export-Import Bank for a loan. The sum of twenty-one million dollars that was advanced in November 1949 was much smaller than the amount originally requested and it carried with it the restriction that the full amount was to be spent on the Helmand Valley project. In November 1953 the Afghans went again to the Export-Import Bank with a request for a nonrestricted loan of thirty-six million dollars. This time the bank granted eighteen and one-half million dollars, making the same restriction, and specifically rejecting the request for permission to use part of the loan to pave the streets of Kabul. Both of these loans had an amortization period of eighteen years and an interest rate of 4½ per cent.

Thus, though the United States was providing funds for Afghan development, the manner in which they were provided evoked more annoyance than gratitude. None of the money, it should be noted, had been in the form of an outright grant, and Afghanistan had never defaulted on an international obligation. The implication that the United States government had so little confidence in the Afghan government was thus looked upon as an insult to its integrity as well as to its intelligence.

In addition, a growing number of Afghans were becoming convinced not only that the Helmand Valley project had been a mistake from the beginning but also that the American government was at least partly responsible for its failure. This has of course been denied; but a number of foreign experts, including some Americans, have concurred, and there is no doubt whatsoever that the plan contained some serious flaws. So far as the execution was concerned, Morrison-Knudsen did an efficient job, far better than the work done in the country by Germans and Japanese. It is true that the project was based upon long-range rather than immediate benefits, and no one is likely to argue against the value of irrigation, reclamation, and hydro-electric development in a country as underdeveloped as Afghanistan. But, with the limited funds available, it is questionable whether giving priority to the Helmand project was wise for Afghanistan in that stage of its development. Eighteen years after its beginning and following the expenditure of one hundred and fifty million dollars (an enormous sum by Afghan standards), the project had a yearly return of ten million dollars. This figure is below the 10 per cent usual on the free market, and does nothing toward amortization.

There are obvious reasons for this comparative failure. Any operation of the complexity of the Helmand Valley project calls for efficient bureaucrats, skilled administrators, and experienced workers, all of whom are scarce in Afghanistan. That the happy notion of settling Afghan nomads on the reclaimed lands would not work out, any anthropologist could have predicted with confidence, had one been consulted. The skills of the nomads have little relation to those of sedentary agriculturists, particularly when it comes to operating an elaborate irrigation system. Many of the Turkomen and Pushtoon nomads brought to the project soon returned to their tents and camels, while those remaining struggled to maintain a marginal existence.[5]

Still more serious than the human failure was the tardy discovery that thousands of acres of the reclaimed land were high in salinity and alkalinity. The poor drainage of the region made the usual practice of flushing out the soluble salts almost impossible. As a result, much of the land proved worthless.

It was at this critical juncture in Afghan–United States relations that Pakistan announced its "one unit" plan, calling for the merger of the provinces of West Pakistan. This could not but disturb the Afghans, to whom the elimination of the North West Frontier Province seemed part of a move to destroy the identity of the eastern Pushtoons. And undoubtedly this was one of the motives behind the plan, for incipient sectionalism remained Pakistan's most serious problem. It is interesting to note that Dr. Khan Sahib, the Khudai Khitmatgar leader, became head of West Pakistan, while his brother, Abdul Ghaffar

Khan, remained resolute in his support of Pushtoonistan and was, ironically, kept under house arrest as a subversive.

It was to an Afghanistan angry with the United States, dissatisfied with its own economic progress, and alarmed over the situation east of the Durand Line, that Nikita Khrushchev came in November 1956, arriving at Kabul on the last lap of his celebrated tour. Several meetings with Zahir Shah and Prime Minister Daoud produced an announcement that caused consternation to American officialdom, namely that the U.S.S.R. was granting a hundred-million-dollar loan to Afghanistan on extremely favorable terms. This money was to be used to advance and hasten the country's program of development, and was to be matched by an equal sum in Afghan currency. Khrushchev added a final touch to this demonstration of Soviet generosity by announcing at the airport that the Soviet Union was presenting the Afghan ruler with an Ilyushin airplane and the people of Kabul with fifty buses for public transportation.

Afghan rulers of the past would have rejected such largesse out of hand, for it was obvious that this sum—by far the largest that the Afghans had ever received from outside sources—would bring to Afghanistan a number of Soviet technicians. The Afghans knew from past experience the double role that such individuals often played. Indeed, for a century it had been their cardinal policy to keep out the nationals of their threatening neighbors wherever possible, and to depend instead upon the presumably less designing Japanese, French, Germans, and Americans. But as we have seen, the new Afghan leaders had confidence in their own ability to keep subversion under control, and were dedicated to bringing progress to their country. They were aware, moreover, that failure to do so might prove more dangerous than any agent of the Kremlin. The "revolution of rising expectations" had come to Afghanistan at last; and no people so volatile and energetic could be expected to remain contented if their country lagged behind while its neighbors forged ahead.

Using the Soviet loan as a base, the Afghans announced the beginning of a five-year plan covering all sectors of the economy. Agriculture, with about 40 per cent of the total expenditure, was to receive priority; transportation and communication would receive 28 per cent, industry 12 per cent, social services (health and education) 12 per cent, and mining 4 per cent. This was, in the opinion of many experts, a wise allocation, since it avoided the common error made by underdeveloped countries, of attempting to establish complex metallurgical or industrial projects.

By 1961 the first five-year plan was declared ended, and a second was announced. As is usual with such plans, not all the goals were reached and the cost exceeded the estimates, but considerable progress had been made. At first the plan had been to finance 75 per cent of the cost from internal sources; but since the U.S.S.R. continued to demonstrate its generosity—in which it was followed belatedly by the United States—over 60 per cent of the expenditures for the program actually came from foreign sources.

There can be no doubt that the beginning of Soviet aid to Afghanistan was what chiefly fostered the interest of the United States in the country, and the creation of what Henry A. Byroade, American ambassador to Afghanistan from 1959 to 1961, has called an "economic Korea." In this new economic battleground of the Cold War, the U.S.S.R. has had the advantages of proximity to Afghanistan, freedom from concern over internal political considerations, and a willingness to support the Afghans against Pakistan. Furthermore, Soviet aid has tended to be more showy than the American variety. For one thing, the U.S.S.R. quickly agreed to finance the paving of the streets of Kabul, a relatively inexpensive project, after the United States had refused to do so. In giving as a reason that the project had no specific relation to economic development, the U.S. policymakers had shown themselves to be woefully unimaginative, for it should be obvious that national morale is basic to national development. Other Soviet projects have been in irrigation and hydroelectric power, petroleum exploration, and highways, including the start of a heavy-duty road from Kushka on the Soviet border through Herat to Kandahar. This has been financed by an eighty-million-dollar grant from the

U.S.S.R., in itself unusual since almost all Soviet foreign aid has been in the form of loans rather than grants.

Another source of satisfaction to the Afghans was the Soviet decision to help modernize the Afghan army. No information on the quantity of Soviet aid in this sector has been released, but the amount must be considerable. The most spectacular feature has been a number of jet fighters and bombers, which now streak through Afghan skies in place of the antique bi-planes. For the first time in Afghanistan's history its army has become an effective support to the stability and authority of the government.

United States aid has been continued mainly in irrigation, transportation, and education; and much of it has gone into the Helmand Valley project. United States funds have also helped launch Ariana, the first Afghan airline, which now operates between the major Afghan cities, with flights to Delhi, Beirut, Mecca, Teheran, Prague, and Frankfort. A grant of $3.6 million and a loan of $1.8 million have gone into the construction of an international airport at Kandahar, a program in which Pan-American Airways participated in return for 49 per cent of the stock. This project may eventually bring considerable air traffic to Afghanistan, since it will reduce the distance of global flights by one thousand miles.

Quite probably the most important contribution of the United States to Afghanistan has been in education. Since World War II the number of Afghan students sent to the United States for advanced studies has increased to the point that by 1962 over one thousand Afghans had received some American education. The records of many of these students in American colleges and universities have been generally better than those from any other Asian country.

These students have been sent to the United States under the auspices of their own government. In addition, the International Cooperation Administration, and such private foundations as the American Friends of the Middle East, with assistance from the U.S. government, have signed contracts with Columbia and Wyoming universities to bring a number of

American teachers to Afghanistan. Some of these were assigned to the Afghan School of Vocational Education (originated by an American, Richard Soderburgh), and others to the University of Kabul, the Technological Institute, and the Teacher Training School.

Even after accepting massive Soviet aid in other fields, the Afghans have been reluctant to employ Soviet nationals in their educational system and have refused persistent offers of Soviet aid. Since it was obvious, however, that Afghanistan could not continue to accept other assistance without some compromise on the issue, in 1961 the first Afghan students were sent to the U.S.S.R. The number has been increasing, particularly in military training, but the overwhelming majority of young Afghans still prefer to go to the United Kingdom or the United States. So pervasive has been the influence of the latter countries on Afghan education that English is now the third language of educated Afghans (along with Persian and Pushto); Radio Kabul broadcasts three English-language programs a day; and an English-language newspaper, *The Kabul Times,* is published daily by the government's press ministry. These competitive programs of aid have brought an unprecedented number of foreigners to Afghanistan, where they have been accepted with equanimity; and thus at last the myth of Afghan fanaticism has ended. A number of airlines, including KLM, Indian Airways, and Sovflot, have established regular flights to Kabul, with the result that tourists may visit the country without making the arduous two-day trip overland from Peshawar.

An especially significant development in Afghanistan's drive for progress took place in 1959, when for the first time since the ill-fated experiment of Amanullah Khan, the women of Afghan cities emerged from behind the purdah, the curtain that had hidden them for centuries. All the leaders after Amanullah had shared his repugnance for this custom, which not only subjected their country to foreign ridicule but injured the health of the women and prevented their participation in the country's economic development. That no attempts had previously been made to breach the practice had been due to the conviction that Amanullah's efforts in this direction had contributed to the revolt against him. Just as in economic affairs and in dealing with the U.S.S.R., the government of Mohammed Daoud was at once more confident of its stability and more impatient with anachronisms than its predecessor. It was thus with satisfaction that the Afghan leaders learned of a plot in the girls' school in Kabul for an attack on purdah. Instead of taking measures to halt the conspiracy—in which, indeed, some feminine members of the royal family were implicated—the government simply alerted the gendarmerie to possible trouble and awaited developments. When finally the girls acted, the courageous eighteen-year-old Mahbuba Musa became the first Afghan city woman of the upper class to appear without the birqa or veil. She was promptly joined by many of her classmates, and the reaction to the move was approval rather than resentment. Immediately the government issued a decree that purdah was no longer required in Afghanistan.

This belated triumph met a temporary setback, however, when the example set in Kabul was emulated by the ladies of Kandahar, the most conservative city in Afghanistan, where a number of reactionary mullahs still had considerable influence. A few of these succeeded in stirring up mob violence, which the government quickly checked by use of troops. The ringleaders were severely punished.

This action dealt a death blow to purdah. Since then an increasing number of Afghan ladies have discarded the veil and moved into positions in the government and in industry. Here, incidentally, they are displaying as much energy as their brothers, if not more—an indication that the presumed subservience of women among the Afghans may have been no less a myth than the reputation for fanaticism.

The attack on the veil increased the popularity of the prime minister among the younger citizens, and marked a major social revolution. It is true, of course, that the majority of Afghan women—almost all of the country folk, the nomads, and the tribes—had never worn the veil; but it had been mandatory for centuries for city women of the upper class, and most educated women belonged to this group. Moreover, these were the wives, sisters, and mothers of men with much actual or potential influence on Afghan affairs—a major reason why the reactionary forces had fought so vigorously to keep them isolated, ignorant, and superstitious.

Through the entire parade of economic and social progress from 1953 to 1962, two things remained unchanged: the Afghan position on Pushtoonistan and the tension between Afghanistan and Pakistan over the same issue. For a time between 1955 and 1958 the tension was eased as General Mirza, who was then president of Pakistan, exchanged state visits with Mohammed Zahir Shah. Pakistan had still made no attempt to incorporate the tribal zones within the framework of West Pakistan, but had continued to deal with the tribes through political officers responsible to the central government. Meanwhile, the Afghans were aware of the alarming internal situation that threatened to end Pakistan's experiment in nationhood at any moment: the irritation of East Pakistan at the domination of West Pakistan, the dislike of all sections for Punjab hegemony in the army and civil service, and the widespread corruption in the government.

For a time in 1958 the Afghans hoped that their desires would be fulfilled, after General Mohammed Ayub Khan had carried out his successful coup. His extralegal position, it seemed to them, might force the new Pakistani government into a more conciliatory attitude toward its neighbors. Besides, since General Ayub Khan was himself a Pushtoon—a Spin Tarin from the Hazara district of Pakistan—he would presumably be more sympathetic toward Pushtoon aspirations than his predecessors. (Ironically, the Spin Tarins came originally from Kandahar, and their ancestor Tarin, according to Pushtoon genealogy, was also the ancestor of the Durranis and the Mohammedzais, the royal family of Afghanistan.)

These hopes proved to have been built on flimsy foundations. On the Pushtoon question, the new government of Pakistan was more adamant than its predecessor. Ayub Khan, for all his Pushtoon background, was British by education and military training, and identified himself with the Punjab. In addition, he was too forceful and aggressive by nature to tolerate any thought of Pushtoon separatism or autonomy.

Soon after the takeover by the Ayub government, tension

between Afghanistan and Pakistan, aggravated by the modernization of the Afghan army and the open support it was receiving from the Soviet Union, reached new heights. In the fall of 1960 and again in 1961 open conflict erupted in the district of Bajaur. The origin of the fighting was a local quarrel, with the Khan of Jandul and the Nawab of Dir sided against the Khan of Khar. When the Afghans came to the support of the first two, Pakistan backed the Khan of Khar. The location of Bajaur happened to favor Afghan intervention, since although it was east of the Durand Line, it bordered on the territory of the powerful Afghan Mohmands and was also inhabited by tribes who had lands in Afghanistan.

Reports of the fighting were confused and contradictory, but Pakistan evidently used several divisions and employed its air force with considerable success. Tribal casualties were heavy, particularly from aerial bombardment, and Afghanistan suffered a reverse when a group of Afghan regulars were captured east of the Durand Line. This, Pakistan contended, was proof of direct Afghan intervention; the Afghans maintained that the soldiers were acting on their own initiative. Apparently the cause of the incident was an Afghan officer's misunderstanding of instructions. At any rate, Bajaur returned to an uneasy quiet with Pakistan in control, although occasional sniping and grenade attacks on Pakistani patrols continued.

On August 24, 1961, shortly after the end of the fighting in Bajaur, Pakistan announced that it was closing its consulates at Jalalabad and Kandahar, and demanded that Afghanistan withdraw its consulates from Peshawar and Quetta. The reason given by the Pakistani authorities for this step was the hostility of the Afghan people toward consular officials—although in fact Pakistani officials had not been popular in Afghanistan for a decade; the actual motive was simply Pakistan's irritation over the Bajaur fighting and its desire to put pressure upon the Afghans. The Afghans, as usual, reacted violently; on September 6, 1961, they broke off diplomatic relations with Pakistan. In any event the Pakistani's demand was ill timed, since it arrived during the Afghans' Jeshan-i-Istiqlal ("celebration of independence"), when their national pride is at zenith.

The end of diplomatic relations closed the border and

blocked Afghanistan's major shipping route, to the satisfaction of no one but the Soviet Union, which thus became Afghanistan's sole means of contact with the outside world—aside from a limited and arduous traffic through Iran. It is an interesting illustration of the apparently unilateral nature of American military and economic aid under the regional defense pacts to note that although Pakistan's actions were bound to be injurious to American interests in the area, its dependence upon United States aid was not sufficient to prevent its persisting in them. Indeed, when the United States government protested the use of its planes and military equipment in the Bajaur fighting, General Ayub Khan rejected the protest curtly in a public speech. Closing the border halted shipments from the United States for its projects in Afghanistan, since it refused to avail itself of the Soviet route, with the result that the U.S.S.R. gained an enormous advantage over the competition in its economic program.

For the first time in centuries the periodic migration of thousands of Afghan nomads into Pakistan was checked. This meant economic hardship for many of these wanderers, particularly for those who had no other winter pasturelands or who depended upon their income as migratory laborers for a part of each year. Pakistan also suffered, because the absence of the migrants meant a labor shortage in the sugar fields, and because Pakistani merchants missed the yearly appearance of the Powindah, or nomads, who supported their trade.

Undoubtedly happy over these developments, the Soviet Union promptly offered assistance and a fleet of fifteen transport planes for daily service to Afghanistan. In this manner the entire fruit crop was successfully shipped to the U.S.S.R., whence much of it was resold at a profit in the markets of northern Europe. At the same time Soviet engineers speeded work on the highways that would connect Afghanistan with the Soviet railhead at Kushka.

XIX

The Present
and the Future

The man never dies who leaves a good
name behind him.—AFGHAN SAYING

AFGHANS in the past have been known as poor followers but
good leaders; they have provided kings for Iran and India, and
their own monarchs, Ahmed Shah Durrani, Dost Mohammed
Khan, and Abdur Rahman Khan, compare favorably with any
of the past rulers of Asia. To these may, perhaps, be added the
name of Mohammed Zahir Shah, the present ruler of Afghanistan.

Zahir Shah, after ascending the throne at the age of nineteen,
was under the tutelage of his three able uncles for twenty years,
and as a result was little known to his people. The resignation
in 1953 of Shah Mahmud, the last of the Mohammedzai
brothers, was, however, an indication that the king intended to
take an active part in Afghan affairs, and it was through his
support that Sirdar Mohammed Daoud, his cousin and prime
minister, was able to reverse traditional Afghan policy and set
the country on the road toward modernization.

Despite the successes and the popularity of Mohammed
Daoud, the king gradually became convinced that the nation's
political structure could not be kept as it was indefinitely. The
constitutions promulgated by Amanullah Khan and Nadir Shah
notwithstanding, it was obvious to all informed Afghans that

277

their government was in reality an oligarchy with power in the hands of the royal family. Admittedly, that government had not been a bad one; on the contrary, considering the circumstances, the amount it had done for the country and the people was remarkable. Its members, moreover, had avoided ostentation to a degree unusual in Asia, and had welcomed persons of lowly family background to high position when they demonstrated ability. This trait was not new in Afghanistan. Ahmed Shah Durrani, Dost Mohammed Khan, and Shir Ali Khan were all noted for the easy informality of their manner, and one of the reasons for the unpopularity of Shah Shuja had been his sullen hauteur. Many people from peasant families had held high place in Afghan governments; several of them had occupied the post of Wazir or prime minister.

Nevertheless, that the government had remained a limited autocracy, with an extremely narrow base of power, was resented by many Afghans, especially the ever-increasing number with advanced and Western educations. The number of previous autocracies notwithstanding, Afghans have a strong democratic tradition, one that was not confined to the people but extended to the rulers. Even that dour tyrant Abdur Rahman Khan had prophesied that the day would come when the "Afghan people would be ruled for their safety by themselves."

In March 1963 the first step was taken in a plan the king and his advisers had been long considering when Sirdar Mohammed Daoud announced his resignation. Daoud had accomplished more for the country in a decade than had been done in a century, and had won wide popularity as a result of the emancipation of Afghan women. But since he and his brother, Mohammed Naim Khan, were members of the royal family, they had become a target for resentment against centralized control—the so-called "family compact" which had dominated Afghan affairs for thirty years.

Daoud, moreover, had close emotional associations with the hard line on Pushtoonistan that had resulted in the closing of the Afghan-Pakistani border and the breaking of diplomatic relations between the two countries. Many Afghan leaders were concerned about the shift of the country's economy from its traditional markets and import sources to the U.S.S.R., for Soviet economic and political policies were one and the same, a truism often repeated by the Russians themselves. Moreover, since the United States refused to avail itself of the routes through the Soviet Union, the closing of the Pakistani border had virtually halted American aid to Afghanistan.

Mohammed Daoud's farewell speech on March 12, 1963 reviewed the progress of the country under his administration and pointed to the problems of the future. His chief message, however, was to call for increased participation by the Afghan people in their government and the separation of its executive, legislative, and judicial powers. This suggestion was promptly accepted by the king (who had undoubtedly had a hand in its formulation), and a committee was appointed to study the question and prepare a new constitution to be submitted to a Loe Jirga for approval.[1]

Without question Mohammed Zahir Shah hoped to move Afghanistan toward responsible government and eventually to establish a constitutional monarchy based upon democratically chosen representation. Considering the low rate of literacy in Afghanistan and the divisive forces that still exist there, this transfer cannot be immediate, but promising steps have been taken and have met with almost unanimous approval. From a comparison of the policy of Mohammed Zahir Shah with those of other royal families in Asia, it is obvious that the Afghan king has acted with wisdom and benevolence, and his popularity has grown as a result. He now enjoys a position of respect and admiration equaled, perhaps, only by Ahmed Shah Durrani and Dost Mohammed Khan in the past.

The new cabinet selected by the king reflected the new policy. For perhaps the first time in Afghan history not one of the ministers was a member of the royal family, although several were connected by marriage. The new prime minister, Dr. Mohammed Yousuf, was a man of relatively humble background who had risen in the government through ability and training (he holds a Ph.D. in physics from the University of Göttingen). Among the other cabinet members, five out of twelve had a doctor's degree, a record hardly to be matched in any other country. Like the prime minister, several came from families with neither prestige nor wealth.

The process launched by the king has continued. In March 1964 the country was reorganized into twenty-nine administrative units. Of the first five governors appointed, the oldest was forty-three; every one had received a master's degree from a foreign university; none owed his appointment to family position.[2] The wisdom of this policy is obvious. Not only are such men better qualified for the work of development in which Afghanistan is now engaged than appointees chosen for their influence or family position, but their advancement demonstrates the possibilities of success to other young Afghans.

This change in government brings the story of Afghanistan down to the present. Concerning the future, a review of the country's past permits a qualified optimism. In comparison with other underdeveloped countries, Afghanistan has both strengths and weaknesses. It has never been a colony, and its people are free from residual feelings of inferiority; they consider themselves the equals of anyone. Their confidence is not easy to analyze; but that they are a people of dynamic energy, fiercely patriotic and determined to prove their worth in the modern world, there can be no doubt.

Moreover, Afghanistan has no serious problems arising from sectionalism or from major ethnic, religious, or racial rivalries. The minorities that do exist, with the possible exception of the Hazaras, have not met with any active discrimination and are not concentrated in specific areas. Some members of minority groups occupy high positions in the Afghan government; Abdul Majid Khan, Afghan minister of finance for a decade, was a Tadjik.[3]

On the other hand, never having been under imperial rule has meant being without the benefits of Western technology, which indeed the Afghans were obliged to resist in their attempt to keep agents of imperial powers from the country. Although in their own eyes the lack was a small price to pay for freedom, it left the nation without a single mile of railway, without industry, without adequate roads or communications, and with an extremely high rate of illiteracy. Fortunately, Afghanistan does not at present have a population problem, although with one of the highest birth rates in the world and the steady increase of medical services, the same may not hold true in the future. Again fortunately, the Afghan leaders have shown energy and foresight in tackling the task of economic development. Resisting the temptation to attempt premature industrialization, they have concentrated on the agricultural and pastoral system that already exists, with attention to the production of such major necessities as textiles, petroleum products, and cement. It is significant that in so doing the Afghans are avoiding the mistakes already made by other underdeveloped countries.

For a time the decision to accept massive Soviet aid caused serious concern in the United States, and led to a spate of articles to the effect that Afghanistan had become one more satellite. Both the concern and the stories were unjustified, and that the U.S.S.R. has gained no political advantage in return is evident from a study of Afghan participation in international affairs. In the United Nations Afghanistan votes with the Afro-Asian bloc, and has shown no deviation from its announced policy of neutralism. The Afghans do not permit any Communist party or activity in the country, and despite vague rumors of a "cell" in Kabul, there is no evidence of any underground apparatus. Soviet nationals in Afghanistan are granted no special privileges; indeed, close personal relations between an Afghan and a Soviet citizen are discouraged, to say the least. Many suggestions by the Soviets have been rejected out of hand, particularly those in sensitive areas. Thus a much-needed aerial survey of the country was done by an American firm, although the Soviet Union was permitted to map the territory impinging on the Afghan-Soviet border.

Foreign observers who still fear that Soviet assistance may woo the Afghans from a traditional suspicion of their powerful neighbor underestimate the political acumen of their leaders. Afghanistan, however retarded its economic development, has existed in a vortex of power politics through most of its history, and its leaders are anything but naive about such matters.

There are no Afghan proverbs about Greeks bearing gifts, but that the generosity of either Soviet or United States aid has little basis in altruism they are quite aware.

Actually the Soviet aid program and the concomitant presence of several thousand Soviet nationals in the country have had a negative effect on the attitude of the Afghans both toward the U.S.S.R. and toward communism. As has been noted, one of the most obvious imperatives in the ethnic character of Afghanistan is a hospitality entailing a generosity and openhandedness that border on the prodigal. Whatever their secret inclinations, Afghans are so impelled by this custom that niggards or misers are rare in Afghanistan, and when they appear are subject to strong social disapproval. As a result of another imperative, Afghans rank high among the world's peoples in the matter of courtesy. They also are extremely volatile; they shout, laugh, talk, and sing at every opportunity, delight in mimicry and ribald humor, and require little more than the clapping of hands to begin a dance.

The behavior of Soviet nationals in Afghanistan, as well as those with whom an increasing number of Afghan visitors have met at home, is almost the exact opposite. The former are apparently under instructions to remain aloof from personal contacts, and exhibit the very conditioning that Russian psychologists are so fond of as a theory. Undoubtedly their incomes are far lower than those of their American counterparts, but their parsimonious habits have not escaped the notice of the observant Afghans—for example, the purchase of clothes that are either of secondhand or of shoddy American manufacture in the bazaars. Outwardly they appear so dull and stolid that if they are enjoying life in Afghanistan, no one would ever guess it. And their manners, although by no means deliberately impolite, indicate that they have little conception of courtesy— either for lack of an elite class to set the pattern or from a desire to embody bluff proletarian virtues.

Afghans who have visited the Soviet Union have returned with a rather low opinion of life in the U.S.S.R. It would be a rare Afghan who had visited both the United States and the Soviet Union and who expressed a preference for the latter.

That Afghans tend to find themselves most at home in California is suggested by the large number of visiting students who apply for admission to the colleges and universities there.

Personal reactions vary, but it would seem that the Soviet Union has failed thus far to convince many Afghans of the merits of communism. Few of them have expressed much interest in collectivization. Perhaps because of historic forces, Afghans are intensely competitive; they will cooperate with their friends or families, but they prefer to compete with all others—an attitude expressed by the ancient Bedouin prayer, "Allah have mercy on me and Mohammed but on nobody else."

This does not mean that the Soviet Union's policies have had no effect upon Afghanistan. The cutting off of the traditional shipping route through Pakistan, and the shift of trade from the West to the Communist orbit undoubtedly did much to alter the Afghans' opinion of their northern neighbor. Communist China, on the other hand, is of little concern. Although the two countries have a common frontier, there is almost no commercial intercourse between them, and the Afghans' attachment is still to the West rather than to the Orient.

So far as orthodox Marxism is concerned, the policy of the Soviet Union toward Afghanistan has been anomalous, to say the least. Theoretically, Afghanistan has not reached what in the Communist lexicon is designated as the "nationalist-bourgeois" stage, and which in *Fundamentals of Marxism-Leninism,* the latest Russian statement of Communist doctrine, is to be supported during the temporary phase of the struggle against "Medieval remnants." Rather, Afghanistan is still in the "monarchic-feudal" stage, in which power is largely hereditary. Nevertheless, there has been no attempt by the Soviet Union to injure or undermine its political structure; on the contrary, Soviet economic and military aid has done much to strengthen it.

There are several immediate tactical reasons for this apparent contradiction between theory and practice. One is a desire to counter the activity of the United States in Afghanistan, where it is a potential threat to the sensitive area of Soviet central

Asia. Another motive is the desire to put pressure upon Pakistan, and thus to render its United States bases more vulnerable. Still another is the desire to build up a more favorable image in the underdeveloped countries of Africa, Asia, and Latin America; and it is significant that since its pioneering application in Afghanstan, the same approval has been repeated in a number of countries.

Soviet aid to Afghanistan is ideologically justified by the revised *Fundamentals of Marxism-Leninism* issued by the Communist Party of the Soviet Union at the Twenty-second Congress in October 1961. According to this view, which is not accepted by the Chinese, however, the struggle in underdeveloped countries is not between the bourgeoisie and proletariat but one between nationalist elements and international imperialism. The underdeveloped countries of Asia, in the Soviet view, are in the first revolutionary phase, the "nationalist," to be followed by the "democratic" and finally the "socialist," the latter to be directed by Communist parties. *Fundamentals of Marxism-Socialism* puts the matter thus: "In the countries of the East, state capitalism in its present form is not a tool of the imperialist monopolies; on the contrary, it stimulates an anti-imperialist movement and is objectively directed against the expansion of these monopolies in the East.[4]

This Soviet evaluation, however, does not explain the extent of Soviet aid to Afghanistan, particularly when the limited amount of "international imperialism" in that country is considered. In the Soviet context this term is usually used to describe capital investment and military assistance. The United States has indeed provided capital to Afghanistan, but this has been in the form of loans and grants rather than capital investment while American military assistance has been negligible.

It seems likely that the extent of Soviet aid to Afghanistan is a practical rather than ideological attempt to tie the developing Afghan economy to that of the Soviet Union. The extent of Soviet aid and the closing of the Afghan export-import route through Pakistan brought about a major shift in Afghan trade with most of Afghanistan's exports and imports going to or through the U.S.S.R. Indeed, some Western observers contended that Afghanistan had become so economically dependent on the Soviet Union that the latter could establish political control if it chose.

This opinion, however, was as faulty as that of *Time* magazine, which characterized Sirdar Mohammed Daoud, then prime minister, as the "red" prince. Afghans have shown in the past that they abhor foreign domination and will make many sacrifices to prevent it. Most Afghans, despite the progress of the past twenty years, still engage in a subsistence economy, and the demand for imported goods, though growing, is still small. Any attempt by the Soviet Union to exercise control by means of economic pressure would be stoutly resisted; and it not only would eliminate whatever good will the U.S.S.R. had developed in the country, but could (and probably would) be countered by the United States with ease.

With the resignation of Prime Minister Daoud, the way was cleared for negotiations with Pakistan through the mediation of Iran. Diplomatic relations were resumed late in 1963 and the export-import route through Pakistan was reopened. And already on March 20, 1963, the United States agreed to construct a highway from Herat to Islam Qala on the Iranian border, as a means of lessening Afghan dependence on the routes through Pakistan and the Soviet Union.

Anyone who has had the opportunity to study the Afghan scene since the close of World War II cannot but be impressed by the remarkable progress made by the country. Schools throughout the country have multiplied many times; the University of Kabul is increasingly able to provide Afghan students with an adequate higher education, and another university is being built in Jalalabad. Despite errors of operation and planning, irrigation and reclamation have placed thousands of acres under cultivation; the dams on these projects have vastly increased Afghan electric power. Highways have been built, improved, and expanded. The country now has an airport capable of handling international jet flights and a number of small but adequate airports for internal use.

The social and political changes since 1950 have been equally extreme. The abrupt end to the seclusion of women was a revolution of enormous proportions, which freed thousands of capable workers for places in Afghan business and education.

Finally, as has already been suggested, the country seems to be moving steadily in the direction of responsible and representative government.

These changes have not solved all the problems of the country; on the contrary, it still faces many serious difficulties. Such divisive forces as the animosity of the Sunnis toward the Shia minority, and the resentment of non-Pushtoon Afghans against Pushtoon hegemony are still present. The conservative and reactionary tendencies have not been destroyed; although they have been defeated and are in retreat, they are still an important factor in Afghan affairs. Despite the advances in education, illiteracy in Afghanistan is inordinately high, and many years of consistent effort will be required to wipe it out.

Economic development has been made possible by large loans from the United States and the Soviet Union, but that development has also brought about new problems. Repayment of the loans will for some time be a burden upon Afghanistan's national income, and development has also led to an inflation which is proving difficult to check.

Perhaps in the long run the most serious effect of these rapid and continuing changes will be on the Afghan people themselves. In the past almost all Afghans, no matter how poor they were, were sustained not only by a confidence that there would be enough to eat and a place to sleep, but still more by a strong sense of identification with a specific group—an extended family, a clan, a tribe, or a village. They had a body of long-established folkways and mores as well as a sustaining religion, whose doctrines they accepted uncritically. All of this gave a feeling of personal worth, one sign of which was the extremely small number of beggars in the country.

Obviously, these things are undergoing rapid change along with the country's economic and social pattern. Clan and tribal loyalties are weakening; the hold of the village is lessening as more and more young Afghans move to the towns and cities or find employment in the developing industries. At the same time, Afghan folkways and traditions are declining as education shows them to be anachronisms in the modern world.

All this is, of course, the same inevitable problem that is faced in equal or greater measure by other underdeveloped countries. But there is reason for encouragement in the achievements of the several thousand Afghans who during the past decade have been visitors to the technological societies of the West, most of them for advanced education.

That the question of Pushtoonistan will remain a primary concern, and will continue as a barrier to good relations between Afghanistan and Pakistan there can be no doubt. Likewise, the final solution of this problem undoubtedly rests not with the rulers of either Afghanistan or Pakistan, but with the Pushtoons themselves. Should Pakistan eventually solve its problems of sectionalism and develop a stronger sense of nationalism, these Pushtoons might become an integral part of it. If the problem is not solved, it would seem inevitable that they must some day be united with the Pushtoons of Afghanistan.

In any event, it is probable that Afghanistan will play an important role in the Asia of tomorrow. Not numerous and without any wealth of natural resources, the Afghans have always demonstrated qualities of spirit and character that have aroused the admiration even of their enemies. Perhaps, after all, the greatest single resource of a country is its people; and in this Afghanistan is rich indeed.

Appendix A

The Pushtoon Tribes

THE population figures that follow are approximations. Tribal qualities are those ascribed by their neighbors.

ABDALIS

Known as the Durranis since A.D. 1747. Subtribes: Barukzai, Achakzai, Popolzai, Alikozai, Nurzai, Ishakzai, and Alizai. Numbering around one million, this is the most important Afghan Pushtoon tribe; the Mohammedzai clan of the Barukzai subtribe is that of the present Afghan royal family. Located in southern Afghanistan, centered around the city of Kandahar.

AFRIDIS

Subtribes: Adam Khel, Aka Khel, Kamar Khel, Kambar Khel, Malikdin Khel, Sipah, Kuki Khel, and Zakka Khel. Numbering about 250,000, these are the historic guardians of the Khyber Pass. Sedentary agriculturists and vertical nomads, the Afridis are a vigorous and aggressive people and one of the more important of Pushtoon tribes. Most of them live east of the Durand Line.

BABARS

A small tribe of less than 5,000 located near Dera Ismail Khan, with their center at Chaudwhan. They are wealthy and respected; many are landlords with non-Pushtoon tenants. Babars are well educated; there is a saying "A Babar fool is a Gandspur sage."

BABIS

A very small tribe of about 1,000 located at Quetta.

BAJAURIS

Also called Tarkanris. Subtribes: Mahmuds, Isazai, and Ismailzai. A large tribe of about 125,000, located mainly in Bajaur. Sedentary agriculturists, they have a good reputation as fighters and have given trouble to Pakistan in recent years.

BANGASH

Subtribes: Miranzai, Samilzai, and Baizai. About 25,000, in the Kohat Valley south of Peshawar. Agricultural; quiet and peaceful. Some of them are Shia in religion.

BANNUCHIS

Centered around the town of Bannu. They number about 80,000, and have a low reputation for bravery. Much mixed with non-Pushtoon stock.

BARECH

About 15,000, some in the Shorawak district of Afghanistan, some in Baluchistan. Small and dark, much like the Baluchis.

BEHRAMZAIS

A tiny tribe, about 1,000; *hamsayah*, under Afridi protection.

BHITANNIS (BATANNIS)

Subtribes: Tatta, Dhana, Uraspan. Located in the hills on the borders of Tank and Bannu, they number about 29,000. Tall and slender, they resemble the Mahsuds but are their bitter enemies.

CHAMKANNIS (CHAKAMANIS)

Subtribes: Haji Kor Para Khel, Khwajak Kol, Bada Khel, and Khani Khel. East of Afridis in Khurmana Valley and on south slopes of Sikaram Range. About 12,000, poor, sedentary agriculturists or vertical nomads.

DAUDZAIS

Subtribes: Mamur, Yusuf, and Manki. About 35,000, just north of Peshawar and south of the Kabul River. Mixed with non-Pushtoon elements. Small and Slender.

DAURS (DAWARS)

About 20,000, located in the upper and lower Dawar Valley. Poor reputation; fanatical; sedentary agriculturists.

DILAZAKS

About 8,000 on the west bank of the Indus near Sarai Saleh. Agricultural; no longer an organized tribe; poor quality.

DURRANIS

See Abdalis.

GADUNS (JADUNS)

About 10,000, on both banks of the Indus. Although some speak Pushto, they can no longer be considered a Pushtoon tribe.

GANDAPURS

About 12,000, west of Dera Ismail Khan. Mostly townfolk or landlords.

GAODARRAS

A very small tribe of about 500 members; *hamsayah* to the Turis and Orakzais.

GHARBINAS

Claiming Arab ancestry, these number about 5,000 and live in the Kurram Valley. Unimportant.

GHILZAI

Subtribes: Hotaki, Tokhi, Nasar, Andar, Tarakhi, Ali Khel, Suleiman Khel. Possibly related are the Shinwari and Wardaks. Numbering over one million, this is the largest Pushtoon tribe in Afghanistan, with the Suleiman Khel by far its largest section. Their center is at Kattawaz in eastern Afghanistan but many of them are Kuchis or nomads. Only the lack of unity in this vigorous and dynamic people has allowed the Durranis to maintain their hegemony.

GIGIANIS

Subtribes: Hotak and Zirak. West of Peshawar, about 20,000; mostly agricultural.

JADRANS

About 60,000, in the southern part of Khost in Afghanistan. Poor but aggressive and warlike.

JAFARS

A small tribe west of the Indus in Baluchistan. About 2,000, much mixed with Baluchis.

JAJIS

About 40,000, living in a forested area between the Peiwar Kotal and Shutargardan Pass. Poor but a vigorous people; hostile toward the Turis, who are probably their distant relatives.

KAKARS

Subtribes: Samar Khel, Sanatias, Targhara, and Sarghara. About 80,000, in Ahib, Loralai, and Pishin. They have a poor reputation; unlike those of most Pushtoons, their chiefs have considerable authority.

KANSIS (KASIS)

A tiny tribe of about 1,000; at Quetta.

KHALILS

Subtribes: the Mattezai, Barozai, Ishaqzai, and Tallarzai. South and west of Peshawar. About 50,000; agricultural. They give much respect to their chiefs, known as Arbabs or lords.

KHASORS

In the Khasor Range. About 5,000. Poor reputation.

KHATTAKS

Subtribes: Teri, Taraki, and Bolak. South of Peshawar and east of Kohat as well as the west of Bannu district. At least 160,000. Noted for their love of music and dancing. Agricultural.

KHETRANS

In the hills above Dera Ghazi Khan. Numbering about 20,000, they are much mixed with Baluchi and non-Pushtoon elements and have almost lost their Pushtoon identity.

KHOSTWALS

Two divisions: the Spin Gundi and Tor Gundi, divided into the subtribes of Ismail Khel, Manduzai, Shamil, Muli, Tarwezai, Saban,

Bakir Khel, and Tani. Living east of the Durand Line in the Afghan province of Khost, they number about 60,000. Most are agriculturists raising rice and tobacco.

KHUGIANI

South of Jalalabad and numbering about 90,000, this tribe claims kinship with the Durranis. Most are agricultural. Despite its size the tribe is not considered formidable.

KUNDIS

Small tribe of about 10,000, near Tank. Peaceful; many are Powindahs, merchants using camel transport.

LOHANIS

A small tribe of about 8,000, near Tank. Wealthy; many are landlords, others are Powindahs.

LUNIS

A small tribe of about 6,000, living in the Loralai district of Baluchistan. Agricultural.

MAHSUDS (MAHSIT)

Subtribes: Alizai, Bahlolzi, and Shaman Khel. Numbering about 50,000, the Mahsud inhabit the center of Waziristan. Primarily pastoral tent-dwellers, they are very democratic and perhaps the most formidable of frontier tribes. They are tall and slender and outstanding as guerrilla fighters.

MAKBALS (MUQBIL)

A tiny tribe of about 1,000, living in the upper Kurram Valley, on both sides of the Durand Line.

MANDO KHEL

Subtribes: Hadizais and Haidar Khel. Numbering about 8,000, they live near Fort Sandeman and Apozai in Baluchistan. They have retained their Pushtoon characteristics.

MARWATS

Numbering about 60,000, they are divided into the "sand" Marwats who live on the plain bordering the Indus River south of Kurram and the "border" Marwats who live on the eastern border of Waziristan.

MISHWANIS (MASHWANIS)

A small tribe of about 8,000, living in the Hazara district and along the northern border of Jandul. Poor.

MOHAMMEDZAIS

Not to be confused with the Mohammedzais of the Durrani tribe, the royal family of Afghanistan. Subtribes: Tangi, Sherpao, Turangzai, Utmanzai, Razar, Charsadda, and Prang. Numbering about 60,000, they live on the west bank of the Swat River about twenty miles south of Fort Abazai. Many are wealthy agriculturists.

MOHMANDS, BAR ("Hill")

Subtribes Tarakzai, Halimzai, Baizai, and Khwaezai. Numbering about 60,000, they live from the Kabul River to the borders of Bajaur and are bifurcated by the Durand Line. Agricultural; unlike those of most Pushtoons, their khans have considerable authority. Belligerent and excellent fighters.

MOHMANDS, KUZ ("Plain")

Subtribes: Kayakzai, Musazai, Dawzai, Matanni, and Sirganni. Numbering about 70,000, and living just south of Peshawar, the Kuz Mohmand have lost contact with their Bar Mohmand kinsmen. Agriculturists.

MULLAGORIS

Just north of Khyber Pass. A small tribe of about 4,000, they have preserved themselves from their predatory neighbors by courage and unity. Oddly enough, they claim descent from an illegitimate child found in a graveyard.

NIAZIS

East of Bannu and west of the Indus River. Sedentary agriculturists numbering about 80,000, they show more kinship with the Punjab than with the Pushtoons, to the extent that Punjabi has almost replaced Pushto as their language.

ORAKZAIS

Subtribes: Daulatzais, Ismailzais, Lashkarzais, Massuzais, Mohammed, and Alizais. Living with them are a number of small tribes that are *hamsayah* under Orakzai protection, including the Ali Khel, Malla Khel, Mishtis, and Sheikhan. A powerful tribe of perhaps 80,000, they inhabit the Khanki, Mastura, Bara, and Khurmana valleys. They have a minority of Shia Moslems.

PANIS (PANRI)

About 25,000, living in Sibi in Baluchistan. Much like Baluchis.

SAFIS

Two sections: the Safis and Kandaharis. About 45,000, living between the Kunar River and Panjshir in Afghanistan. Probably converted Kafirs, they are considered somewhat fanatical in religious matters. Often florid in complexion with light eyes and hair.

SAM RANIZAI

In the range of hills on the border of lower Swat. Much mixed, perhaps not a distinct tribe. About 10,000.

SHILMANIS

A small tribe of about 4,000, living north and east of the Afghan town of Dakka. They claim relationship with the Mohmands.

SHINWARIS

A powerful tribe of about 80,000, living in the Jalalabad valley west of the Safed Koh up to the Kabul River. Divided into four sections: the Mandehzai, Sangu Khel, Sipah, and Ali Shir Khel. Many are prosperous farmers with Tadjik tenants. The Shinwaris are well-armed and have an excellent reputation for bravery. Their rebellion in 1929 helped bring about the overthrow of Amanullah Khan.

SHIRANIS

Subtribes: Largha and Bargha. Numbering about 45,000, they live around Dera Ismail Khan and the Zhob district. They have a low reputation among other Pushtoons. Like the Orakzai, they have a Shia minority.

TARINS

Two groups: the Tor Tarins and Spin Tarins. The Tor Tarins, numbering about 5,000, live south and east of Chaman; the Spin

Tarins, also about 5,000, live to the east and south of Loralai. In addition, about 3,000 Spin Tarins live in the Hazara district of Pakistan.

TURIS

Numbering about 25,000, they live in the Kurram Valley as far as the Durand Line. They are the only Pushtoons who are entirely Shia in religion.

URMARS

An odd group, probably not of Pushtoon origin. About 3,000 live in Laniguram in the center of Waziristan; about 6,000 just south of Peshawar; about 3,000 in the Logar Valley near Kabul. The last two sections speak Pushto, but those at Kaniguram speak a language called Urmari or Bargista, apparently a separate tongue although of the Iranian language family.

USHTARANAS

About 7,000, sedentary agriculturists living between Fort Sandeman and the Indus River.

UTMAN KHEL

About 40,000, living north and west of Peshawar on both sides of the Swat River. Agricultural.

WAZIRIS (DARWESH KHEL)

Subtribes: Utmanzai and Ahmedzai. Over 100,000, living in Waziristan, the Utmanzai in the north, the Ahmedzai in the south. About 15,000 live in Afghanistan near Birmel. An exceedingly formidable tribe, mostly pastoral, the Waziris would challenge their neighbors the Mahsuds as perhaps the most powerful and aggressive of the border Pushtoons.

YUZUFZAIS

Divisions: the Mandanr and Yuzufzai. Oddly, the Mandanr Yuzufzai are usually referred to as Yuzufzais, while the Yuzufzai section is often called by the name of the territory they inhabit—as, for example, Bunarwals. A very large tribe totaling perhaps 500,000, they live to the north of Peshawar, in Swat and Bunar. Living among them, usually as workers or tenant farmers, are at least as many non-Pushtoons.

ZAIMUKHTS

About 9,000, on the south slopes of the Zawa Ghar Range.

ZMARAIS

A small tribe of about 2,000, living in the Lorala district of Baluchistan.

Appendix B

Afghan Dynasties

THE SADDOZAIS (Shahs)

Ahmed Shah	1747–1773
Timur Shah	1773–1793
Zeman Shah	1793–1799
Mahmud Shah	1799–1803
Shah Shuja	1803–1809
Mahmud Shah (*return*)	1809–1819

CIVIL WAR

THE MOHAMMEDZAIS (Amirs)

Dost Mohammed Khan	1835–1839
British invasion and occupation	1839–1842
Dost Mohammed Khan (*return*)	1842–1863
Shir Ali Khan	1863–1867
Afzal Khan	1867–1868
Azim Khan	1868–1869
Shir Ali Khan (*return*)	1869–1879
Yakub Khan	1879–1879
Abdur Rahman	1880–1901
Habibullah Khan (*assumed title of Shah*)	1901–1919
Amanullah Khan	1919–1929
Revolution	1929–1929
Mohammed Nadir Shah	1929–1933
Mohammed Zahir Shah	1933–

Appendix C

The New Afghan Constitution

ON September 9, 1964, the Afghan Loe Jirga unanimously adopted a new constitution for Afghanistan. This was the work of a seven member committee appointed by the king; it shows many influences from the United States; and it marks a major political change in Afghanistan.

Under the new constitution the executive, legislative, and judicial branches of the government will be separated. The throne is hereditary in the line of Mohammed Zahir Shah according to the rules of primogeniture. The king appoints the prime minister who, in turn, selects his cabinet. The prime minister, however, may be removed by a two-thirds vote of the People's Council, the lower house of the Parliament, and no member of the royal family may serve as prime minister.

Legislative authority will be in the hands of a bicameral parliament consisting of a People's Council and a Council of Elders. Members of the People's Council will be selected by secret ballot in open elections for four-year terms. One-third of the Council of Elders will be appointed by the king; one-third selected by Provincial Councils; one-third elected.

Judicial affairs will be in the hands of a Supreme Court of nine members, headed by a Chief Justice and appointed by the King. No member of the royal family may serve as Chief Justice.

Another, and extremely important, provision of the new constitution is the specific authorization of political parties as long as they do not contradict the spirit of the constitution; a proviso that excludes any Communist Party.

Appendix C

This new constitution marks a long step forward in the direction of responsible and representative government. Promulgation of a constitution and its implementation are separate matters. But it seems evident that the Afghan leaders, specifically Mohammed Zahir Shah, have begun a program of political evolution that is wise and farsighted.

Notes

1. Afghanistan has not had a census or an adequate survey. All figures are estimates.

2. The name was first explained in the writings of the fourteenth-century Moroccan Arab, Mohammed ibn-Abdullah ibn-Batutah. *The Travels of Ibn Batuta* (London, 1829).

3. Felix Howland, "Crossing the Hindu Kush," *Geographical Review,* xxx: 272–278.

4. Syed Mohammed Qasim Rishtya, "The Rivers of Afghanistan," *Afghanistan* (Kabul), I (1946).

5. Mohammed Ali, *A New Guide to Afghanistan* (Kabul, 1958).

6. A slab was purportedly found here in A.D. 1480 with the inscription, "This is the tomb of the lion of Allah and his saint, Ali, brother of the Apostle of Allah." Non-Afghan Moslems scoff at this claim, and insist that Ali is buried in the Meshed Ali near Kufah.

7. The region is variously known as Sakasthan, Sijistan, Seistan, and Sistan, and was also once called Nimruz ("midday").

8. P. Yetta, "The Horse as a Factor in Early Chinese History," *Eurasia Septentrionalis Antiqua,* XXXIX: 231.

9. Topographical and geologic information on Afghanistan is still scanty. For available material see Donald N. Wilber, *Annotated Bibliography of Afghanistan* (New Haven, 1956), pp. 13–47.

CHAPTER II

1. Carleton S. Coon, *Caravan, The Story of the Middle East* (New York, 1951), p. 169.

2. *Pathan* is an Indian corruption of *Pushtoon.*

3. *Hudud-al-Alam (Regions of the World)*, translated by V. Minorsky (Cambridge, Mass., 1937), p. 91.

4. Abu Raihan Mohammed Ibn al-Biruni, *Alberuni's India,* translated by Dr. Edward Sachau (London, 1910), p. 208.

5. Hon. Mountstuart Elphinstone, *An Account of the Kingdom of Caubul* (London, 1819), Vol. I, p. 242.

6. *The History of Herodotus,* translated by George Rawlinson (New York, 1928), p. 379.

7. The first known record of these traditions, shared by all Pushtoon tribes, is in the writings of Niamatullah (A.D. 1612) a scribe at the Moghul court of Jehangir. Niamet Ullah, *Makhzan-i-Afghan,* translated by Bernhard Dorn (London, 1839).

8. Mohammed ibn Najib Bakran, Istakhri, and al-Khwarazmi.

9. Ibn Batuta, p. 128.

10. Major H. Raverty, *Selections from the Poetry of the Afghans* (London, 1867), p. 187.

11. Adam Olearius, *The Voyages and Travels of the Ambassadors* (London, 1669), p. 65.

12. Elphinstone, p. 400.

13. For the Pushtoons see Olaf Caroe, *The Pathans: 550 B.C.–A.D. 1957* (London, 1958).

14. Carleton S. Coon, *The Races of Europe* (New York, 1939), pp. 634–638.

15. On the Turkic peoples of Afghanistan see Gunnar Jarring, *On the Distribution of Turk Tribes in Afghanistan: An Attempt at a Preliminary Classification* (Lunds, 1939); also Waldemar Jochelson, *Peoples of Asiatic Russia* (New York, 1928).

16. On the Hazaras see Elizabeth E. Bacon, *Obok, A Study of Social Structure in Eurasia* (New York, 1958); H. F. Schurmann, *The Mongols of Afghanistan* ('S-Gravenhage, 1962), pp. 110–158.

17. Josiah Harlan, *Central Asia* (London, 1939), p. 82.

18. Schurmann, pp. 49–73.

19. George S. Robertson, *The Kafirs of the Hindu-Kush* (London, 1896).

20. See Appendix A.

21. Because of the drive for modernization now being conducted by the Afghan government, the next few years should witness the publication of more accurate ethnic investigation in Afghanistan. Serological studies, for example, are just beginning.

CHAPTER III

1. Many of the regions of Afghanistan are mentioned in the Avesta under names that are still recognizable. To the Indo-Aryans the name of the country was Eirene-Veejo or Aryanum Vijoo.

2. A. T. Olmstead, *History of the Persian Empire* (Chicago, 1948).

3. Afghans claim Zoroaster as a native, but he was apparently born in northwestern Iran close to the Caspian Sea.

4. Herodotus, *ed. cit.*, p. 379.

5. W. W. Tarn, *The Greeks in Bactria and India* (Cambridge, England, 1938).

6. Mohammed Qasim Ferishta, *History of the Rise of Mohamedan Power in India till the Year 1612* (Calcutta, 1908).

7. William Montgomery McGovern, *Early Empires of Central Asia* (Chapel Hill, N.C., 1939).

8. Procopius, *History of the Wars* (Cambridge, England, n.d.) Book I, p. 13.

9. Guy Le Strange, *Lands of the Eastern Caliphate* (Cambridge, England, 1930), p. 416.

10. Wilhelm Barthold, *Turkistan Down to the Mongol Invasion* (London, 2nd ed., 1928).

11. Mohammed Habib, *Sultan Mahmud of Ghaznin: A Study* (Bombay, 1927); also Muhammad Nazim, *The Life and Times of Sultan Mahmud of Ghazna* (Cambridge, England, 1931).

12. M. C. Defrémery, "Histoire des Sultans Ghourides," *Journal Asiatique* (Paris) IV série, II (1844): 167–200.

13. C. D'Ohsson, *Histoire des Mongols depuis Tchinguiz Khan jusqu'à Timour Bey ou Tamerlan* (4 v., La Haye et Amsterdam, 1834–1835). Still the best general history.

14. The Kurts owed their position to the favor of the Mongol Il-Khan Ghazan. They ruled the territory around Herat from A.D. 1245 to 1389.

15. *Mulfuzat Timury, or Autobiographical Memoirs of the Moghul Emperor Timur, written in the Jagtay Turky Language turned into Persian by Abu Talib Hussyny* (London, 1830). Whether Timur wrote this purported autobiography is doubtful.

16. Mohammed Zahir-ud-din Baber, *The Babur Nama in English,* translated by A. Beveridge (London, 1921), Vol. I, p. 199.

17. Laurence Lockhart, *Nadir Shah: A Critical Study Based Mainly on Contemporary Sources* (London, 1938).

CHAPTER IV

1. Ahmed Ali Kohzad, "Two Coronations," *Afghanistan* (Kabul), V, 3 (1950): 38–40.

2. Abdul Karim, *Murarbak-i-Satatin-i-Durrani* (Cawnpore, 1847), p. 9.

3. The title of Sirdar (Persian for leader or chief) is now reserved for male members of the royal family.

4. See Muhammad Jafar Shamly, Takrikl-i-manazelu Futuh in *The History of India as Told by Its Own Historians,* translated by Sir H. M. Elliott and Professor John Dowson (London, 1867–1877).

5. *Ibid.*

6. Many of the Afghans rode horses from Badakshan, famous for speed and endurance.

7. Ellsworth Huntington, *Mainsprings of Civilization* (New York, 1945), p. 425.

8. Alexander Dow, *The History of Hindostan* (London, 1768), Vol. II, Appendix, p. 81.

CHAPTER V

1. This action did not increase the Afghan's regard for Shah Timur.

2. G. T. Vigne, *A Personal Narrative of a Visit to Ghuzni, Kabul, and Afghanistan* (London, 1840), p. 376.

3. Ibid., p. 8.

4. As the title of Haji indicates, he had made a pilgrimage to Mecca.

5. Charles Masson, Manuscript papers (India Office Library), Vol. III p. 31.

6. Munshi Mohan Lal, *Journal of a Tour through the Panjab, Afghanistan, Turkistan, Khorasan, and Part of Persia* (Calcutta, 1834), p. 243.

7. Lieut. Arthur Connolly, *Journey to the North of India* (London, 1834), Vol. I, p. 289.

8. John William Kaye, *History of the War in Afghanistan* (London, 1878), Vol. I, p. 111.

9. Major D'Arcy Todd and Sir J. W. Kaye, *Lives of Indian Officers* (London, 1887), Vol. I, p. 346.

10. Sir Henry Marion Durand, *The First Afghan War* (London, 1879), p. 40.

CHAPTER VI

1. The march of Alexander of Macedon impressed Bonaparte and his British opponents, both of whom failed to consider the nature of Alexander's army.

2. C. U. Aitchison, *A Collection of Treaties, Engagements and Sanads Relating to India and Neighboring Countries* (Calcutta, 1933), Vol. XIII, pp. 45–60.

3. A Persian ambassador to India was killed in a fight between his escort and some sepoys. The embarrassed British paid an indemnity so respectable that a wag at the Persian court commented if they would be as generous in the future that they might kill any number of envoys.

4. Aitchison, pp. 46–49.

5. John McNeill, *Progress of Russia in the East* (London, 1835), p. 135.

6. John Howes Gleason, *The Genesis of Russophobia in Great Britain* (Cambridge, Mass., 1950), p. 204.

7. Viscount Mersey, *The Viceroys and Governors-General of India* (London, 1949), p. 57.

8. Mohan Lal was liked by the Afghans despite his religion and the knowledge that he was a British agent.

9. Josiah Harlan, *A Memoir of India and Afghanistan* (New York, 1842).

10. J. P. Ferrier, *History of the Afghans* (London, 1858), p. 262.

11. Certainly an amusing comment.

12. Sir Auckland Colvin, *John Russell Colvin* (London, 1895), p. 124.

13. Charles Masson, *Narrative of Various Journeys in Belochistan Afghanistan, and the Panjab* (London, 1842), Vol. III, p. 401.

14. W. K. Fraser-Tytler, *Afghanistan* (London, 1953), p. 317.

15. W. Massalski, "Pierwazy Polak W. Afghanistanie" *Prezeglad Geograficzny* (Warsaw), VIII: 155. (More precisely, Witkiwicz was a Lithuanian.)

16. Masson, Vol. III, p. 462.

17. An explanation that did not convince the British.

18. *The Chronicle,* London, May 10, 1840.

CHAPTER VII

1. Major W. Hough, *A Narrative of the March and Operations of the Army of the Indus* (Calcutta, 1840), p. 242.

2. J. C. Stocqueller, ed., *Memorials of Afghanistan* (Calcutta, 1843), pp. 37–43.

3. William Taylor, *Scenes and Adventures in Afghanistan* (London, 1847), p. 163.

4. Todd and Kaye, p. 350.

5. Captain John Wood, *A Journey to the Source of the Oxus* (London, 1872), p. 4.

6. This was the only time in which Christian missionaries have worked in Afghanistan. The impression they made was very unfavorable and drew critical comments from Burnes and Macnaghten.

7. Lt. General Sir George MacMunn, *Afghanistan from Darius to Amanullah* (London, 1929), p. 139.

8. Shahamet Ali, *The Sikhs and Afghans in Connexion with India and Persia* (London, 1849), p. 295.

9. Mohammed Hayat Khan, *Hayat-i-Afghan* (Lahore, 1874), p. 41.

CHAPTER VIII

1. John William Kaye, *History of the War in Afghanistan* (London, 1846), Vol. I, p. 536.

2. Letter from Mohan Lal to J. R. Colvin, *ibid.,* p. 250.

3. *Ibid.,* Vol. II, p. 72.

4. Lady Sale, *A Journal of the Disasters in Afghanistan 1841–2* (New York, 1843), p. 1.

5. Vigne, p. 112.

6. Major General Sir Vincent Eyre, *The Kabul Insurrection of 1841–2* (London, 1879), p. 234. The Afghans claim that Macnaghten drew a sword from a cane he was carrying.

7. Kaye, Vol. II, p. 156.

8. *Ibid.,* p. 72.

9. Lieutenant Vincent Eyre, *The Military Operations at Cabul* (London, 1843), 4th ed., p. 227.

10. Eight men were in this group. This desertion of their comrades drew a great deal of critical comment at the time but it seems that General Elphinstone approved of their departure. Kaye, Vol. II, p. 233.

11. Kaye, Vol. II, p. 216.

12. Dispatch to Sir Jasper Nicholls, March 15, 1842.

13. Rev. I. N. Allen, *Diary of a March through Sinde and Afghanistan* (London, 1843), p. 311.

14. *Ibid.,* p. 319.

15. G. W. Forrest, *Life of Field-Marshal Sir Neville Chamberlain* (London, 1909), p. 144.

CHAPTER IX

1. Kaye, Vol. II. p. 98.

2. Aitchison, p. 237.

3. *Ibid.,* p. 238.

4. H. W. Bellew, *Journal of a Political Mission to Afghanistan in 1857* (London, 1862), p. 299.

5. *Correspondence Respecting the Relations between the British Government and that of Afghanistan* (London, 1878), p. 3.

6. Abdur Rahman, *The Autobiography of Abdur Rahman* (London, 1900), Vol. I, p. 63.

7. Stephen Wheeler, *The Ameer Abdur Rahman* (London, 1895), p. 40.

8. *Parliamentary Papers* LVI (1878): 464.

9. Sir Henry Rawlinson, *England and Russia in the East* (London, 1875), p. 283.

10. *Afghanistan Blue Book* (London, 1878), No. I, p. 118.

11. Lady Betty Balfour, *Lord Lytton's Indian Administration* (London, 1899), p. 8.

12. *Ibid.,* p. 54.

13. *Ibid.,* p 86.

14. Bosworth Smith, *Life of Lord Lawrence* (London, 1893), Vol. II, p. 629.

15. Balfour, p. 255.

16. W. F. Moneypenny and G. E. Buckle, *The Life of Benjamin Disraeli, Earl of Beaconsfield* (New York, 1913, 1920), Vol. I, p. 382.

17. Balfour, p. 313.

18. Aitchison, p. 240.

19. Rahman, Vol. I, p. 152.

20. Joshua Duke, *Recollections of the Kabul Campaign* (London, 1862), p. 81.

21. Howard Hensman, *The Afghan War of 1879–80* (London, 1882), p. 174.

22. *The Second Afghan War: Official Account* (London, 1908), p. 496.

23. Major R. C. W. Mitford, *To Cabul with the Cavalry Brigade* (London, 1881), p. 195.

24. The "white-clad Ghazis" so frequently mentioned by the British press and authors like Kipling were simply Afghan tribesmen wearing their usual clothing, almost invariably white in color.

CHAPTER X

1. Elphinstone, Vol. II, p. 254.
2. Rahman, Vol. II, p. 6.
3. *Ibid.*, p. 169.
4. *Ibid.*, p. 217.
5. *Ibid.*, p. 251.
6. *Ibid.*
7. *Ibid.*, p. 262.
8. Elphinstone, Vol. II, p. 253.
9. Rahman, Vol. I, p. 277.
10. George Scott Robertson, *The Kafirs of the Hindu-Kush* (London, 1896).
11. Rahman, Vol. I, p. 291.
12. Frank A. Martin, *Under the Absolute Amir* (London, 1907), p. 157.
13. Any insult to his foreign employers was punished by the Amir in sanguinary fashion.
14. The display of military power by which Abdur Rahman was so little impressed was a customary feature of the visit of any potentially trouble-some visitor to India in the nineteenth century.
15. Rahman, Vol. I, p. 240.
16. *Ibid.*, p. 196.

CHAPTER XI

1. Baron A. Meyendorff, *Correspondance diplomatique de M. de Staal* (Paris, 1929), Vol. I, p. 26.
2. *Parliamentary Papers* LXXV (1873): 709.
3. Charles Marvin, *The Russians at Merv and Herat* (London, 1883), p. 709.
4. Lieutenant A. C. Yate, *Travels with the Afghan Boundary Commission* (London, 1888), p. 336.
5. Angus Hamilton, *Afghanistan* (London, 1906), p. 402.
6. An odd circumstance, considering the general accuracy of Burnes's observations.
7. Wheeler, p. 186.
8. Colonel Sir T. Hungerford Holdich, *The Indian Borderlands* (London, 1901), p. 285.
9. Dharm Pal, *The North-West Frontier 1843–1947* (Bombay, 1947), p. 34.
10. Arnold Keppel, *Gun-Running and the Indian North-West Frontier* (London, 1911), p. 52.

11. Abdur Rahman, Vol. I, p. 156.

12. *Ibid.,* p. 158.

13. Captain H. L. Nevill, *Campaigns On the North-West Frontier* (London, 1912), p. 211.

14. *Parliamentary Papers* LXIII (1879): 122–123 (C8714).

CHAPTER XII

1. A number of Dalai Lamas died as they approached manhood in the nineteenth century. Murder by their advisers is probable if unprovable.

2. A. H. Grant, "A Winter at the Court of an Absolute Monarch," *Blackwood's Magazine* CLXXX (Nov. 1906).

3. Aitchison, pp. 282–283.

4. "They put the Turk on a horse and he killed his own father" is an Afghan proverb.

5. Lady Betty Balfour, *Letters of the Earl of Lytton* (London), Vol. II, p. 64.

6. Oskar von Niedermayer, *Unter der Glutsonne Irans* (Dachau, Munich, 1925).

CHAPTER XIII

1. Hamilton, p. 362.

2. Siraj-ul-Akbar (Kabul), Feb. 19, 1919.

3. Lord Hardinge of Penshurst, *My Indian Years* (London, 1948), p. 105.

4. L. F. Rushbrook Williams, ed., *India in 1920* (Calcutta, 1921), p. 38.

5. H. C. E. Zacharias, *Renascent India* (London, 1933), p. 193.

6. Sir Michael O'Dwyer, *India As I Knew It* (London, n.d.), p. 312.

7. *The Third Afghan War: Official Account* (Calcutta, 1926), p. 23.

8. *Times of India* (Delhi), May 12, 1919.

9. Sirdar Ikbal Ali Shah, *Modern Afghanistan* (London, 1938), p. 118.

10. *Ibid.,* p. 120.

11. Aitchison, pp. 287–288.

CHAPTER XIV

1. *Digest of International Law* (Washington, D.C., 1938), p. 195.

2. *The Times* (London), June 13, 1919, p. 12.

3. Sir Michael O'Dwyer, Address to Central Asian Society, June 15, 1921.

4. Aitchison, p. 288 ff.

5. Said Alim Khan, *La Voix de la Boukharie opprimée* (Paris, 1929), p. 22.

6. Ikbal Ali Shah, "The Federation of the Central Asian States under the Kabul Government," *Journal of the Central Asian Society.* VIII, Pt. I (1921): 29–48; also, Lt. Col. P. T. Etherton, *In the Heart of Asia* (Boston, 1926), p. 235.

7. Essad Bey, *OGPU* (New York, 1933), p. 190.

8. In 1919 alone, 1,153 persons were killed, wounded, or captured.

9. Mohammed Ali, *Progressive Afghanistan* (Lahore, 1933), p. 6.

10. For the German's story see G. Stratil-Sauer, *From Leipzig to Cabul* (London, 1923). The Afghans have another and probably more accurate version.

11. Mohammed Yunus, *Frontier Speaks* (Lahore, 1942), p. 157.

12. *Times of India* (Delhi), Jan. 8, 1929.

13. "The Real British Attitude toward Afghanistan," *The Journal of the Royal Artillery* (Woolwich), Jan. 1929: 477.

CHAPTER XV

1. Robert Graves and Alan Hodge, *The Long Week End* (New York, 1941), p. 233.

2. F. Taillardot, "La fin du voyage du roi Aman Ullah," *Bulletin Asie Française,* Oct. 1928: 326.

3. Sorab K. H. Katrak, *Through Amanullah's Afghanistan* (Karachi, 1929), p. 106.

4. *Report of the Air Operation in Afghanistan between December 12th and February 25th, 1929* (London, 1930).

5. Amir Habibullah, *My Life from Brigand to King* (London, 1930).

6. Arnold Toynbee, *A Study of History* (Oxford, 1939), Vol. VI, p. 103.

7. *Times of India* (Delhi), March 3, 1929.

8. Ghani Khan, *The Pathans* (Bombay, 1947), p. 48. The author is the son of Abdul Ghaffar Khan.

9. *Aman-i-Afghan* (Kabul), Jan. 2, 1929.

10. Peter Fleming, *News from Tartary* (London, 1936), p. 313.

11. Lieutenant Colonel H. C. Birdwood, *A Continent Experiments* (London), p. 132.

CHAPTER XVI

1. S. M. Shah, *Trade with Afghanistan* (Lahore, 1943), p. 51.

2. Lieutenant Colonel Sir Kerr Fraser-Tytler, "The Great North Road," *Journal of the Royal Central Asian Society* XXIX (April 1942): 129.

3. Mohammed Qasim Rishtya, "Education in Afghanistan," *Afghanistan* (Kabul), I (1946): 38.

4. *Islah* (Kabul), July 7, 1932.

5. Flash floods, common in Afghanistan, destroyed many of the bridges constructed by Germans.

6. J. Castagne, "Les relations Nippo-Afghanes," *France-Japan* (Paris), April 1935: 88.

7. Ernest F. Fox, *Travels in Afghanistan* (New York, 1943).

CHAPTER XVII

1. Mohammed Kabir Ludin, then minister of public works, was a graduate of Cornell University.

2. Mohammed Hayat Khan, *Hayat-i-Afghan* (Lahore, 1875), p. 35.

3. Sir William Barton, *India's North West Frontier* (London, 1939), p. 57.

4. *Times of India* (Delhi), Aug. 17, 1947.

5. Sir George Cunningham, "The North West Frontier and the Tribes," *Sunday Statesman* (Delhi), May 29, 1949.

6. *Intelligence Reports Concerning the Tribal Repercussions in the Punjab, Kashmir, and India* (Lahore, 1948).

7. *Islah* (Kabul), April 12, 1949.

CHAPTER XVIII

1. Most of the information in this and the following chapter is based upon conversations with Afghan leaders.

2. Although quite different in temperament, Mohammed Zahir Shah and Mohammed Daoud have been close personal friends for many years.

3. Conversation with the author, Aug. 19, 1956.

4 The Safis won several battles with Afghan regular troops and captured a general.

5. A number of Turkomen were brought to the project from north-western Afghanistan.

CHAPTER XIX

1. See Appendix C.

2. *Kabul Times,* March 14, 1964.

3. Mohammed Wali Khan, prime minister in the time of Amanullah Khan, was also a Tadjik.

4. Jan F. Triska, ed., *Soviet Communism: Programs and Rules* (San Francisco, 1962).

Selected Bibliography

THE following bibliography is intended for those seeking additional information on particular aspects of Afghan history or ethnology, or on Afghanistan in general. The works listed are thus mainly in English. Scholars should refer to Donald N. Wilbur's *Annotated Bibliography of Afghanistan,* Human Relations Area Files (New Haven, 1956) or to Mohammed Akram's *Bibliographie analytique de l'Afghanistan,* Centre de Documentation Universitaire (Paris, 1947).

GENERAL AND DESCRIPTIVE

AHMAD, JAMAL-UD-DIN, and MOHAMMED ABDUL AZIZ. *Afghanistan, A Brief Survey* (Kabul, 1313 A.H.).

AITCHISON, C. U. *A Collection of Treaties, Engagements, and Sanads Relating to India and Neighbouring Countries,* Vol. XIII (Calcutta, 1933).

ALI, MOHAMMED. *A New Guide to Afghanistan* (Kabul, 1958).

FERRIER, J. P. *History of the Afghans* (London, 1858.).

FRASER-TYTLER, W. K. *Afghanistan* (2nd ed.; London, 1953).

IVEN, H. E. *Das Klima von Kabul* (Breslau, 1933).

MACMUNN, GEORGE FLETCHER. *Afghanistan, from Darius to Amanullah* (London, 1929).

MALLESON, COLONEL G. B. *History of Afghanistan* (London, 1879).

PAZHWAK, RAHMAN. *Aryana* (London, 1953).

SYKES, SIR PERCY. *A History of Afghanistan* (2 v.; London, 1940).

VAVILOV, N. I., and D. BUKINICH. *Agricultural Afghanistan* (Leningrad, 1934).

WILBER, DONALD, *et al. Afghanistan, Its People, Its Society, Its Culture* (New Haven, 1962).

AFGHAN ETHNIC GROUPS

BACON, ELIZABETH C. *Obok, A Study of Social Structure in Eurasia* (New York, 1958).

CAROE, OLAF. *The Pathans 550: B.C.–A.D. 1957* (London, 1958).

COON, CARLETON STEVENS. *The Races of Europe* (New York, 1939).

HERLICH, ALBERT. *Land des Lichtes* (Munich, 1938).

JARRING, GUNNAR. *On the Distribution of Turk Tribes in Afghanistan* (Lunds, 1939).

ROBERTSON, GEORGE S. *The Kafirs of the Hindu Kush* (London, 1896).

SCHURMANN, H. F. *The Mongols of Afghanistan* ('S-Gravenhage, 1962).

VOIGT, MARTIN. *Kafiristan* (Breslau, 1933).

PRE-ISLAMIC AFGHANISTAN

The Cambridge History of India, Vol. I (Cambridge, 1922).

GROUSSET, RENÉ. *In the Footsteps of Buddha* (London, 1932).

KONOW, S. *Saka Studies* (Oslo, 1932).

McGOVERN, WILLIAM MONTGOMERY. *The Early Empires of Central Asia* (Chapel Hill, North Carolina, 1939).

OLMSTEAD, A. T. *History of the Persian Empire* (Chicago, 1948).

RAWLINSON, SIR HENRY. *Bactria: The History of a Forgotten Empire* (London, 1912).

STEIN, SIR AUREL. *On Alexander's Track to the Indus* (London, 1929).

TARN, W. W. *The Greeks in Bactria and India* (Cambridge, 1938).

ISLAM TO A.D. 1747

BABER, MOHAMMED ZAHIR-UD-DIN. *The Babur Nama in English,* translated by Annette Susannah Beveridge (London, 1921).

BARTHOLD, WILHELM. *Turkestan down to the Mongol Invasion* (2nd ed.; London, 1928).

BATUTA, IBN. *Travels in Africa and Asia,* translated by H. A. R. Gibb (New York, 1929)

BROWNE, EDWARD G. *A Literary History of Persia* (2 v.; London, 1908).

DOLLOT, RENÉ. *L'Afghanistan* (Paris, 1939).

FORBES, ROSITA. *Forbidden Road* (New York, 1937).

FOX, ERNEST F. *Travels in Afghanistan* (New York, 1943).

FURON, RAYMOND. *L'Afghanistan* (Paris, 1926).

MAILLART, ELLA K. *The Cruel Way* (London, 1947).

MAYNE, PETER. *The Narrow Smile* (London, 1955).

SHAH, SIRDAR IKBAL AL. *Modern Afghanistan* (London, 1938).

SHAH, S. M. *Afghan General and Commercial Directory* (Karachi).

SHAH, S. M. *Trade with Afghanistan* (Lahore, 1943).

SHOR, JEAN BOWIE. *After You, Marco Polo* (New York, 1955).

WATKINS, MARY BRADLEY. *Afghanistan, Land in Transition* (Princeton, 1963).

Index